CONDUCT OF THE NEW DIPLOMACY

CONDUCT OF THE

NEW DIPLOMACY

James L. McCamy

Harper & Row, Publishers

New York, Evanston, and London

CONDUCT OF THE NEW DIPLOMACY

by James L. McCamy   Copyright © 1964

Printed in the United States of America. All rights reserved. No part
of this book may be used or reproduced in any manner without written
permission except in the case of brief quotations embodied in critical
articles and reviews. For information address Harper & Row, Publishers,
Incorporated, 49 East 33rd Street, New York 16, N.Y.

C-P

Library of Congress Catalog Card Number: 64–12789

For Julia

For John

CONTENTS

Part III Personnel

Part IV Changes Needed

LIST OF TABLES

ACKNOWLEDGMENT

For seventeen years the University of Wisconsin, and the colleagues who teach or administer and set its tone, have given me the best job I can imagine. For time off to write and the pay of a research assistant, I thank the Graduate School's Research Committee, a faculty group. For more time off, I thank equally the College of Letters and Science. Behind the scenes for much good that has come my way, including time to think, has been William H. Young, a fellow political scientist and assistant to the president.

The Carnegie Corporation supports the National Security Studies Group at the University of Wisconsin. Some additional help came from this part of the university. I thank the Carnegie Corporation.

Part of Chapter 16, on the need for a new policy staff, appeared as an article in *Harper's Magazine*. Otherwise the book is all new, and all my responsibility, of course; for no one else can be associated with its views or its errors.

JAMES L. MCCAMY

Madison, Wisconsin
January, 1964

PART ONE THE RELEVANCE OF ADMINISTRATION

CHAPTER 1 THE STATE

OF AMERICAN DIPLOMACY

THE PROCESS BY WHICH A DECISION IN FOREIGN policy is made is intricate almost beyond analysis. It involves many conditions and agents inside and outside the government, inside and outside the nation itself. Behind each telegram of consequence signed by the Secretary of State, behind each statement of the President, behind a decision of strategy in the Joint Chiefs of Staff, behind each vote in a Congressional Committee that deals with foreign affairs is a matrix of facts, forces, and agents that work on each other.

The nation starts its foreign policy from facts. Its geographical location in relation to other nations effects a whole set of facts. Its power in relation to the power of other nations is made of facts. One fact of power is the amount of natural resources. Another is the number of people related to the supply of food and water—and the skill of those people. Health and education have become as much a part of national power as guns and missiles.

Events and social circumstances at home and abroad are facts. The actions of other governments affect American foreign policy. Poverty and wealth, feelings about race and colonialism, religious beliefs, and the states of the arts and sciences in other nations and in our own affect foreign policy.

A vast labyrinth of facts about the stability and the competence of the political and economic system of the nation keeps political scientists and economists busy describing and analyzing things in motion. The stage of technology matters; so does the willingness to spend money for research and development, for this willingness reflects the nation's attitude toward change based upon scientific discovery. Skill depends upon the acceptance of scientific attitude, including the habit of self-analysis and the acceptance of change when it is indicated. This is true of both natural and social sciences, both industrial and military skills, both economic and political organizations. And of course the skill of the institutions available for analysis and recommendation—the universities, government research staffs, industrial laboratories, research institutes—also enters into the nation's power.

Another set of facts is composed of the ideas held at home by a nation. Not nearly as much attention is paid to these facts as to technical, economic, and political ones, perhaps because relatively the former seem so obvious. Yet ideas are just as strategic as any economic or political condition. Thus religion can encourage or frown upon and hinder change. Ethics adds to or subtracts from the efficacy of a political and economic system, for a nation's goals can be reached with much less delay when honesty prevails than when numerous blocks have to be introduced to stop losses from dishonesty. A system that operates on credit and the easy handling of bank checks works faster than the one that demands cash and distrusts everyone who writes a check. Politicians and civil servants who are honest save time and money, compared to those who assume that their positions entitle them to graft. Military officers from a society of high ethical standards will see that rations and medicines get to the men who need them, and are not diverted for selfish gain. The ideas of charity and tolerance also will shape a nation's foreign policy. The complex of religious-moral-ethical facts is just as much a part of the background of any policy decision as the collection of economic, political, and technical facts.

For each decision the many-sided facts get expressed by agents—groups of men who enter either in plain sight or obliquely, through mass media, in the minds of the public and private groups of men who assume responsibility for making the decision. A catalog of such influential agents (and their media) would include:

I. The newspapers, magazines, television, radio, and the book presses, with their components
   A. The newsmen who report events and opinions.
   B. The editors who state opinion on editorial pages and the columnists and commentators who interpret events and opinions.
   C. The editors who choose what to publish.
   D. The publishers and other owners of media, including advertisers on radio and television, who set the tone of news and opinion.
II. The public, subdivided into
   A. The mass public, reflecting cultural traits and moods.
   B. The smaller attentive public of any issue.
   C. The smaller expressive public of any issue.
   D. The electorate for any election, which may or may not be attentive to issues.
III. Organized interest groups that make themselves heard on particular issues.
IV. Individuals, business firms, and private institutions that publicly take a stand on particular issues and are influential.
V. Congress operating as
   A. A whole.
   B. Committees that deal with proposals and investigations.
   C. The individual members of House and Senate, or
   D. Those persons who work for members either in their offices or in the staffs of committees.
   E. Party leaders.
VI. The Executive, composed of
   A. The President.
   B. Political chiefs who head departments and agencies.
   C. Political aides who work for the President and his political chiefs.
   D. The permanent staffs of both military and civil establishments.
VII. The officials of other nations, both when they act at home and when they negotiate in Washington.

For one person in one book to try to deal with all these agents—representing all the facts that enter a decision—would be as foolish as it would be impudent. Many reporters and analysts are working on specific aspects of the facts and agents. The bibliography at the back of this book shows only part of the results of their work; a selected list, it covers only books, not articles, and then only those books most relevant to an understanding of the conduct of American diplomacy, omitting others that deal with the nature of foreign policy itself.

II

Our concern in this book is with the way the Executive Branch is organized and staffed to carry out its part in deciding and executing foreign policy. The way the Executive Branch works is more important than most Presidents and Congressmen would appear to think. Some students of administration believe the nation can be threatened by flaws in the machinery of government; it can neglect, fumble, and muddle its way into second place.

In government no situation is ever perfect; there is always room for improvement. Since 1836 the State Department has been growing more unmanageable; or, some would say, less competent. In that long-ago year Secretary John Forsyth reorganized the Department to put all similar jobs together in as few units as made sense. By this simple rule he tried to have as few subordinates as possible reporting to the Secretary. His was the last neat chart, the last proximity to what his successors today would call a streamlined department, as if the whole institution were hurtling against the wind.

Later reorganizations—and there have been many—resemble those microscope slides of swamp water, where movement never stops yet nothing ever gets any better. Cell division too takes place in the State Department. Secretary Hamilton Fish in 1870 divided six units into thirteen, which is one better than nature can do. Since his triumph, bureaus have multiplied, similar jobs have been separated, and more people report to the Secretary. Joseph Kraft, in *Harper's Magazine,* November 1961, could write accurately that the State Department's organization "is diagrammed less by an orderly row of boxes than by a topographical map of a chain of folded mountains," and quoted a recent Secretary, Dean Acheson, as saying, "Nobody has been able to run the Department in a hundred and fifty years."

If the State Department needs remodeling, the military needs reconstruction. It is now a full partner in making decisions and executing foreign policy and will continue to be so as long as nations use latent force in bargaining. The American military, divided into four services (Army, Navy, Air Force, Marines) and three departments (Army, Navy, Air Force), and under the supervision of the Secretary of Defense and a canopy of mixed civilian and military offices called the Department of Defense, resembles a weird monster from science fiction, perhaps a throbbing mushroom.

Above both the State Department and the military, the Presidency has evolved into what may be the most serious problem of all. The President himself knows his job, of course, and would not be in it if he could not handle it. But the man is no longer the whole of the Presidency and has not been for years. Every President since Herbert Hoover has used assorted offices and individuals to do his work. These helpers sometimes give orders, sometimes cajole, and sometimes make final decisions, which have the same force as if the President himself had made them. A central apparatus of many able men has grown without definition of what it is supposed to do and how it is supposed to do it. One theory is that these men only advise the President, in person, but there are too many doing too much for this to be true. Still no one has given them the authority to command.

In the confusion, the President tries to handle the big issues, hoping that his immediate staff and his numerous subordinates in the other agencies are happily on top of all the lesser issues. Presidents are taken by surprise fairly regularly. The Russians reached into space before the Americans, and President Eisenhower found that his rocket-missile enterprise was about as big a mess as Washington had ever known. Cuban exiles tried a foolishly planned invasion to seize Cuba, and President Kennedy discovered that the Central Intelligence Agency was neither secret nor competent to manage the invasion. The most conspicuous failures of the plan were its lack of secrecy and of accurate intelligence. Either President could have been tripped by the U-2 affair, which will be analyzed later as an illustration of the way organization and people relate to the state of our foreign affairs.

III

Of course the record is not all error. If it were, we would have lost long ago. The United States has made more sensible moves than wrong ones. Its most striking success is military. The strategy of deterrence, of piling power on top of power on top of power until Russia dares not start a major war, which would do more harm than good to both nations, has confined wars and saved much of the world from misery ever since the Second World War.

The military power of the United States has also allowed us to succeed politically in those remarkable alliances, the North Atlantic Treaty Organization, the Organization of American States, and the Southeast Asia Treaty Organization. Other nations welcomed such alliances in which they could be protected by strong arms.

Military deterrence coupled with regional alliances proved dramatically successful when the Russians tried to place offensive missiles in Cuba and met a showdown with the United States and the Organization of American States in the autumn of 1962. This was another episode in a conflict of power, but it was closer than Korea or Berlin, and threatened to give Russia enough new strength to tip the balance. It showed near at hand the meaning of military deterrence as a foreign policy. For the experienced men of government, the firm stand against Russian bases in Cuba was part of the pattern of force, perhaps more risky than Korea or Berlin but not clearly so, for those episodes also ran great risk of setting off unlimited war.

The Cuban episode demonstrated another strength, combined

with weakness, of the American method. A strong President who takes personal command will make sensible decisions quickly. For him the machinery springs to life and delivers both analysis and action. This is strength. When the President does not take a subject into his own hands—and he cannot possibly take all of them—the machinery is much less proficient. When a strong man holds the office, the power of the President is a strength of administration; but the fact that he is apparently so essential to a successful outcome is a weakness. No man can keep enough reins in his own hands to make the decisions that must be made on all the subjects that are important. A competent organization, filled with competent people, is more necessary than ever. We cannot escape this fact by tossing the easy slogan that all the nation ever needs is a good President who will take care of everything.

IV

The point in this book is this: American diplomacy is holding its own, in many cases doing very well indeed, but it could be much more successful if it were better administered in the executive branch.

The nation has not failed. It succeeded notably in its military strategy of deterrence; no nuclear blow has been struck. It succeeded in facing down the Soviet Union in Cuba. It succeeded in the politico-economic dealing with Western Europe after the war, and may still have a chance to succeed in Latin America and South Asia.

Always one may ask whether his government could not get more and better results. This is the critical question in the conduct of diplomacy, especially now that American diplomacy has changed so much from the time when its traditions were established and its tasks first defined. National safety rests in arms, attitudes, and skills. Without skill in foreign affairs, we can fail to do the best possible job despite good arms and the best of attitudes.

CHAPTER 2　THE U-2 CASE

A CASE WILL SHOW THE RELEVANCE OF AD-
ministration to foreign policy. Camp David, U-2, and the summit
are related in one event usually called the U-2 affair.

Nikita Khrushchev came to the United States in September of
1959 at the invitation of President Eisenhower. Diplomatically, as
always, the motives on both sides were mixed and not all by any
means under control. If Mr. Khrushchev wanted to come, there
was not much the United States could do to stop him. To say that
we could not guarantee his safety would be a glaring lie when our
own President is so carefully protected from harm. To say that we
simply did not want him would have been so churlish that all
other nations would have been shocked.

On the other hand, we could use the visit for some ends of our
own. We could show the Russian people, through the Soviet
reports of Mr. Khrushchev's triumphal procession, that we were
peace-loving and not war-mongering, to use the symbols of that
time. We could show the man our strength. As a good Marxist
theologian, he believed that communism would bury capitalism.
Now he could see how much had to be buried. He could learn
how remote was any revolutionary spirit among the American
proletarians, whose like had not been foreseen by Marx. Not least,
the people of the United States, by being themselves, had a
chance to convince this hostile chief that he need not fear a war.
It was unlikely that Mr. Khrushchev's mind would be changed by
anything he saw. He was shielded by his faith from all facts that

did not conform. The most we could do was to show him the facts of our system at work.

Being ourselves was the real rub. In the exposure of Mr. Khrushchev to Americans and their ways our government took a great risk. Some Americans were Hungarian, Polish, or Czech Americans with a grudge against all Soviet communists. Other Americans hated foreigners, and most of all communist foreigners. These formed a fringe of extremists that might make more noise than the calm and friendly majority. Even the majority would have to be reminded to be courteous. For twelve years their leaders had been telling them that Soviet Russia and communism were implacable foes. Now they must be told that the Enemy-in-Chief was to be an honored visitor.

The visit went off pretty well. Mr. Khrushchev, a charmer himself, was treated well by most Americans. He ignored the few protesters in the street crowds. Only for a few hours did Americans who were not on the extremist fringe annoy the visitor. A boorish movie executive berated Mr. Khrushchev at a social affair in Los Angeles. Mr. Khrushchev was taken to see a can-can dance at a motion-picture studio in the same city. This was as much a violation of Russian good manners as if the French had arranged a public visit by President Eisenhower to a strip-tease show in Paris. But this was Los Angeles. Mr. Khrushchev's secret agents surely had told him about Los Angeles. From the large number of volunteer counter spies there, one can deduce that the city was crawling with Soviet spies. The Russians may well have known more about Disneyland than we thought.

In San Francisco Mr. Khrushchev met the only other trouble he had. Top leaders of American labor unions held a small private conference with Khrushchev. To a communist, American labor leaders are worse than capitalists. In Marxist-Leninist doctrine the only sensible and moral role of a labor leader is that of a Communist Party member dedicated to revolution. So to Khrushchev the men who met him in San Francisco were either dupes or traitors to the revolution. And to them, he was no more than a party politician who rose to power not from any real concern for workers but from the age-old desire of certain men to be supreme. Mr. Khrushchev knew what he thought about capitalistic union leaders, and what they thought of him, before he entered that conference with them. No damage was done.

To offset the bad manners of Los Angeles and the rancor between American and communist labor leaders, other hosts were agreeable. Businessmen welcomed Mr. Khrushchev at high-priced banquets. Most people in the streets were friendly. So were managers and workmen in the enterprises he visited.

In foreign policy, the result of the tumult was "the spirit of Camp David." This was no small thing. When the chiefs of the two most powerful nations on earth met in a weekend retreat and agreed to try to get along together, it was a turning point. If the amity had lasted, it might have been the beginning of an easier life for all.

In the new atmosphere the United States agreed to a summit conference, that old device with a new name. And Mr. Khrushchev invited Mr. Eisenhower to Russia for a social visit. For imperfect man, who should never expect to get all he wants, the future looked good that year.

II

Then an American U-2 plane was captured inside Soviet territory. The U-2 is a high altitude craft useful for either reconnaissance or weather observation. We used it for both purposes. When the Russians first announced that they had the plane, they said nothing about its capture almost intact and nothing about the uninjured pilot who talked a lot. The National Aeronautics and Space Administration announced that one of our weather planes was missing and might have strayed into Russia.

Mr. Khrushchev then told his Supreme Soviet the full story with photographs. The plane had been brought down twelve hundred miles inside Russia. Its pilot was provided with the usual tools of the spy, cameras, suicide dose, various nations' moneys, and trade goods (wrist watches and gold rings in this case) with which to buy protection and information if he got the chance.

The Russians had us.

We now said that the plane was probably spying. Such planes had been making flights "along the frontiers of the free world for the past four years."[1] Our excuse was that Russian secrecy made it necessary for us to spy against the danger of surprise attack. This much confession was in a statement from the State Department's press officer. The same statement added this untrue, and as it turned out hurtful, remark: "As a result of the inquiry ordered by the President, it has been established that, insofar as the authorities are concerned, there was no authorization for any such flights as described by Mr. Khrushchev." This statement was made in the afternoon of May 7, 1960, after some members of the State Department knew the Russians had the pilot, part of the plane and equipment, and film from the camera. It was made with the knowledge of Christian Herter, the Secretary of State, who was himself one of "the authorities" who had authorized just such flights as we now denied. Mr. Herter later told the Senate Foreign Relations Committee that this statement "was still partly cover."

Experienced spies have gained skill in such matters. For one thing, once a cover story is used, don't change it. But the cover story, to be convincing, must be plausible and must cover all possible developments. This one, pulled from the file, hardly explained how a weather plane in trouble drifted twelve hundred miles. Another rule is, don't acknowledge the charge. Instead, just ignore the accusation and the event. In this case, once the "weather flight" story was used, we should have stopped talking. There is a good deal of practical custom about espionage, recognized by all civilized agents just as protocol is accepted by their overt colleagues. Cover stories are part of ritual. They may have no more relation to truth than the rite of a girls' school Maypole dance

[1] All direct quotes and other statements of fact used here were taken from the Report of the Committee on Foreign Relations, U.S. Senate, June 28, 1960, "Events Relating to the Summit Conference." (Government Printing Office.) Two news reporters, David Wise and Thomas B. Ross, dug out additional information from anonymous interviews and records and wrote an enthralling book that makes better reading than most thrillers. It is recommended for accuracy and perception as well as for its interest. David Wise and Thomas B. Ross, *The U-2 Affair* (New York: Random House, 1962).

has to the fact that it is spring, but they allow both sides to ease out of a mistake. (As a result of custom in the civilized practice of espionage our captured spy, Francis Gary Powers, was exchanged in February, 1962, for a Russian spy, Col. Rudolf I. Abel, whom we had imprisoned.)

Mr. Herter and other top authorities seemed to forget some of the routines of secret intelligence.

III

We had been making such flights with U-2 planes for four years. Khrushchev himself said that he had known of one high altitude flight over Russia in July 1956 but had decided not to protest at the time.

The big question for us had been whether to continue the flights after the Camp David meeting. If the Russians knew about them, or if a pilot had an accident or was shot down, these snooping forays could be used to kill the spirit of Camp David. Normally no top man would know of a particular flight, so none could be expected to stay the one that got caught. Decisions of when and how to get particular information would be made in the subordinate ranks and in the field. All that could be expected at the top was that someone decide that all our actions that might give the Soviets a good public reason to break the new amity should be reviewed and possibly stopped. No one decided this.[2]

When he should have played dumb, Mr. Herter issued on May

[2] In fairness, the high officials who testified before the Senate Committee claimed that there was a particular reason for the flight on May 1. The reason was so secret they would not reveal it. Some newsmen at the time said that we were expecting the Russians to demonstrate a new missile in celebration of May Day. Messrs. Wise and Ross in *The U-2 Affair* say the immediate purpose of the flight was to photograph some construction that was suspected of being the first Soviet base of intercontinental missiles. (p. 10.) They conclude, however, that the main reason for sending a flight so near the date of the summit conference was a fear on the part of the technicians of secret intelligence that a new friendship might come from the conference and stop the flights entirely, hence a desire to get one last flight across. (p. 259.) Wise and Ross do not give specific evidence for this conclusion but present it as their analysis of all available evidence, including their interviews.

9 a statement that set the embers ablaze. He said the United States would continue to seek information that might lessen the danger of surprise attack. Although Mr. Herter said later that he did not mean to say that U-2 flights over Soviet territory would be continued, this was what, of course, news reporters and Russians alike assumed that he meant. His language could be so interpreted:

I will say frankly that it is unacceptable that the Soviet political system should be given an opportunity to make secret preparations to face the free world with the choice of abject surrender or nuclear destruction. The Government of the United States would be derelict to its responsibility not only to the American people but to free peoples everywhere if it did not, in the absence of Soviet cooperation, take such measures as are possible unilaterally to lessen and to overcome this danger of surprise attack. In fact the United States has not and does not shirk this responsibility.

Next Mr. Herter threw a bomb in the fire. He said *the President* had ordered that information be gathered "by every possible means."

In accordance with the National Security Act of 1947, the President has put into effect since the beginning of his Administration directives to gather by every possible means the information required to protect the United States and the Free World against surprise attack and to enable them to make effective preparation for their defense. Under these directives programs have been developed and put into operation which have included extensive aerial surveillance by unarmed civilian aircraft, normally of a peripheral character but on occasion by penetration. Specific missions of these unarmed civilian aircraft have not been subject to Presidential authorization. The fact that such surveillance was taking place has apparently not been a secret to the Soviet leadership and the question indeed arises as to why at this particular juncture they should seek to exploit the present incident as a propaganda battle in the cold war.

The President was thus made personally responsible for secret operations in other nations. He did not know of each specific mission. He did know in general what he had ordered. Two days later in a press conference the President confirmed, by acquiescence, that he was indeed going to take the responsibility. He referred to secret intelligence as a "distasteful but vital necessity."

Now that the Chief of State had accepted the responsibility, there was no way to bargain. He could not blame a scapegoat. He could no longer say the flight was a mistake. Presidents do not make mistakes. Certainly he could not apologize now that an apology would have to come from the President and would mean loss of face for the nation. If an orator gestures full length with both arms, there is no more room for interpretation. He has used all there is.

One possible theory was that our officials were trying to get the Russians to scuttle the Summit Conference and the President's visit to Moscow. They had used the capture of the plane to affront Khrushchev, this theory ran, so that he would be disgraced at home if he continued to deal with Eisenhower. After all, the Russian people, and, more important, Mr. Khrushchev's colleagues in power, would wonder about two aspects of the U-2's capture. How could it penetrate twelve hundred miles before it was shot down? And how could a President who had been called a friend at Camp David order such penetration? Border incidents are common between Allied and Soviet forces. They are settled quietly except when one side or the other wants to use such an incident consciously, or is left no way out.

If our officials were capable of such guile, they hid their skill with even greater performances when they testified before the Senate Committee on Foreign Relations. There they appeared to be men who simply knew little about international politics and secret intelligence. We had to drop as unreasonable the idea that these men were clever and turned the episode to serve an end of their choosing.

IV

This much should be said to their credit. After the week of stumbling, our men kept their heads for the next few amazing days in Paris, where the Summit Conference was due to open on May 16. They made the Russians force the issue and appear to scuttle the conference, as indeed the Russians may have meant to do from the beginning, although there is only opinion and no fact for this.

Mr. Khrushchev set his demands high. Before he would join the conference, he said, the United States would have to denounce the U-2 flights, promise not to repeat them, and punish those responsible for them. The United States had already announced that the President, our Chief of State, was responsible for the flights. He could not apologize save in national shame. He could not punish himself. The only part of the condition that he could meet was to cancel future flights, and this Mr. Eisenhower did. Insiders knew that the flights had to be called off anyway, for once a method of espionage is compromised, it is no longer useful. In this case allies too were compromised because they had lent air bases to the enterprise. They would not want to continue the risk. The American gesture, however, looked good to the world.

Mr. Eisenhower proposed anew that both nations allow aerial inspection, an idea that was called the "open-skies policy" in the shorthand of the day. He was also ready to talk with the Russians on the side while the main conference went along. Mr. Khrushchev had taken a stance so remote that Mr. Eisenhower was not speaking in a voice that approached him.

The conference ended. Mr. Khrushchev withdrew the invitation to Mr. Eisenhower to visit Russia. Each side blamed the other.

One unexpected break in propaganda fell to America and her allies. Mr. Khrushchev apparently forgot that he was in the West and misbehaved at a press conference. He was vituperative, belligerent, and absurdly undignified. Sitting at his side, and prominent in photographs and movies of the spectacle, was a Soviet marshal whose presence added a tone of military threat. Mr. Eisenhower and his department heads took the line that the Russians had meant to stop the Summit Conference from the beginning. They used the U-2 disclosure to do so. This was our official line. It could neither be proved nor disproved. Largely because Mr. Khrushchev behaved so badly at his press conference, the American leaders were not challenged much at home or abroad.

Both sides showed poorly. Richard H. Rovere, one of the most

acute reporters of the day, summed it up in *The New Yorker* of
May 28, 1960:

> If entries were being made in a ledger, more red ink would be needed
> on Chairman Khrushchev's page than on President Eisenhower's.

Still, the essential thing is that no black ink was required for either
Americans or Russians, and few American onlookers could fail to conclude or afford to forget that we had served ourselves and our allies very
badly indeed at a most critical moment. The government had told a
preposterous story and been found out; trapped, it had sought a haven
in the truth and found that there was no haven there. (To the President
and the Secretary of State, the ultimate in irony must have been the
outrage of the American press, which everlastingly demands the truth
and professes to retail it at a nickel or a dime a day, when the two of
them at last told it.) Then, in Paris, the government moved from truth
and falsehood to baloney. Once it became apparent that there would
be no meeting, our people began to say that they had known right along
that Khrushchev was coming to Paris for the express purpose of wrecking the conference, and that they had made their plans in accordance
with this knowledge.

The Senate Committee on Foreign Relations concluded:

> It is more difficult to answer with assurance the question of whether,
> given the U-2 incident, Khrushchev's behavior in Paris would have
> been significantly different if the incident had been handled differently.
> Here one can only speculate. It seems reasonable to suppose, however,
> that the Soviet reaction was greatly intensified by two aspects: (1) the
> interpretation that the flights were going to continue; and (2) the
> assumption of personal responsibility by the President.
>
> It can be argued, as Secretary Herter did at some length, that it was
> unreasonable to interpret the statements of May 7 and 9 as implying a
> continuation of the flights. Nevertheless, the fact is that Khrushchev, as
> well as many of the free world's newspapers, did so interpret the state-
> ments. Thus, by the time the President announced the suspension in
> Paris May 16, the Soviet position had already been set and Khrushchev
> did not depart from it.
>
> In the end, one is left with the same two questions with which one
> started: (1) Should the U-2 flight have been sent at all on May 1? and
> (2) Once the flight failed, should the United States have reacted dif-
> ferently?
>
> In regard to the first question, the committee is handicapped . . . by
> its lack of knowledge of the specific mission of the U-2. In looking

back, if one accepts the conclusion that the failure of the mission furnished an excuse for Khrushchev's wrecking of the summit conference, then, in the absence of compelling reasons to the contrary, there is good reason to conclude that the flight should not have gone.

In regard to the second question, . . . it seems that the U.S. reaction to the failure of the U-2 complicated the problems which resulted from that failure.

Relations between the two strongest nations remained bellicose for the rest of Mr. Eisenhower's days in office. Assuming that the Russians had long planned to wreck the conference, and to find some way to cancel the Eisenhower visit, as our officials argued, we had to conclude that the American actions helped the Russians succeed. We had to admit that American officials in the highest posts appeared to be deceitful and indecisive, if not just plain foolish.

CHAPTER 3 U-2, AN EXAMPLE

OF ADMINISTRATION

Here in the U-2 episode was a result of government, a product of administration. It can be examined for purpose, organization and coordination, the quality of personnel, and responsibility.

From the beginning, our purpose was unclear. In the large sense, did we want a summit conference or not? Did we want to negotiate or not? Reasonable arguments could be found for either position. The one unreasonable position for a nation was to have no position. In the short range, did we intend to continue the U-2 flights or did no one remember to stop them? Once caught, did we mean to make the President responsible and so close the door to all compromise? Or was this done without thought of consequences?

These are questions of purpose, of foreign policy basic and applied. They will not be answered unless the executive apparatus is working. In this case, they apparently were not answered at any time.

II

Next consider the organization and coordination in this case. At most, two jobs were present. One was to collect intelligence against a surprise attack. This is a routine task of the military. The other was to prepare for a summit meeting. This is a task for the State Department.

As the government executive branch is organized, these two missions required the coordination of no less than twelve separate agencies or persons—twelve instead of the two agencies and two persons to be expected from the two objectives.

Although the intelligence sought was military in nature, its collection was in the hands of the *Central Intelligence Agency*.

Because the Central Intelligence Agency works covertly, it used the *National Aeronautics and Space Administration* as a cover for these flights. (The Space Administration in turn had a contract with the Lockheed Aviation Corporation to make the flights, and the pilot who was captured was on the payroll of this private firm. I do not count the aviation firm as part of the government apparatus.)

The Space Administration collected weather data for the *Air Force* and pretended that these flights were for this purpose.

Because it is a canopy over the four branches of the armed forces, the *Department of Defense* was involved, for three reasons. (1) The Air Force was part of the cover, and overseas bases were used. (2) It was military intelligence that Central Intelligence Agency was collecting. (3) The Department of Defense, or the entire military establishment, is concerned with foreign policy in this day when military power is at the center of much policy.

For this matter the *Secretary of Defense* (Thomas Gates at the time) as a person, as well as head of the Department of Defense, was busy. He represented the whole military establishment, and he acted as a close member of the Eisenhower Administration.

The *Department of State* is responsible for general relations with other countries. With a reservation that the point is often confused by other agencies, it is also most responsible for the assembly and conclusion of foreign policy when the President himself does not do this.

Representing the Department of State and also acting for himself as an adviser to the President was the *Secretary of State*.

Within the Executive Office of the President the *National Security Council* at the time recommended to the President decisions of foreign policy for those matters that came to its attention. Its members are the President, the Vice-President, the Secretary of

State, the Secretary of Defense, and the Director of the Office of Emergency Planning. This matter came to its attention, loudly and informally, without the stately progression of papers and regular meetings. One gets the impression that the members were on the telephone a lot, and when they got together, they did so in haste.

The Staff Secretary to the President (at this time Brig. Gen. A. J. Goodpaster) dealt for the President with policy while it was developing.

The President's Press Secretary (then James C. Hagerty) is on the spot with reporters whenever news is breaking at this high level. He reveals the President's actions and views. Nothing could have been much hotter news than the U-2 capture and summit conference.

At this time the Vice-President (Richard M. Nixon) was heeded by the press because he was clearly to be the next Republican candidate for President. He justified the secret intelligence flights in a television interview that was quoted in newspapers.

The President was involved, of course, in such shaking events. Subordinates spoke for him part of the time. In a press conference at home and at the first, and last, session of the Summit Conference in Paris he spoke for himself.

I have not counted the persons within the agencies who were involved in these decisions. The Department of Defense is not one man, nor is State or the Space Administration. It is a safe guess that no less than fifty persons had this episode first in their work while it was happening. They were all men who contributed to policy, heads of agencies, deputies, advisers, all in the upper levels of the pyramid.

The profusion of tasks among too many agencies and people was one fault of organization. Every hour of every day, year after year, it holds true that the more people involved, the more uncertain become control and coordination. It was true when Moses admitted that he could not administer the Israelites alone and chose deputies to handle all except the hard causes, which the deputies brought unto Moses. It was true when the U-2 fell on Mr. Eisenhower.

What is more, when organization is diffuse, the wrong people take up all the time and the right people never get consulted. It happened in this case. So many chiefs and deputies were talking to each other that no one had time to ask advice of the specialists. Any bright graduate of a military intelligence school would have handled more ably the statements after the plane was compromised. Any able foreign service officer could have handled the statements with more foresight as to the other nation's political use of them.

There is no reason to expect high officials to think as junior officers think. When high officials act outside their competence, however, there is reason to expect them to ask the advice of specialists. In this case it is hard to understand the decisions made by our chiefs unless we assume that they simply did not know much about the conduct of secret intelligence and diplomatic negotiation.

Poor organization created too many chiefs who had to reach agreement. They conferred on a mountain top remote from the level where lesser men had met such crises before. No wonder the chiefs looked silly.

III

One other fact of organization set the outcome of this affair. By the Defense Act of 1947 we placed the Central Intelligence Agency in the Executive Office of the President. This put the President in direct command of American espionage. There is no ignoring the fact that the agency collects secret intelligence—and arranges treason in other lands, as all such agencies do when they use a citizen of another country to get secret information or to commit sabotage. I do not mean to draw a moral tone here. All nations that need it and can afford it will get secret intelligence. The Congress of Vienna which made official and binding some of the central etiquette of modern diplomacy was so spy-haunted that historians can always get some good paragraphs from the telling.

The United States openly lists its secret agency as directly subordinate to the Chief of State. Other nations can buy charts and manuals that show this, and the agency itself has not been shy about publicity favorable to itself, all of which is reported home by any embassy that reads the American papers.

From 1946 through 1960 the Central Intelligence Agency by its present and former names is cited each year in *Readers' Guide to Periodical Literature* and *The New York Times Index*. The number of magazine articles ranged from one in 1949 to eleven in 1960, the year of the U-2 crash. One paradoxical but revealing title was "We Tell Russia Too Much," by Allen W. Dulles, Director of the Central Intelligence Agency, in *U.S. News*, March 19, 1954. The agency appeared thirteen times in *The New York Times* in 1946 and twelve times in 1960. Its big year of prominence was 1954, when it appeared forty-five times, following twenty-eight times in 1953 and preceding twenty-seven times in 1955 and twenty-six times in 1956.

The late, reckless Senator Joseph McCarthy was responsible for some of the publicity in 1953 and after. Except for his charges against personnel, however, other news and magazine discussion carries the appearance of having been published with the tacit consent of the agency and sometimes with the open help of Mr. Dulles. Great secrecy is demanded by the Central Intelligence Agency when its budget or competence are questioned. Favorable publicity is not suppressed, including good words said by the President at a public ceremony to lay the cornerstone of the Agency's new building.

Such conspicuous effort in secret intelligence in one way made it necessary to label the President responsible for the U-2 flights. The charts of organization showed that he was truly responsible. If we had claimed that he was not, that some subordinate had erred, the Russians might well have put the lie to us again.

IV

Changes to get away from such faults of organization as those shown in this case are obvious. The units involved in the U-2 flights and their aftermath could have been confined to the Departments of Defense and State, and their Secretaries, plus the President if the issue became so big that he had to get involved. The key is the object of the flights. It was to collect military information by reconnaissance from the air. Our military services are not strangers to secret operations overseas in peacetime, as thousands of able veterans know. They do not need to turn to the Central Intelligence Agency for some rare skill at high altitude. They can set up their own civilian cover to avoid the charge that the spy, if caught, is a military aggressor.

Once the cat was out of the bag, the object of administration was to save the Summit Conference, still assuming that our leaders were simply not sinister enough to plan the whole thing to wreck the conference. The State Department at this point would have taken command in a well organized government.

As for the location of the Central Intelligence Agency in the Executive Office of the President, a change should have been made years ago. The President needs coordination of intelligence, not its collection. He needs evaluation of the information. This evaluation is as much a function of policy-making as it is a function of intelligence work. He can keep a staff for coordination and evaluation and transfer the large apparatus of collection to some less conspicuous place in the executive branch, perhaps as a division of an existing department. It should always be remembered that the military also collects secret intelligence, and the State Department's missions abroad are not unaware of secret as well as open intelligence. Only the Central Intelligence Agency stands out as devoted primarily to the collection abroad of secret intelligence, and only it is located in the Executive Office of the President.

V

Unless people are competent, the best organization cannot insure good results. Government needs the same kind of good people as private enterprise needs for the same kind of work. Staff and executive work in a federal department is not very different from such work in a corporation. Some men study problems and give advice. These do staff work. Other men listen to advice, apply all the factors, including both logical and non-rational elements, and make decisions. These are executives. In government the staff men are usually permanent civil servants and the executives are partisans who change with elections. We are concerned with the quality of both kinds.

In the U-2 sequence there was little chance to measure the quality of permanent staff. If its members were not consulted, they could not be judged. And apparently they were not consulted as much as they could have been. Probably we will never be able to judge the ability of American intelligence workers. They hide their failures behind the claim of secrecy and allow only their successes to show. We can only go to results and guess backwards.

The results in this case were mixed. No one could ask for better collection of information. The fact of an American camera plane high over the Soviet Union, penetrating twelve hundred miles, must have startled most Russians as much at it did Americans. On the other hand, all of us could expect more grown-up handling of policy after the plane was discovered. Because the political executives handled the case themselves, they must be called to blame.

The competence of political executives had to be questioned. No one could possibly say with any proof that these men were not qualified. They had all shown superior ability for years in or out of government. I think we conclude that good men were trapped by poor organization and thereby made the mistakes that made them appear to be incompetent.

VI

Responsibility is easier to advocate than to define. Our system assumes that our executives will do what we want done. We cannot tell them what to do each day. Our representatives in Congress cannot tell them how to make immediate decisions.

So far, there is no question that responsibility was served. All our men did what they thought was best for the whole nation. They were not biased for any special interest nor devoted first to the selfish advancement of themselves. It would have been excusable, in an election year, if they had tempered their decisions to reflect most favorably their party and its up-coming candidate. But they didn't. They followed their course in non-partisan spirit until the effect, if any, was harm to the Republican reputation.

This leaves unanswered a big question about responsibility. Does it also mean that our chiefs must be wise and correct to be responsible? Or are their good intentions enough? Should results be measured to decide whether executives have served us responsibly?

At this point theory and practice part company. In theory, of course public officials have to be competent to fulfill their responsibility. In practice we Americans, as our English cousins, do not hold officials responsible except in the most general way. If the economy goes to pot, we vote a president out. At least we did in 1932.

President Eisenhower and his political executives tried to repair the U-2 disclosure, tried honestly and ineptly. The result that gave the Soviets an argument to use against the United States and its President, and to accuse us for the failure of the Summit Conference, was not held against the officials. They may have erred. So the nation had to support them.

VII

The contention so far is that the results of government depend upon the quality of administration. Such plebeian matters as organization, personnel, and responsibility can make the difference between skillful handling or blundering in such episodes as Camp David, U-2, and the Summit Conference.

The quality of administration depends upon organization and the people who use organization. Structure of organization is to administration what a house is to the life of the people in it. It is an arrangement of units in relation to each other. When units are properly arranged, the work to be done—and the heart of this work will be the making of decisions, of which U-2 was a set of examples—can be done with more foresight, acumen, and accuracy than when the units are arranged cumbersomely. No structure, whether it be organization or dwelling, can substitute for talented people, but good people need good structure. By analogy, when the U-2 was captured, honest, and surely able, officials had a harder time trying to cook two meals in twelve kitchens than if they had been able to use only two kitchens. Their talents were held down by the burden of coordination that could have been avoided.

PART TWO ORGANIZATION

CHAPTER 4 PRESENT
ORGANIZATION

To BE IN THE SWIM THESE DAYS ONE MUST TALK about defense posture, as if a nation had knees, shoulders, chin, and fists. Well, the defense posture of the federal executive is a sprawl.

One way to see it is to imagine the President looking outward from his lonely desk. He sees first his immediate assistants, some 25 of them working on whatever he tells them to do but always specializing too in such subjects as press relations, military affairs, daily appointments, or foreign policy. These are the closest aides to the President. They are loyal to him first and always, unlike heads of departments, who must be loyal to their departments as well as to the President.

Assistants to the President, according to one of our myths, do not make decisions nor interfere with the heads of departments. In practice they do, as everyone of experience knows. They have only to recommend or suggest to get the same results as if they had commanded. Everyone knows that they are likely to be closer to the President than anyone else. All they need do is to make their ideas known, always reflecting the interest and the personal policies of the President as if he were himself making the decision. "I always found a powerful magic," one of them told me once, "in the mere words, 'this is the White House calling,' spoken by the telephone operator. Heads of departments, governors, mayors,

31

heads of corporations and labor unions all assumed from the sheer magical aura that the President himself was on the line with me or, at least, had told me to call."

Next beyond his personal aides the President thinks of agencies within the Executive Office of the President, a big and growing adolescent that lives in part next door to the White House in the old State-War-Navy building. Here in this next circle are the Bureau of the Budget, the Council of Economic Advisers, the secret Central Intelligence Agency (in its own much publicized building), and the Office of Emergency Planning. He sees the heads of these fairly regularly. They work directly for him.

In the next circle are the elaborate departments headed by members of his Cabinet: State, Treasury, Defense, Justice, Post Office, Interior, Agriculture, Commerce, Labor, and Health, Education, and Welfare. The heads of these departments see the President in a group perhaps once a week and as individuals as often as possible—but seldom as often as they would like. They compete with each other and sometimes with him. Their own jobs are almost as complex and as tense as his own; their ambitions keen; their sense of importance well honed by the deference they get everywhere except in the White House. While they are in office and very important people, few cabinet members contemplate that history will forget them. So they count themselves important enough, and they are, for the President to have to bargain with them. They are part of the intricate executive politics by which a President leads and commands, a process well defined by Richard E. Neustadt in *Presidential Power, the Politics of Leadership*.

In another belt, beginning to be remote, are the agencies whose heads are not members of the cabinet; for example, the National Aeronautics and Space Administration, Veterans Administration, Atomic Energy Commission, United States Information Agency, or Federal Aviation Agency.

And on the outer rim are what some humorless artist of gobbledygook labelled "multi-headed agencies," the boards and commissions. They live, each in its own cave, on the fringe of government; such free and remote political creatures as the Interstate

Commerce Commission, Federal Power Commission, or the Securities and Exchange Commission. No President can keep close watch over the multi-heads.

II

The number of units whose heads the President sees is only the beginning. The Executive Branch is a labyrinth. Channels connect rooms in so vast a net that no man can know the whole. A letter addressed to the President about some small matter flows outward to a department, to a bureau within the department, to a division within the bureau, to a section within the division, to a unit within a section, to a person within the unit, who will prepare a reply. If an answer is needed from the field a channel leads there too, from Washington to a region, to a district, to a local office, or, if the matter is international, to an office in another country. The names given to units and areas vary, but the principle is always the same. Federal offices of many kinds are located literally around the globe, from the Distant Early Warning line to Antarctica, from the District of Columbia around the world to Beltsville, Maryland, next door.

Decisions are made in bureaus, divisions, sections, and units, as well as in departments and the White House.

It is not enough to say that the President has to deal with eighty very important people in the Executive Branch, for that was the absurd number in 1962 after those inside the Executive Office of the President were added to the heads of departments and agencies outside. His work load comes from the thousands of sub-units as well. Of course he long ago stopped any real supervision for all but two types of decision, one the decision that is brought to him by his very highest subordinates and the other the very rare decision that he initiates himself. He would be foolish to try for anything more. His great task as an executive is to set a tone for all subordinates, then deal with only the most important decisions. And being an executive is only one of his several jobs; he cannot spend his full time at this alone.

III

The trouble comes when coordination is needed. One of the central duties of an executive is to coordinate all the policies, actions, and equipment, wherever available, to the purpose at hand. A failure of coordination was at the heart of the U-2 affair. The policies and actions of Camp David and the Summit Conference were not coordinated with the policies and actions of the Central Intelligence Agency and the National Aeronautics and Space Administration.

Pinned down, it was a failure of the President to perform as an executive. No one was in charge. In this case only the President could be in charge. As the Executive Branch is now organized, only he could coordinate the Secretary of State and his department, the Central Intelligence Agency of the Executive Office of the President, and the National Aeronautics and Space Administration. Only the President can ever under our Constitution coordinate the armed forces and the State Department and other civil units. Only the President is Commander in Chief.

The difficulty of coordination increases with each added unit that deals with a subject. For two subjects in the U-2 affair, intelligence and summit conference, twelve units got involved. Now the impressive fact is that this number is not at all unusual. A news story (March 5, 1961) says that President Kennedy met with his chief advisers on disarmament. Eight people besides the President had to be present for minimum coordination. Four assistants to the President were at work on this subject. Four others represented the State and Defense Departments, the Joint Chiefs of Staff, and the Atomic Energy Commission. Another news story (October 29, 1961) tells of plans to send a high level group to Japan to discuss trade and other international economic affairs with high officials of Japan. Five Cabinet members, an undersecretary, and two of the President's aides were to go. And still another news story (February 8, 1962) says the President had appointed a committee on the stockpile of critical material, some of the most strategic being available only from other countries. The heads of seven agencies made up the committee. Such news is common in any year.

IV

The sprawl shows as clear as anywhere in the organization for the conduct of foreign affairs. No corset of soothing words can possibly hide it.

There were in 1962—and the number varies little for any other of twenty years—26 persons and agencies involved consistently in foreign affairs, 12 in the Executive Office of the President and 14 outside.[1] The President is not included in this count. Inside the Executive Office of the President were the Central Intelligence Agency, Bureau of the Budget, Office of Emergency Planning, and the interagency committees that might be called agencies in their own right when they meet, the National Security Council, and the National Aeronautics and Space Council. Also inside the Executive Office of the President were these individuals: a Special Assistant for National Security Affairs, a Military Adviser, the Military Aide, who has much more responsibility in military liaison and policy than the title implies, a Special Representative and Adviser on African, Asian, and Latin-American Affairs, a Special Assistant and Food for Peace Coordinator, a Special Representative for (foreign) Trade Negotiation, and a Special Assistant for Foreign Aid. When these titles and persons disappear, others will take their place if the pattern of the past twenty years continues.

Outside the Executive Office of the President, these departments and agencies are consistently engaged in foreign affairs: the De-

[1] Here, as elsewhere, the figures for a particular year are used only as illustration of a general point. The shape of the federal Executive Branch changes constantly but slowly. Figures for 1962 are not precisely true for every month of 1962 and certainly not precisely true for 1952 or 1972, but they illustrate the general condition of the federal executive for any year since 1940, when the new emphasis on foreign affairs began. Unless the pattern changes drastically, the figures will illustrate the point ten years hence.

partments of State, Defense, Treasury, Justice, Agriculture, Commerce, and Labor and the Atomic Energy Commission, National Aeronautics and Space Administration, U.S. Information Agency, the Export-Import Bank, U.S. Tariff Commission, Foreign Claims Settlement Commission, and, just to be complete, the American Battle Monuments Commission.

Two departments, State and Defense, had semi-autonomous units within them whose heads could (in some cases by law and in others by the weight of their work and prestige) almost be counted as additional separate agencies. State technically encompassed on a chart, but held doubtful control in fact, over the Agency for International Development, the Peace Corps, and the Arms Control and Disarmament Agency. Defense had within it the professional military heads in the Joint Chiefs of Staff, who could always give advice to Congress, although most of the time they were good soldiers and accepted the decisions of their civilian superiors in the Executive Branch, the Secretary of Defense and the President.

The phrase "consistently engaged in foreign affairs" needs definition. Some agencies, such as the U.S. Information Agency, are just as full time as the State and Defense departments in this work. Others, such as Treasury, are first concerned with domestic work but have as well such a steady task in foreign affairs that they contain permanent subdivisions that do nothing else. Examples in 1962 were the Office of International Finance in the Treasury, the Immigration and Naturalization Service of Justice, the Foreign Agricultural Service of Agriculture, the Bureau of International Programs and the Bureau of International Business Operations in Commerce, the Bureau of International Labor Affairs in Labor, the Division of International Affairs of the Atomic Energy Commission, and the Office of International Programs of the National Aeronautics and Space Administration.

Some other units are engaged part-time in foreign affairs as steady work. Some examples in 1962 were the Bureau of Customs in Treasury, the Public Health Service of Health, Education, and Welfare, or the Narcotics Bureau of Treasury. There were 40 such part-time units in 1962.

Those individuals and agencies who deal with the President are still only the beginning of the sprawl. Each main department has a sprawl within itself.

The Secretary of State, for example, in the summer of 1961 had 24 subordinates who reported to him. He also had to deal rather steadily with American ambassadors overseas, in addition to his subordinates in Washington.

Almost as difficult is the job of the Secretary of Defense. He had 16 reporting to him in 1961. They included such eminent and complicated chiefs in their own realms as the Joint Chiefs of Staff (counted as one) and the Secretaries of Army, Navy, and Air Force.

Surely all the units that are directed by law to do something in foreign relations, either full or part time, make close direction and coordination difficult if not impossible. The search then is for some organization that will allow the President and a few subordinates to control what happens under their responsibility.

CHAPTER 5   RISKS AND

PURPOSES OF ORGANIZATION

ORGANIZATION FOR ITS OWN SAKE IS ALWAYS A threat and too often a fact. It stops good work in favor of busy-work; all energy is spent in coordination, with none left for the attainment of dreams. Administration becomes an end itself instead of the means to an end. People spend so much time deciding what to do and how to do it that they never get much done.

The growth of organization for its own sake, and of coordination as an end in itself, was malignant in the conduct of diplomacy by 1960. Committees were one sign of it. Each time a committee was created in the hope of curing sprawl, manpower was wasted in attending meetings. As the number of committees increased, the same man became a member of several committees. Because the important matters were discussed in committees, it became a matter of prestige to belong to committees. Agencies sought to place representatives on committees. Individuals felt, with cause, that their merit would be measured by their number of assignments to committees. The more pungent souls remarked all this. Walking away from one meeting a group of us once passed an open door and looked upon another meeting. "There's a conference I was not invited to," said one man. "I must be slipping." And a forthright Army officer assigned to the Secretary of Defense in 1960 told me in Wisconsin, "The only way I get any real work done is to come on field trips. In Washington all I do is attend committee meetings to discuss what we should do and how we would do it if we ever got started."

Other apparatus added signs of strangulation. Staff meetings became too large and too frequent. Meetings once a week became once a day. Two or three chairs grew to ten or thirty. By Harry Truman's time, the President began his day with a meeting of six to twelve or more of his immediate aides. He faced later meetings with larger groups. Bodies such as the Cabinet and National Security Council turned out in meeting to be more than the number of legally ordained members. The Budget Director, the Director of Central Intelligence, presidential assistants, the Ambassador to the United Nations and others were added for the sake of fuller coordination. Sometimes an outfield ring of subordinates was added to the participants. These too needed to be kept informed. They were to listen but not speak unless spoken to. Again there was prestige in attending staff meetings, even as a silent spectator, and men sought the honor. Perceptive executives had to be vigilant to hold the numbers down.

The mimeographed news sheet, circulated to those who need to know what is happening and what others are doing, is in one way the saddest confession of sprawl. A busy man who is doing something should not spend his time reading about what others are doing. He should be making news, not reading it. If a man is inexperienced, unperceptive, or plain lazy he can, on the other hand, find a good excuse to do little more than keep up with what is going on. The flow of inside bulletins grew in the conduct of diplomacy.

II

A day of 1959 in the life of the State Department's Assistant Secretary for Policy Planning will illustrate the disease. This man headed the Policy Planning Staff. Its job is to propose long-term programs, to anticipate problems, to study and report on broad politico-military problems, to evaluate current policy in the light of the future, to coordinate all planning in the Department—in sum, to be in charge of looking ahead and to recommend moves for the future. When international relations consist of move and counter-move, the staff charged with planning should be the heart of the matter.

Our greatest weakness, and the same is true of our allies, is that we still live by the creed which says that a diplomat reports events and a Chief of State decides what to do about them but no one makes events happen. Such a passive acceptance of fate can be suicidal when communism has built into its doctrine the urgency of planning. We are satisfied with our ways. The communists want revolution, and all revolutionists are planners by their very nature. So we live in anxiety. The communists are always doing things to stir up the water. We like quiet water. They want a storm. When they stir up the water, we respond with plans to quiet the waves. We almost never look ahead.

We did not look ahead in China in the 1940s to adjust to the total victory of the communists—or else to enter with our own force to kill off the revolution—and we now live blindly with our most dangerous adversary. We did not look ahead in Africa in the 1950s, or in Southeast Asia, or the Western Hemisphere of all places. For the world's most powerful democratic nation to allow a revolution to be taken over by communists in a nation less than a hundred miles away because we had not looked ahead and planned action is so preposterous that men of the future will find it hard to believe.

A need for looking ahead produced the Policy Planning Staff in 1947. Only at times has it been respected by the higher-ups who make policy. Secretaries Marshall and Acheson listened, if not to the Planning Staff at least to someone who looked ahead enough to propose the containment policy and the Marshall Plan. Secretaries Byrnes and Dulles marched to no drums save their own. These four set and deployed our strength for the Cold War. On the whole we have been on the defensive. Such rare large policies as contain-ment and the Marshall Plan were still defensive. We were keeping the bear at bay, trying to keep him from taking more neighbors than he had already eaten.

Once we had adopted policies, we failed to look ahead within those policies and make adjustments to change. When a time came to step up political and economic weapons in the containment policy we were not ready. One result was a thumping setback in the Middle East, where for pique over an upstart, bad-mannered dictator we withdrew support for the Aswan Dam and made life harder for ourselves in the long run. Nor were we ready with a military alternative. When our allies the British and French used force in their plan to get rid of the dictator, we refused to join them, denounced them, and self-righteously bewildered them.

The Policy Planning Staff ideally would have plans ready for such main events as the victory of communism in China, the rush to independence in Africa, Castro's inclination to take comfort from communists, and the unabashed guile of Nasser in Egypt. A staff can anticipate only if it is free of routine operations, as intended when the Policy Planning Staff was established.

No contemplation is allowed when organization and coordination become the end and not the means.

III

The Assistant Secretary of State for Policy Planning in 1959 arrived at his desk at 8:45 A.M. and began a day filled with keeping up with what was going on, as reported by Robert Ellsworth Elder in *The Policy Machine.* There was little time for quiet analysis. On the Assistant Secretary's desk when he entered the office was a four to five page "Daily Staff Summary." This gave in brief the most important cables that arrived in the Department during the night and a list of all decisions made the previous day by the Secretary of State and the undersecretaries. Selected news items from the Department's Office of News were also on the desk with the summary.

Thirty minutes later, at 9:15 A.M., the Assistant Secretary for Policy went to the Secretary's daily staff conference. Here the Director for Intelligence and Research gave an intelligence briefing. Then members of the group raised problems for discussion.

Several times a week members of the Policy Planning Staff attended staff meetings in the various bureaus of the Department, held just before or just after the Secretary's staff meeting.

At 10:15 A.M. each day the Policy Planning Staff had its own meeting for thirty minutes. Members briefed each other.

It was now 10:45 A.M. "With this background of information," Mr. Elder reported with a straight face, "they are ready to begin the day's work."

Perhaps 10:45 A.M. is about as early as a planner should begin to contemplate large issues and main trends. There is no magic hour. One truth, however, is established in the human experience: If a thinker waits until 10:45 to start work, he should be left alone before then. He needs time to straighten the junk on his desk, to drink coffee, to pull his ear, to read a newspaper, and to slide gradually into his day. He should not be expected to trot from one meeting to another to keep up with the transient actions that make up the routine of government.

Those who organize such business fail to see that planners need to see patterns and not current events. A mind cluttered with records of routine daily decisions is crippled for the perception of world patterns. It is filled with what happened yesterday in the Congo and not with the Congo as part of the whole web south of the Sahara and the great decisions that the United States should make concerning the new Africa.

There remained before lunch one and three quarter hours, time to talk or write or think. We can rule out the lunch hour as time for planning. Usually nothing but indigestion is produced in Washington luncheons. The reasons for such luncheons are always the same, and none is related to thoughtful discussion. Somebody wants to line up an associate for some plan, or wants his support in a fight. A subordinate wants to sell his boss some pet idea, or needs encouragement for the sake of his morale. A friend from outside the government wants a favor, or wants to tell the government man how silly his policies look to the outside. A man without enough work to do simply wants to "keep in contact" with another man who hasn't enough work. The only civilized behavior at table in Washington takes place after 7 P.M. It is rare even then. The men of government usually want to talk shop. Their wives, bored spouses of ambitious men who think first of their work, could not care less and gather in their end of the room to discuss children.

By 1:30 P.M., to get back to Mr. Elder's report, the "Daily Secret Summary," accompanied by the "Daily Opinion Summary" from the Bureau of Public Affairs, and a report on legislative matters from the Congressional Relations Staff had arrived. We are not told what the "Daily Secret Summary" is, and this is reasonable if it really needs to be kept secret, but we are told that it was prepared by public affairs officers in the geographic bureaus. These were public relations men. They were concerned with the Department's appearance in this country and with the nation's public relations abroad.

Their job was, in part, to collect answers to possible questions that might come up in the Secretary's press conference. The official position to be given the public, in other words, was assembled by public affairs officers. In a sense the press conference is the American version of British questions in the House. It is just as important for all officials to know the American policy as for members of the Government to show unity in Parliament.

Equally it is important for officials to be left alone when they are not directly concerned. Once this notion of coordination by mimeograph gets loose, there is no check for the spate that can follow. Busy men probably don't read the stuff. (They cannot avoid staff conferences; their bosses and associates expect them to be there.) Lazy men welcome it as an excuse for being. Certainly, policy planners need not keep up daily with answers to press questions, clues to public opinion in the United States, and the status of bills in Congress.

The flow of paper was not ended. By 3 P.M. the Assistant Secretary received the "Afternoon Staff Summary." This was a late edition of the summary which began the day. It was now six or seven pages long and now contained a list of decisions made by Assistant Secretaries and others of equivalent rank.

In addition to all these bulletins and staff meetings, it should be understood, came special memoranda and conferences. Papers had to be written on demand, and requests came from several sources including the National Security Council, which worked then by an elaborate system of papers on each topic considered.

Coordination ate up the time that should have been spent in planning. In different words, the same could be said for any part of the Department and government.

IV

The first step in planning any organization should be to ask what is it to do, what is the job, what purpose is to be served?

In the conduct of diplomacy the central purpose is to make *foreign policy* in the broadest sense, including planning to make events happen. Another purpose is to carry on *foreign relations*. The first consists of deciding what to do. The second means the array of contacts between nations through embassies and consulates, other civil offices, military forces, delegates to international conferences, and chiefs of state. Such contacts range from alliances in war to checking ships in and out of port. Private foreign relations in business, education, the arts, entertainment, sports, and tourism are also relevant, but in free nations they are taboo to government direction. It is unthinkable that any government give orders to the British or American tourist, and probably just as well, considering how unpredictable some tourists are.

We are plagued in the West by a refusal to distinguish between foreign policy and foreign relations. There is reason of long standing for the confusion.

The difficulty begins when experienced people see truly that issues arise in foreign relations and the settlement of the issues constitutes policy. They say that policy is made in the cables. Policy is made by answering the mail. Such foreign policy is bound to be sporadic in change, unplanned, and no more than the expression of American reaction to the mail that other nations wrote. We react to the issues that others raise.

All this is normal and to be expected. It is what career diplomats do in their profession, and it calls for knowledge, skill, and poise.

The error starts when we assume that this is the whole of foreign policy. It is only that portion that we cannot avoid making. The mail must be answered. In theory such policy from foreign relations should be made under the guidance of larger policy. A professional diplomat would say this larger policy should come from his political chief, repeating the refrain that has persisted in career diplomacy since the time when dukes and kings made their own plans and used diplomats only to report, represent, and negotiate.

In the modern state political chiefs are executives who head large and complex institutions. The President and Prime Minister cannot keep the peace by arranging a betrothal. They are besieged by subordinates who want decisions on the issues that come from foreign relations. A Secretary of State or a President could find all their time absorbed in answering the mail. After some years thoughtful and worried people will begin to say that we have not defined our national goals. They may even try to make systematic the common hope for peace, prosperity, and the pursuit of happiness.

Noble generalities that result from the frustration of being swamped by the mail are, however, only the beginning of foreign policy. They have to be refined to decisions of what we want as the end result in such monotonous places as China, Africa, Latin America, and the Middle East. Once the large policies are decided, then issues raised in the daily mail can be settled in a way to serve the long-range plan.

The big purpose to be served by organization is, then, to make long-range foreign policy as well as to make the daily, routine decisions of foreign relations. This isn't easy. Long-range policy should reflect national purpose. It should also blend political, economic, military, cultural, and administrative considerations, and these occur in many different parts of government. The machinery for making the blend can be constructed; it is not beyond the reach of man; but it is not easy.

The next purpose of organization is to make sure that policy changes to keep up with needs. One great, overshadowing threat in large government is always that once a course is adopted it is never questioned again. Only when outside events come crashing through the walls of a tunnel, to draw an image from a building contractor friend who thinks the biggest burden of the human race is what he calls tunnel vision, will some policies ever be changed. In terms of organization and management, staff work provides the questioning that ought to be applied to all policy, large and small, old and new.

A third purpose is to provide efficiently all that is needed to make and carry out policy. This means information and analysis, money and travel, people, posts and equipment, and all the other necessities of international relations. Need it be said that to stop with this purpose alone is to stagnate? The work of research and management exists only to enable people to make policy and then to question it for change. Management for itself alone can become the most burdensome of all busywork.

Should it be necessary to say that the mere provision of units labelled to do certain work is not all the answer? The Policy Planning Staff in 1959 was a ludicrous contradiction of the bureaucratic credo that to solve a problem one creates a new unit. This Staff was not alone. Others too spent their time at busywork, and the chart was sprinkled with the shells of units once created but never abolished. Men have to be supervised after they have been organized. Executives are hired to supervise men. The executives fail when staff units, created for good cause, begin to work in order to appear to be doing their work. In 1959 the Policy Planning Staff, and all others of its same frustration then and now and in the future, could have been directed by a competent executive to stop keeping up with what was going on and start planning something.

V

A less obvious purpose of organization is to provide counterbalances in the interplay of human nature that exists whenever people are organized, or, for that matter, whenever people meet in any circumstance. Not much can be done about human nature. Men of good will accept it genially. Men of bad will try to manipulate it for their own ends and win too often for comfort.

Most humans are unaware of human nature. In group conference they will skip from foible to foible and never realize that this is not the only way to think. If an aware member of the group questions certain assumptions he is marked a time waster or an odd one.

Something more has to be said about the incongruities that come from human nature. Organization can alleviate the trouble caused by human nature, as we can note in some examples. At the same time, it is obvious again that organization by itself is no solution. It is no more than an apparatus in which people behave as people. They can get more done with more ease in a well designed organization than in a poor one. This was said earlier. There is no need to expand here.

Human nature, as a hypothesis, leans on assumptions that are accepted by most members of a group, whether or not the assumptions have been tested. "The exchange of students creates international understanding." Here is an assumption widely held inside and outside government. No one really knows whether it is true. No one has questioned the assumption in the degree needed. Foreign students have been coming to the United States for generations. Many of them became leaders in their own lands. Did their policies as leaders show love or hate? What difference appeared between those of color, who had to endure American prejudice, and those of white origin? Or between Latins and Arabs? A staff unit could test the assumption.

We hold some other assumptions. Is it really true, or only an article of faith, that technical assistance to the people of underdeveloped nations will make them favor freedom? It could make them jealous and resentful. Is it true that business cartels are bad and international trade would be healthier if the whole world had antitrust laws? Most other free nations do not agree. Is it true that the reluctance of private firms to invest in underdeveloped countries is due mainly to fear of political instability? Perhaps American firms are making all the profits they want in mature nations and simply do not want to be bothered by the excessive and erratic regulation that is typical of new, jealous, and immature nations.

We know so little about our assumptions. We spend billions to carry them out and spend nothing for the research that would test them. It is human nature, it seems, for groups to make policy by stereotypes. It is good administration to break up such a fantasy world by staff work that questions stereotypes.

Organization can provide critics of the group product, persons set up in separate units and told to examine all proposed decisions for change. Let's face it; a free thinker has a legal but not a real right to say exactly what he thinks. If he wants to be accepted as normal, as most of us do, he must say what is expected by his normal fellowmen. This is as true in government bureaucracy as it is in church, business, profession, or club.

For in bureaucracy the center of decisions is the small group. And the associations in a small group are about as intimate as humans ever get outside of living together or fighting side by side in battle. Each member of the group depends upon the other members for something. He needs to be liked. He wants to earn more and rise higher, and promotion depends upon what associates think of him. He believes in the same purposes as his associates. He enjoys company and wants respect. He wants prestige. He knows that the quickest way to get a job done is to reach reasonable agreement. A member who raises questions that are not readily understood and answered threatens to delay a decision. Anyway, the others say, he is a minority because no one else thinks that his question is important.

Above all, a member of the bureaucratic group is eccentric if he questions the basic assumptions. Literally, the other members will not listen to him. They will think that questioning assumptions is a waste of time. The assumptions are fundamental policy. They are the starting point. You don't tear out the foundations just to re-arrange some furniture in a room upstairs. Never mind that the foundations were never tested for soundness. They are the foundations we have. Everyone has agreed to use them.

The staff unit that is created to be critic, to ask questions about either assumptions or conclusions, will be itself subject to the unreality produced by human nature. Its members will form a group to themselves, and will behave according to human nature in their own group. But the big difference made by organization is that the critics will not depend upon the favor of the members of other groups whose reasoning they criticize. Of course the critics will be unpopular. Staff units usually are. They are outsiders who ask questions about matters that are already settled for the insiders. But they are needed as a check upon the errors of human nature that appear in other groups.

VI

Organization can, to take another example, supply institutional memory, an element usually missing because human nature seems to ignore the past. We of this group and this moment are responsible and competent and we do not think of what went before. Few humans, faced with a problem to solve, can remember that other people were here before they arrived. It may be just as well. A world run by elder statesmen is unthinkable. But time could be saved, and mistakes avoided, if bold new men had a quick reference service to show them the past. This much should not slow them or cloud their inventiveness.

Usable records do not exist now. As a nation we have allowed the technique of keeping records to lag far behind the creation of records that have to be kept. Files are usually incomplete; the essence of what happened is so often verbal and unrecorded that it is not left in the files. The papers that do get into the files are haphazardly selected, and reading them is at best a search for something helpful, not a sure source of light. All who have ever called for a file know how little to expect.

Is the answer then to keep persons on the job longer so that institutional history is carried forward in the heads of those who make it? This is the idea of all those who deplore the fast turn-over in personnel, both career and political, in the conduct of American diplomacy. An argument for using career men to carry memory forward is standard in America, and the practice is long established in Great Britain. Career men are expected to provide continuity when new political chiefs enter and old ones leave in the tides of elections.

The theory is unarguable. Old men know more about the past than young men. In practice, however, this solution is clouded. Old men are also more protective of the past than young men. When change is faster and faster, to check the past only as the first step to meet the future is wiser than to try to preserve the past, as old men do.

The theory falls too on the hard fact that we simply cannot expect good men to stay put in one place. Fast change means new needs for good men, and needs that outrun the supply. In the West, and especially in the United States, we have been changing so rapidly, under the usual acceleration, that we have been short of high-quality executives and staff men in both public and private affairs since 1930. This does not mean that the quality of the men who managed affairs after 1930 was low. To say this would be clear error. Those who fought the Depression, war, and Cold War from 1930 on were as competent as any nation could hope to produce. But there were never enough of them to satisfy the demand. Not even during the Depression, when men sought government work, were there enough good men already trained.

The problems of that time required such new thinking that a whole new kind of talent had to be found. Business was in bad shape and in bad repute. It called for executives who could navigate the new stream of committees, public relations, labor relations, research, and more influence by government. No longer could a rough-handed master of finance, production, and sales run a firm. In his place appeared groups of young men, college trained, more aware of the whole society, often able to switch back and forth easily from private to public bureaucracy. Such young men were not listed as unemployed during the Depression; they had to be found and developed. As war and Cold War followed depression, and change accelerated, they remained relatively in scarce supply.

What was true of business was also true of government. The public service, faced with the Depression, could no longer rely alone upon either civil servants who were too addicted to routine or on political executives who knew how to conserve votes but not how to plan new programs. Old-time civil servants and old-time politicians alike saw with consternation the invasion of new-thinking lawyers, professors, social workers, and intellectual businessmen into public posts. Again, the new kind of public servant was in short supply. The same type was—and is—wanted by both public and private enterprise. In a bureaucratic society, the new men skilled in bureaucratic decision are as scarce as ever and probably always will be so long as acceleration continues to bring change faster and faster.

When there are fewer people than needed for the top jobs, competition sets in. It matters little whether the job is private or public. In either case a group in conference will decide to try to get a good man from where he is to where they need him. In private enterprise they persuade him with their purpose, their group friendliness, more pay, more status, and such intangible tangibles as options to buy stock, pension funds, and expense accounts. In government they persuade him with the same arguments except for stock options, pension funds, and expense accounts.

So long as competition exists, men in a free society will change posts. It seems a forlorn hope that we can ever in this kind of fast change keep the same good men in the same posts long enough to provide in them the institutional memory that should be checked before new decisions are made. That is, assuming that we want to carry history along through the succession of aging men, which is doubtful.

Written administrative histories have been tried as a way to transmit institutional memory. They are written about agencies or about episodes, even about particular decisions and called case studies. In neither Great Britain or the United States are they the answer. Valuable they are, certainly, as records of what happened and as the basis for contemplation.

But only by accident do they deal with a problem that is close kin to one faced later. Only rarely can the historian recapture the subtleties of all that went into a past decision. Those present at the time are not all aware of the same things and will tell a historian different versions in the few times when he can interview participants. All too often the later group faces a problem that is so different from the one its predecessors faced that administrative history is not truly relevant. This is, alas, the fate of policy-makers in accelerated change; they can seldom find any prints to follow.

More in tune with this speedy time is electronic filing, which has already been adopted by some agencies in Washington, including the State Department. Facts are coded into machines for storage. Later when someone wants all the facts on a subject the code for that subject is run through. It will produce from storage all the items under the code.

Decisions of policy can be coded and filed electronically, provided someone states them briefly, concisely, and clearly, not always qualities admired by most members of the human race. When some later group faces a decision on some matter of Latin American politics, for example, the machine can deliver the references and the facts. Of course it is difficult and costly to use the new machines, and the catalog of facts in a machine is only as adequate as the skill of the skull-bound man who made the program.

The results should be worth the cost. We do not seem now to pull things together. We decide for the future without checking the past. We might save much error if we had institutional memory. A staff unit of organization, specializing in electronic records may be the way to serve memory.

VII

No single formula of organization answers all questions. Diplomacy is but another product of government and is therefore in part a product of administration. To satisfy its purposes, some rules can be followed, as we shall say in the next chapter. The rules will be modified to suit particular circumstances, as always when human nature is imperfect, as it has been since Eden. Politics will affect the extent to which the rules are followed. Humans act politically in nearly all their affairs—in business firms, churches, interest groups, social groups, and in government. For some reason they do not call it politics when they put a useless cousin in a private job that otherwise would not be on the chart of organization.

The big question is not whether politics enters but whether the rules of good organization are followed far enough to create a sound design in which political men can accomplish with the least possible trouble the ends they choose.

CHAPTER 6 A JUDGMENT
OF PRESENT ORGANIZATION

A RATIONAL ORGANIZATION OF THE EXECUTIVE branch has to meet, then, these demands, all of which have been discussed before this point and are listed here in review:

1. It must allow easier coordination among agencies, so that the sad chaos of the U-2 affair will not be repeated.

2. Organization should prevent the malignant growth of co-ordination as an end in itself. Housewives in a well designed house need not live only to keep the house clean and serviceable. Officials in a well designed government, executive branch, need not spend more than fractional time at coordination, certainly not as much as in the present State Department. The virus of over-administration, of excessive growth, of circular monkey business threatens all human enterprises. It can be controlled best by tight, economical, easily arranged coordination.

3. Organization should serve the purposes for which it exists. In the case of diplomacy the most noticeable purposes are: (a) to make long-range foreign policy, (b) to make changes in policy, (c) to manage routine foreign relations, (d) to handle all the usual chores of administration so necessary for the pursuit of all other purposes, and (e) to reduce the waste due to human nature.

II

There are rules for organization. In both government and teaching I find that six rules, principles, dogmas, guides, whatever they are called, cover all the most common questions. When the rules are violated, trouble begins; when they are followed, the work goes ahead with little delay due to faults of organization. Simple and unscientific but true, the rules are:

1. Tell each executive clearly what his responsibility is. This means clean-cut assignments of duties, without ambiguity or double meaning. For example, tell an ambassador plainly whether he is responsible for *all* American activities in the country in which he represents the President. Don't tell him and others, as we do now, that he is responsible for American foreign policy in his country without defining the term policy. Few terms are as slippery.

2. When an executive is made responsible for some activity, give him the authority he needs to carry out the responsibility. Wise old bureaucrats never accept a duty unless they know that they also have the necessary authority to go with it.

3. Don't put any person under more than one boss for the same job. (If a person fills more than one job, he may have a separate superior for each, but he should keep his lines straight. This is known as wearing two hats. For one hat the wearer should have only one boss.)

4. Provide staff services; such as budget, personnel, planning, and housekeeping, for each executive as he needs them. Executives up and down the ladder need staff aid according to the size and complexity of their responsibilities.

5. Give each executive only as many immediate subordinates as he can supervise. The number will vary by the volume and kind of work and the quality of subordinates; routine work requires less supervision than new work, and smart, well trained less than stupid, poorly trained people. Duties have to be analyzed to reach the best number.

6. Put together in one unit all activities that are alike. This implies that the units will be defined by the nature of the work. If the job is to deal with commodities, for example, put metals in one unit and grains in another. If it is foreign relations, put Latin America in one unit and Western Europe in another. Don't have two or more units doing the same principal work. (Of course some work, such as typing or accounting has to be done in all units, and

only analysis should decide whether such duties can be done better in one place or scattered. These are not principal but supporting activities. The division into units should be made according to principal activities.)

All these rules can be applied in the structure of organization, in the choice of units and their linking together. The architect applies rules when he plans only one kitchen for a small house. A designer of organization applies rules when he draws the chart of a new organization or a plan of reorganization. After learning to think of organization as a structure, filled with people who behave like people, any experienced observer can look at a chart and see whether these six rules have been followed.

I want now to illustrate the pertinence of these rules to present organization for the conduct of diplomacy. Experts will recognize the sketchiness of this exercise and will, I hope, pardon the audacity. I am not trying to write a deep analysis. What I want to show is the possibility that administrative disorder can be cleaned up, that man's experience has taught him some truths that can help, if used. All the studies and recommendations that political scientists make in depth are file fodder unless political chiefs and legislators do something about them. I am oversimplifying deliberately because I hope to show that policy-makers can do something if they have a mind to.

III

For the first rule, that each executive should be told clearly what his duties are, take the Secretary of State as example. Once, in the beginning, he was clearly in charge of all foreign relations for the President, and the image was created properly that in this area he was chief administrator and sole adviser to the President. The military was an instrument of foreign policy. In the extremity of war the Army and Navy were diplomats by other means but in peace they were quiet servants waiting to be called. Commercial foreign relations were private; the government helped with some services and never dreamed of foreign aid, which by another definition is the export of goods and services by government. Cultural relations were unplanned and unheeded by government beyond the usual consular services to travellers.

No one conceived that foreign policy would soon demand for each decison the intricate composition of political, military, economic, and cultural point and counterpoint. Few realize this yet, to tell the truth. No one thought about it at all in the old days. Diplomats were general practitioners, very general, and the Secretary of State was truly responsible for all foreign relations until the shooting began, when the military took the field for combat.

Herbert Hoover, hailed for his skill at administration, began the modern confusion of duties for the Secretary of State. When Mr. Hoover was Secretary of Commerce under Harding and Coolidge, he established representatives of the Commerce Department in overseas missions separate from the State Department's foreign service. Next the Department of Agriculture established its own agents and offices overseas. The Commerce and Agriculture men were never numerous as compared to the State Department's foreign service, and they were absorbed by the State Department in 1939, although the agricultural men were returned to their own department in 1954. These separate agents for Commerce and Agriculture set three precedents. First, Congress and the President recognized that other civil agencies than the State Department had full-time work in foreign relations. Second, they decided that specialties, in this case commercial and agricultural reporting and promotion, would be handled by specialists. Third, they allowed other agencies than the State Department to open offices in foreign lands alongside the diplomatic and consular missions.

War and cold war extended the precedents. During the Second World War the new agencies were thought to be temporary. They were so in name and were disbanded at war's end. Before long they were back under new names that changed from time to time but always reflected the same activities. The wartime Office of Strategic Services was gone; the Central Intelligence Agency was new, and thriving, in the age-old work of espionage and subversion. The Office of War Information disappeared; the United States Information Agency appeared to conduct propaganda abroad. The Foreign Economic Administration disbanded; the Agency for International Development evolved to manage civilian foreign aid. Theaters of war, where the military ruled over civil agencies, became, first, zones of occupation and, finally, areas where American forces were stationed, as in Germany and Japan. And forces were by international agreement stationed too in such places as Great Britain, Western Europe, and the Philippines. The specialties of secret intelligence, propaganda, economic aid, and military operations were established for keeps.

None could argue that the Secretary of State had clear responsibility. He was vaguely assigned to foreign relations. So were the heads of the other agencies. From 1942 on this lack of clear-cut assignment was debated. Studies and executive orders too numerous and too repetitive to catalog here were issued in the hope that words would make the vagueness disappear. Words failed. No President and Congress were willing to say that only the Secretary of State was in charge of foreign relations. The best they would give him was a statement that he was in charge of general foreign policy and the specialists had to conform to it. Since general foreign policy is made up of the proper blend of specialties, the Secretary in his strongest hour could do no more than be chairman of a group that included the new specialists.

The peak of decision by consensus was the National Security Council under Presidents Truman and Eisenhower where the Secretary of State, the Secretary of Defense, and the Director of Emergency Planning, a specialist in economic policies, had equal voices. It was easy to suspect that the chief of secret intelligence also shared equally although he was legally a servant of the Council. One could also surmise that under Truman and Eisenhower the Secretary of the Treasury also carried weight, although not a member of the Council.

IV

Rule two, that adequate authority should go with responsibility, is almost certain to be violated when responsibility is left unclear.

Few officials in foreign affairs are given firm authority. Such phrases as "in collaboration," "subject to approval," "in consultation with" are common in the definition of authority in this field. They reflect a reluctance to give clear assignments and emphatic authority. If an executive's superior, at whatever rank, supports him in the use of authority, the words on paper, and words unwritten, make little difference. Authority in a bureaucracy comes not from the word but from who supports whom how far. But in this case authority is diffused in support by executives as well as in the word of law. Franklin D. Roosevelt wanted his executives to compete. John F. Kennedy appeared to like confused authority. Harry S Truman and Dwight D. Eisenhower were neater than Roosevelt and Kennedy but never so neat as to give any subordinate the sense of assurance. Mr. Eisenhower pointedly expected what he called teamwork, without often acting as boss of the team, and without direction a team will ooze instead of hit the line hard.

If diffusion and variety are true on Olympus where very important persons get through their days, it is just as commonly true on the slopes. Almost never can an executive in the federal government make a decision on his own authority. He must check with another executive whose unit is also concerned, or with a staff office such as budget or personnel, or with his superior to see if that eminence is still hitched.

Charlton Ogburn, Jr., once patiently recorded the moves required to reach a policy on a hypothetical telegram.[1] Our ambassador to X, a country in Western Europe, had reported that relations would be strained if the United States failed to vote with X in the United Nations against consideration of a question about one of X's colonies. The action copy of this telegram went to the desk officer for Country X, whose superior was the officer in charge of the section, whose superior in turn was chief of the office of Western European Affairs, whose superior was the Assistant Secretary of State at the head of the Bureau of European Affairs,

[1] "The Flow of Policymaking in the Department of State," in *The Formulation and Administration of United States Foreign Policy*, by the Brookings Institution, 86th Cong., 2nd Sess., Senate Committee on Foreign Relations, 1960, pp. 172–177.

whose superior was an Under Secretary of State or the Secretary. This is the way authority is distributed on a chart of hierarchy. The responsibility for deciding American policy toward X could be located in any of these executives. The important thing is to give the responsible man enough authority to make the decision.

In the tortured day of Washington the telegram failed to take such a simple route as the one up and down the hierarchy. Information copies went to at least ten people in the State Department other than the desk officer and to at least two other agencies, the Department of Defense and the Central Intelligence Agency. Any person who received a copy was supposed to give his advice if he had any to give. Information copies are distributed to get such advice, as well as to keep the right people informed.

The desk officer conferred with his superior before drafting a reply. Together they conferred with their next superior, the Assistant Secretary for European Affairs. Such conferences before action are usual for any matter of importance, as this was. So far they are confined within the one line of both authority and responsibility for Country X. The desk officer prepared a telegram to say that if X dragged its feet on a colonial issue, the communists would gain strength in the colony. This was no bold statement, but it could be read by our ambassador to X to mean that the United States would not support X in the United Nations.

Before that telegram could go out, it had to be approved by three separate, coordinate bureaus. These three were not responsible for relations with Country X, but they shared the authority. The Bureau of Near Eastern and South Asian Affairs was given its share of authority because it dealt with a part of the world where colonialism was a hot issue. The Bureau of African Affairs entered because the colony in question was in its territory. The Bureau of International Organization Affairs deals with American representatives to international conferences. It was included in this authority because the issue upon which Country X wanted us to join against the colony was to come up for a vote in the General Assembly.

When one says that a bureau approves a telegram, one means that some unit within that bureau, perhaps an individual but more likely two or three in conference, decide to try for a change from the original draft that came from the point of first responsibility. More conferences follow. When the debate is finished over which version is to be used, the telegram has to travel in each bureau through layers of approval. It also has to travel sidewise to all the other bureaus that are involved. In an extreme sense authority in this case was divided not only among four bureaus but among all the individuals in each bureau who spoke their pieces on the policy.

The telegram brought the next move from our ambassador in X. That country, he said, will fight to avoid a United Nations question about its colonial affairs. What exactly will the United States do and how far will it go to get supporters? Now a position had to be taken toward the discussion of X and its colony in the General Assembly. To reach this position four new units were added to the four already mentioned. They were the Policy Planning Staff, the Bureau of Public Affairs (to advise on the effects in propaganda), and two Offices of Research and Analysis (intelligence), one for Western Europe and the other for the Near East, South Asia, and Africa. By now eight units, each subdivided into individuals and groups, shared the authority to make the policy. But the X desk officer and his line of superiors still had the responsibility for American relations with X.

As all people who can quote a little Donne know, no man is an island, and executives of government should not expect to be left alone to do as they please. We are not considering such extremity. Experience with organization means only that if a man is given a job, he should be allowed to do it. He is so allowed only when he is given the authority to go with the responsibility.

V

On the charts very few persons have more than one superior and the third rule is followed on paper. Violation comes in fact because authority is divided in fact, as we have just seen. When a man drafts a telegram that must be approved by a half dozen or more persons superior in status to himself he thinks twice. He is not under the command of all, but he has to get the agreement of all, and this in its way is compulsion. The demand for consensus can be just as heavy as the hand of a single commander. If authority is matched with responsibility, as required by rule two, the unwritten duplication of superiors is also avoided. Because our culture loves discussion and esteems consensus, multiple superiors are common in fact though not in the charts.

VI

Rule four says to give each executive all the staff services he needs. In Washington obedience to this rule is overdone for some services and underdone for others. All that busywork in the State Department, all those internal bulletins about what was happening and what officials were deciding, illustrates overdone staff service, in this case too much undigested inside intelligence. Too little planning is an example of underdone staff services. Too little evaluation of intelligence is another.

One way to estimate whether staff services are overdone, or underdone, is to compare the number of employees devoted to such services to the number devoted to carrying out the main functions of the agency.[2] The main functions of the State Department are to shape foreign policy and to conduct foreign relations. Employees who serve these functions directly are in the Office of the Secretary and Under Secretary, with some exceptions, in the Bureau of Intelligence and Research, the Bureau of Educational and Cultural Affairs, in the five regional bureaus, in the Bureau of International Organization Affairs, the Bureau of Economic Affairs, the Bureau of Security and Consular Affairs, and in the mission to the United Nations and the Boundary and Water Commission.

Staff services are of two kinds. Some provide planning, the review of policy and operation, the provision of internal information,

[2] This is no scientific way to measure staff services. It is only the handiest. Needs vary from one agency to another with the kind of work, the geographic spread, the quality of people, and other factors. A count of personnel is indicative, however, especially when other signs, such as the overdose of mimeographed intelligence described earlier, also suggest that too many people are helping other people do their work.

legal advice, public relations, and Congressional relations. These are called, for want of better terms, general staff services. Others assemble the budget, keep the accounts, handle all the paper and other jobs that come from the hiring, care, and retirement of personnel, and the handling of all the many other essential services, from delivery of the mail to the provision of office space and equipment. These are called management staff services.

In the State Department people who perform general staff services are in the Executive Secretariat and the Office of Protocol, partly in the Offices of Secretary and Under Secretary, in the Office of Inspector General for Foreign Assistance, in the Policy Planning Staff, the Legal Adviser's staff, the Bureau of Public Affairs (public relations), and in the office of the Assistant Secretary for Congressional Relations. People who perform management staff services are in the Office of the Deputy Under Secretary for Administration and in the Bureau of Administration.

The same sort of separation can be made for the Agency for International Development and for U.S. Information Agency, the other two civil agencies most prominent and full-time in the conduct of foreign affairs. Unfortunately the figures are not clear for the Defense Department. The number of civilians can be had readily, but the number of military men and women assigned to work alongside civilians in departmental and headquarters work cannot.[3]

When the numbers are added for the two kinds of staff work and cast as percentages of the whole number of employees, the results are startling. They are shown in Table 1.

Something strange goes on here. These figures say that one of every two persons employed by State and the Agency for International Development is engaged in staff work. For every person who does the main job of foreign policy and foreign relations another person helps with either general or management staff services.

[3] All figures used in this analysis are taken from "Organization of Federal Executive Departments and Agencies," data as of January 1, 1962, to accompany committee report No. 22, U.S. Senate Committee on Government Operations (Washington: Government Printing Office, 1962). This informative chart and report are issued annually. Change is constant but never very large, so the figures for 1962 can be accepted as typical of any recent year.

TABLE 1. PERCENTAGES OF EMPLOYEES ASSIGNED TO STAFF SERVICES

	Percentage of All Employees in General Staff Work	Percentage of All Employees in Management Services	Total in Staff Services
State Department	8.5	36.8	45.3
Agency for International Development	7.4	51.2	58.6
U.S. Information Agency	7.3	18.5	25.8

Narrowed to management services alone, one in three in the State Department and one in two for the Agency for International Development serve the main work. It is as if for every two cooks assigned to make the broth, one man for State and two for the Agency make sure that they are budgeted, accounted, recorded, paid and pensioned, transported, housed, and supplied.

Some questions rise immediately. Are these proportions unusual for the federal government? Do the high percentages come from the fact that these agencies have staffs and offices overseas?

The first can hardly be answered except in the broadest sense. No two executive departments or agencies are really comparable. How can the State Department be compared to Post Office or Agriculture? Or how can State even be compared to the Agency for International Development? The first is a policy-making center and conductor of foreign relations. The second is known as an operating agency. Having made this crippling qualification, comparison becomes not evidence but no more than the satisfaction of idle curiosity. Using the same definitions of general staff and management services, a count shows that of the departments only Commerce approaches the same emphasis on staff work. It spends 19.4 of its personnel on general staff and 12.1 percent on management services, or a total of 31.5 percent. Labor is next with 8.9 percent devoted to general staff and 11.0 to management services for a total of 19.9 percent. The others have much lower percentages for staff work: Interior, 6.2; Health, Education, and Welfare, 4.9; Agriculture, 4.4; Treasury, 2.6; and Post Office, 0.7. The Departments of Defense, Army, Navy, and Air Force are not compared at all because, as said before, the extent to which military personnel is used is not given in the source used here. Anyway, the military function is so different from civil functions that comparison is more unreal than for other departments.

Do missions overseas make the difference? The answer appears to be no, unless all jobs are being done twice, once in the mission and again in Washington. Each mission has its own staff services. In a large embassy the chief administrative officer supervises all the usual management services found in the State Department, then adds some, such as rentals and purchasing, that would be done by General Services Administration for a department in the United States. Missions for the Agency for International Development and U.S. Information Agency also have their own management staffs. In theory all management staffs abroad also help each other.

The truth may well be duplication. Observers have long gossiped about the difficulty of getting anything done in the State Department because of the convolutions of management. Men in the missions have long endured and damned restrictions from Washington, restrictions which usually meant duplicate effort, paper, and responsibility.

The bulge is in management services. All three of the agencies wholly devoted to foreign affairs use much more of their personnel for management than other departments, and more than most organizations whether public or private. It is in management services that duplication, needless clearance, too meticulous rules can always develop, often in the name of economy when no one asks whether it is false economy. (It took some thirty years for the General Accounting Office to agree that auditing every item of expenditure cost more for the small items than a few losses would cost and to begin a spot check of certain expenditures.)

Not only the devil finds work for idle hands. Good people, many of them churchgoers, find work for their own idle hands. They see work that can be done, and they do it. They think up extra cautions to protect the public interest. Pieces of mail get duplicated in more copies so that more people can be informed and involved, until coordination becomes the end in itself and not the means for larger ends. The more people assigned to management services, the more work they will find to do. Soon work that was never thought necessary before gets established as a routine and begins to grow within itself, demanding more people to do it. All this was axiomatic long ago to students of administration. C. Northcote Parkinson in good humor and accurate wit had only to call it his law for all to recognize that Parkinson's law described what really happened.

Staff services of the wrong kind are exorbitantly provided in the State Department, Agency for International Development, and, to a lesser degree, the U.S. Information Agency. Management services eat up the budget. Rule four is followed too extravagantly and too blindly for management services. For general staff services, the rule is followed reasonably so far as numbers go. We shall see later that, so far as the kind of general staff work is concerned, more emphasis, not more numbers (in Washington at least), is needed in planning.

VII

Rule five is that each executive should have only as many subordinates as he can supervise. It has no universal meaning. Its interpretation depends upon the facts of each case.

Observers for twenty-five years have found that generally in the conduct of diplomacy top executives have too many subordinates reporting to them.

This begins at the top with the President. The subordinates he supervises bring to him matters of immeasurable complexity and risk. They head departments that are in themselves intricate and engaged in complex work. The President can never assume that he faces a routine—except perhaps in some of his interminable signing which he does while his mind is on something else. He is not, to be absurd, a supervisor of dressmakers at piece rates. If he were, perhaps he could deal adequately with the number of immediate subordinates who now claim his attention.

The President in 1962 had 80 people reporting directly to him. Of these, 30 were either heads of agencies in the Executive Office of the President or aides immediately at his service in the White House Office, and 50 were heads of departments and agencies outside the Executive Office of the President. He could not begin to give each of 80 top officials all the attention they wanted or that he should have given them to insure his control of policy. Back in 1937 the Brownlow Committee recommended that a reorganization of the Executive Branch should leave the President with no more than 24 immediate subordinates, 12 inside the Executive Office of the President and 12 heading departments of government. At the time this recommendation was made, the President supervised 49 persons, and that was considered too many. Twenty-five years later, he supervised 31 more than he had supervised when the Brownlow Committee tried to reduce his load. He has steadily lost his grip over the policies and actions for which he is to be held responsible.

Among the 80 subordinates who reported directly to the President, 26 were involved consistently in foreign affairs, 12 in the Executive Office of the President and 14 outside. They were introduced in Chapter 4 and need not be repeated here.

The President's load of supervision in foreign affairs alone is about the same as that of the Secretary of State who spends all his time on the one subject. The Secretary of State in 1961, it may be repeated, had 24 subordinates who reported directly to him, not counting ambassadors.

For comparison of the main agencies wholly involved in foreign affairs with departments primarily in domestic affairs, Table 2 shows the numbers of subordinate executives who reported directly to the heads in 1961:[4]

[4] Counted from charts of organization in *United States Government Organization Manual, 1961–62*, revised as of June 1, 1961, prepared by Office of the Federal Register, National Archives (Washington: Government Printing Office). An exception is Agency for International Development. Its number was counted from a separate chart obtained from the agency, dated March 30, 1962.

TABLE 2. NUMBER OF SUBORDINATES WHO REPORT DIRECTLY TO HEAD OF DEPARTMENT OR AGENCY, 1961

State	24
Agency for International Development	21
U.S. Information Agency	19
Defense	16
Army	9
Navy	17
Air Force	15
Treasury	17
Justice	20
Post Office	10
Interior	9
Agriculture	11
Commerce	10
Labor	16
Health, Education, Welfare	17

Only five of these can be held as models for a President who wants to command. They are Army, Post Office, Interior, Agriculture, and Commerce. All the others exceed a reasonable span. For while one cannot be rigid about exactly how many men an executive can supervise, one can reasonably assume that no executive at the head of a federal department can supervise adequately fifteen or more subordinates, each of whom in turn is responsible for matters of great complexity. Any decision, any supervision at this level is high policy.

The Secretary of State, these figures show, has the most difficult span of control in government after the President. Next come the Director of the Agency for International Development and the Director of U.S. Information Agency; only the Attorney General equals these officials in the sprawl of his dominion. The conclusion is that while most federal departments and agencies are too loosely organized, the civil agencies engaged wholly in foreign affairs are more so. Their heads have so many subordinates who report directly to them that close command is impossible. So does the Secretary of Defense, for that matter.

VIII

Rule 6 says to put together in one unit all activities that are alike. In a way the violation of this rule causes more inefficiency and downright failure than any other fault of free nations. And in another way a strict obedience of the rule is undesirable, if not impossible in a free society.

No free nation, however, needs to violate integration as much as we do now. Any president is absurd when he tries to deal with 25 subordinates in the one activity of foreign affairs. Mr. Eisenhower saw the results of too many people involved in one mission when his plans caved in because one of our spies was caught. For the two activities of military intelligence and a summit conference, twelve persons and agencies, remember, were involved. What was true in the U-2 case is true all the time in nearly any other case. The difference is that U-2 espionage exploded in the President's face as he was about to leave for the Paris conference, while the damage from similar cases is constant, erosive, and accepted. Too many interagency committees, too much paper to be passed around for initials, too many staff meetings with too many attending, too many jurisdictional arguments are all endemic in government and all symptoms of the failure to put like things together.

The big question is why are mergers so rare, when the need for them is so plain. Surface answers are easy. Separate agencies, such as Treasury, Agriculture, and Commerce got established in foreign activities before foreign policy was so all-inclusive, and, once established, they fight to keep their foreign activities. Such old departments are strong in the jurisdictional politics of Washington. The State Department, lacking support in the grass roots, is weak. It must rely most on the good sense and conscience of President and Congress, who will not insist that the Department of Agriculture give up its foreign activities when farm lobbyists insist that it keep them. Or Commerce, when business associations can be stirred to say they prefer to deal with their own department. But some President and Congress will have to insist on merger someday if the nation is to be assured in its conduct of diplomacy.

Another reason for dispersion and failure to merge was the reputation of the State Department. Whether deservedly or not, the State Department for years inspired distrust among those who realized that a new diplomacy had appeared in which military, economic, and cultural factors were equal with political. State was dominated by those trained in traditional diplomacy. They were not accustomed to foreign aid, military advice, haggling over requirements for goods or the prices to be paid.

One of the sternest rules of their tradition was that a diplomat was a guest; he must not interfere with the affairs of the host. All the new programs required interference in the affairs of other countries. No nation will give aid without placing conditions on its use. To promote trade or to distribute propaganda is to bring pressure. The polite vocation in which reporting and representation were the main purpose, and negotiation when it had to be done was stately, was invaded by ruffians who demanded changes while they waved promises of supplies, arms, and loans. As soon as the new men discovered the reluctance of the State Department to accept them and their boldness, they lost respect for State. So did Congress.

One non-rational argument helped to spread the distrust in the years when change was imminent. Professional diplomats were disliked in America until a few years ago. No evidence was examined; truth was irrelevant. The cliché was often accepted that diplomats were dilettantes whose main interest was in social life. Today few rank and file career Foreign Service Officers ever dress formally, but they still have to deny that they wear striped pants. Some members of Congress are always ready to challenge funds for entertainment. They dislike cookie-pushers. Career diplomats have to explain again and again that parties are a way of work and not recreation as for most people. (They leave unsaid the fact that cookies are seldom present but booze is an occupational hazard.) Unjust as it is, the cliché of the dilettante was strong in the minds of some of those who spread foreign affairs among so many agencies. It enhanced the distrust of the State Department.

Another fact stood regardless of the non-rational charges. State could not take on some of the new functions and did not want to. It could not be expected to carry on traditional diplomacy and simultaneously bring pressure on the host governments. Instead other agencies such as the Office of War Information and U.S. Information Agency, the Foreign Economic Administration and Agency for International Development, were created to perform the new kind of diplomacy. For the most extreme interference with the affairs of another country, espionage and subversion, the Office of Strategic Services served during the Second World War and the Central Intelligence Agency afterward.

When the work that might be unpleasant was given to new agencies, traditional diplomacy could carry on even when the new diplomats were rash. But the traditional men also lost their exclusive role. They saw, in fact, the new functions become so important that the complexion of the career diplomatic corps changed as more specialists entered to deal with the new diplomacy created in part by the new agencies. Still no one pressed for complete merger.

Perhaps the strongest surface force against merger was the rise of the armed forces as constant agents in foreign affairs. Where once they had stood by in readiness, they now, after the Second World War, spoke their piece in all decisions of foreign policy and placed their agents in many friendly lands. They began their full-time engagement with the occupation of liberated countries and conquered countries. They spread their wings in military aid, accompanied by Military Assistance Advisory Groups of American armed forces to show the other countries how to use the aid. More significant still was the fact that the containment of communism depended upon military force, as was shown in Korea, negatively in Indochina, and, later, in Laos, Vietnam, and Cuba. The men with the guns had to be asked to the conferences on foreign policy.

No civilian agency could hope to make decisions without knowing whether the nation had the force to carry them out. Equally, no civilian agency could hope to absorb the armed forces. For a long time the armed forces had been left out of policy discussions, had developed their own ways and professional career men, and they were not ready to contemplate any course save one in which they remained independent within their specialty. Now their specialty was the heart of foreign policy.

No one suggested that the armed forces should merge with civilian agencies for still another reason. In Anglo-American doctrine, the civil and military functions are kept separate, and civilian political chiefs are in control. An American politician would as soon recommend polygamy in a nation of monogamous women as to say that professional soldiers should manage foreign policy. He admits the military as partners, who come from their special province and return to it when they have been heard. Civilian political chiefs of the armed forces are theoretically in charge of whatever is said, and at the top a civilian is Commander in Chief, so the tradition of civilian supremacy is served. We want it this way, for the good reason that we don't want a military state. Nor does the military want to be in control.

Below the surface, a strong cultural force works against merger of civilian or military units. We say that in diffusion there is protection. Officials with too much power are dangerous. Spread the power. If spreading means less efficiency, the gain is worth the loss. It is better to be free than efficient. Then, as justification, we add, without thinking very much, that competition is a good thing. When we spread the power, and the work, we set agencies to competing with each other, we say, and thus get better results. The trouble with this is that, in contrast to private enterprise, government agencies do not compete for profits but for survival and growth. Their method of competition is not to produce more efficiently but to succeed at the political maneuvers that are so common inside government, as in other large organizations.

No matter the arguments, diffusion of work has been much commoner than merger in American government. Some separation of units and functions is necessary and desirable. Government cannot be a blob. It must have structure and channels, authority and delegated authority, and a separation of the work into parcels for assignment. In the organization for the conduct of diplomacy we have more diffusion than is necessary. Some merger is urgent.

CHAPTER 7   RATIONAL
ORGANIZATION:
THE EXECUTIVE BRANCH

Reorganization is the way out of the labyrinth. Everyone agrees to this much. The arguments begin when a particular reorganization is suggested. Congressmen argue that their favorite multiheaded agencies must remain independent and not be merged into related departments. Each department has loud reasons why all its bureaus should remain with it. The paid representatives of private interests turn their pressure against any change that would upset their relations with agencies upon which they depend. A President has to anticipate a battle, fought, as they say, with everything in the book, whenever he decides to reorganize any small part of the sprawling structure that surrounds him.

Despite the jugular tendencies aroused, reorganization occurs all the time in the federal government. Periodically, it reaches crests stirred up by the proposal for a central budget office, the Brownlow Committee report, and the first Hoover Commission report. During these times of flood, agencies shift from one department to another and new departments are born, as the Department of Health, Education, and Welfare was born. The federal executive began with the Departments of State, Treasury, and War. Reorganization produced all the other major departments and all the many added subdivisions inside departments and all the independent agencies.

Nor is reorganization always big. It also occurs quietly. Work is transferred from one unit to another; units are transferred from one agency to another. More of this occurs than most people realize. If it did not, the government would have bogged down years ago. Minor fights and agonies accompany this small reorganization too, but they do not create the storms of big change.

The most common occurrence in the growth of administration is not reorganization, however, but failure to pay much attention to organization. A new agency is created. It is made independent without much talk about whether it should be put into an existing department. The President gets another subordinate whom he will not be able to supervise. More coordination is required. The need for reorganization is made more urgent every time Congress and President ignore the fundamental subject of organization.

II

In the conduct of diplomacy both types of evolution appear. Flood crest reorganization produced the present Defense Department. Quiet reorganization moved the Agency for International Development to supervision by the Secretary of State and moved the Agricultural Attachés away from his jurisdiction to that of the Secretary of Agriculture, in a reversal of an earlier move which put the Agricultural men under State. Indifference to the rules of organization earlier had set up the Development Loan Fund as an independent agency, alongside Treasury, State, International Cooperation Administration, and the Export-Import Bank, all of which are concerned with international loans and development. Reorganization later combined the Development Loan Fund and the International Cooperation Administration in the new Agency for International Development. Such back and forth change produces a federal language of initials to refer to agencies. One testimony to the constancy of reorganization is the fact that after a year away from Washington anyone who once knew the language can no longer speak it accurately but must ask what new initials mean.

No reorganization has gone far enough to make order of the disorder that exists in the conduct of diplomacy.

Take the reorganization of the military departments in 1947 as an example. Most thoughtful and unbiased officials looked at the lessons just learned in the Second World War and decided that unification of the services was a good thing. In the crisis of war, unified commands were created; joint decisions were made possible in Washington by the formation of committees at many levels, and in the field by theater commanders. When hot war turned to cold war the need for unified decision continued, and the way to get it was to make unified command an institution—in other words to follow the rules of organization.

The reorganization did not attain the end sought. Jealousies, pressures, meanness, and the nobility of honest conviction diluted any policy that was indicated by the evidence. Military men, when threatened, turn out to be Navy, Army, Air Force, or Marine men with small regard for each others' services. More accurately, they turn out to be submarine men, or long-range bomber men with little concern for other branches of their own service. Members of Congress and private interests support their favorites. I once was told of an effort to make the Army and Air Force use the same length cartridge of a certain caliber ammunition at a saving of $20 million a year. All the technical evidence showed that one specification would serve without danger to national security. The ammunition could be shot from airplanes, tanks, trucks, or emplacements without any variation in the length of cartridge. Both the Army and Air Force fought any change. Their arguments were so weak that they might have lost before any forum of common sense. They were saved because the Congressman who was chairman of the subcommittee for appropriations had in his district a manufacturer of the ammunition for one of the services. This company did not want to change to a new specification. The Congressman agreed. (No doubt in his next campaign he preached economy in government; he was a conservative Republican.)

We went into the reorganization with two military departments, War and Navy. We came out of it with four, Defense, Army, Navy, and Air Force. The unified military command was not a man but the Joint Chiefs of Staff, the commanders of the Army, Navy, Air Force, and Marines (when questions that affected the Marines were considered), and a chairman without authority who was added to make five heads instead of one. Twelve years later the conscientious men caught in this maze were still trying to get their work done. Those in Defense tried to form policy and co-ordinate activities that were common to all services. Decision by consensus was the order of the day. It flowed through all the Pentagon, and it produced compromises in all the works. Even such a common purpose as hygiene went through debate before the same measures could be used by all services, as if bacteria noticed differences in uniforms.

A few changes were made, it is true, and some money may have been saved, though no one knew much about the true costs of the military and how much was unnecessary. On the whole, however, the conduct of military affairs was more diffused after the Second World War than during it. There was no assurance at all that foreign policy recommended by the military would be the most sensible that could be based upon the evidence. It was more likely to be a compromise in which each service got some part for its favorite strategy and weapon.

Not until 1961, fourteen years after the Defense Department was created, did a new man, Secretary Robert McNamara, try for clear control and systematic coordination by executive action instead of committee action. He used the budget, and his effort will be discussed later. But Mr. McNamara still had to deal with the five-headed commander of the armed forces, and there was no assurance that his successors would be as smart and as tough as he.

III

The failure to unify the military was the most prominent example of shallow, compromise reorganization in the conduct of foreign affairs, but it was not the only one. Civil activities were shuffled by a succession of dealers in the executive and Congress. Within a span of fifteen years foreign economic aid was located in the State Department, in an independent agency, and in both. Overseas propaganda was located in the State Department, in an independent agency, and in both. The responsibility for general foreign policy was located in the State Department, in the National Security Council, and in two or three members of the President's staff.

Deep and rational reorganization has been needed desperately for too long in the conduct of diplomacy. It is needed equally for the Executive Branch as a whole, for each of the main agencies, and for the Executive Office of the President.

IV

Some assumptions have to precede any talk of reorganizing the whole Executive Branch. Some theory is needed. Looking back over years of talk about reorganization, I find that all of us floundered. We did not think enough before we decided what to propose. We accepted the blocks that lay scattered on the floor and tried to fit them together, without an idea of what we wanted beyond a rearrangement of the existing agencies. Always we who talked reorganization were too considerate of politics, and we tried to propose changes that would offend as few people as possible yet improve administration to some extent. A few lamentably sought through reorganization to enact their own political biases. I recall being interviewed by a friend who was about to write a recommendation for reorganization. When I told him that a certain division of the State Department should be abolished because it duplicated work done elsewhere, he replied that, in his view, it should be kept because it was the only liberal influence in that Department. Strong political chiefs reorganize according to the evidence, then get the kind of staff with the views they want; they need not expect a student of administration to get what they want through prejudiced organization.

All talk about reorganization for the conduct of diplomacy should start from these assumptions:

1. Foreign relations at one time or another will enter into

every agency of government, but it will be the full-time concern in only a few. Weathermen are sometimes engaged in negotiations with other nations, but this is incidental to their main work. Department of Agriculture men who deal with the distribution of surplus food to other nations are full-time in foreign affairs. A reorganization should make the distinction and provide for both partial and complete involvement. The weathermen have to be coordinated; the surplus food men have to be supervised.

2. While foreign affairs have come to dominate all other questions in the advanced nations, these nations still behave as if they live alone with their internal concerns first in mind. The executives of national states are organized to take care of segments of internal governance; for example, interior, agriculture, welfare, and commerce. A foreign office and armed forces are set up especially to deal with other nations. This habit of dealing with other nations through a pipe will continue so long as nationalism lives, and nationalism is a strong faith.

3. In the United States and other developed nations, the military forces will continue to be managed separately from civilian agencies. Military professionals have to be consulted in the decision of foreign policy, but they are not given the control over decision in any mature nation.[1] Reorganization will have to continue separate apartments for civil and military foreign relations and provide too a common room where they can meet.

4. The President will be held responsible in the United States for all that happens, so far as anyone is held responsible. He alone can be held responsible at the polls, for he is the only federal executive who is elected, with of course his stand-by the Vice-President. Other nations' chief executives can find in cabinets and parliamentary majorities some company in their responsibility. The American President stands alone.

5. Because he is alone in responsibility, the President will want personally to control the main decisions for which he must answer. A President who does not try to be a strong executive is naive, in-

---

[1] In the underdeveloped nations the military often controls all policy, and is sometimes the strongest force for honesty and competence.

different, ill, or lazy. One who thinks he can operate as a mere chairman of the board is doomed to fail.

6. Coordination in the conduct of foreign affairs has to come from the President. He alone can give orders to both civil and military units. His power goes further. Only the President can command all the units which will from time to time be involved in foreign affairs. Coordination by any other means than the President means debate, compromise, uncertain decision, and appeal to the President.

7. The President as one man, confined by the physiology and custom of his kind, cannot handle his job alone. He cannot alone make all the decisions for which he will be held responsible. Nor will advisers and secretaries alone make it possible for him to stay on top. They only bring work to him in partly digested form. They do not relieve him of work; if anything, they increase his load because they require his time. As the outcome of the increasing demand on the one man, the Executive Office of the President grows in size and authority. Despite theories that his staff members should not have authority, they do, and they make decisions for him in his aura. We have in fact a presidential institution that mixes staff work with magic authority. At no time can one say whether advice or authority is represented by that powerful signal: "This is the White House calling." Soon, I think, we will openly have to adopt deputies for the President, officials who will consciously exercise his authority.

V

These assumptions will shape a reorganization of the whole Executive Branch. If it is accepted as fact that foreign affairs will be the occasional concern of all agencies and the constant concern of some, then we can consider two different treatments for two different categories. Part-time agencies are one thing; full-time are another. The part-time can be coordinated; the full-time can be integrated. If it is assumed that the military will remain separate from the foreign office, then we can leave it separate in our thoughts of reorganization. We need not argue that the armed forces should be put under command of the Secretary of State. It simply would not happen anyway in the United States or other advanced nations where civilian political chiefs long ago learned to govern honestly and responsibly and where seizure by the military has small promise.

One assumption is that nations will continue to deal with each other through special offices for this purpose. In our case the State Department is our specialist in international relations. It is not alone. Twenty-five others, 12 in the Executive Office of the President and 13 outside, also consistently spend time in decisions of foreign policy and in the conduct of foreign relations. By all the rules of organization, this should cause confusion and does.

In Washington cumbersome schemes are now devised to reach the compromises that displace decisions based on evidence. In another country the United States presents more differences than unities in spite of all our efforts to maintain abroad the teamwork that burdens Washington. An American ambassador on paper has general supervision over all American activities in his country. In practice he has more a chairman's authority. If he gives unwanted orders to the head of one of the American missions, he must be prepared to fight his cause back in Washington, where the Ambassador's power depends upon the support he gets from the State Department and the other fellow's power is equal because his agency also reports to the President. I recall a Consul General, not experienced at dealing with the Army and unable to get the quarters he wanted, who threatened to go all the way to the President. The President, he said, would make the Army give the Consul General a certain house. A Colonel drew up huffily and said, "And I, sir, will go to the Secretary of the Army, who will go to the Secretary of Defense, who will go to the Commander in Chief who gives me my orders. And until the Commander in Chief tells me to give you that house, you, Mr. Consul General, can go to hell."

Here in thankless jobs, far from ultimate authority, both conscious of duty, these two men showed in a nutshell the difference between theory and reality. The Consul General took seriously the scrap of paper that said the Ambassador, his superior, was in charge of American activities in the country. The Colonel knew that he had authority over that house. Both knew that their particular issue was not important enough to send to Washington. Both men would have looked ridiculous if they had asked for top-level orders on the small question. Their only recourse was to negotiate, to argue with each other, to persuade, to agree. Neither had more real authority than the other, no matter what a paper said. One pound of personal compatibility in an overseas mission is worth a ton of executive orders. It is negotiable. The paper is not.

VI

For the sake of simplicity, and we need all we can get when so many experts make their living by making things complex, the easiest answer for reorganization of the Executive Branch is to put into the State Department all those units that work full-time in foreign affairs. If we have to deal with other nations through one pipe, let's have one pipe instead of twenty-six. Right off, however, we retreat from part of the solution. We cannot put the military under the State Department for reasons of tradition and the Constitution which makes the President Commander in Chief. Once the military is left out, the President must coordinate the military and State Department.[2] The President will need a stronger Executive Office of the President than now, a point to be discussed later. So we also leave outside State the twelve persons and units now engaged full-time in the Executive Office, for later handling.

We are left with civilian units to be transferred to the State Department. One of them, the American Battle Monuments Com-

[2] This represents a change of view from *The Administration of American Foreign Affairs* (New York: Alfred A. Knopf, 1950), pp. 153–155. Then I thought that the State Department should specialize in political affairs, at which it was then more competent than any other group. The President's staff would coordinate all executive agencies. Since 1950 the military has become so important as a full partner, and so competent at political as well as military affairs, that a change of proposal results. Now the President's staff will have its hands full if it coordinates no more than one major civil department of foreign affairs and one major military department.

mission, which maintains war cemeteries and other memorials overseas, is closer related to the military and can more sensibly be transferred to the Defense Department.

Now these units remain for transfer to State. They are:

Office of International Finance, Department of the Treasury.

Office of Alien Property, Department of Justice.

Immigration and Naturalization Service, Department of Justice.

Foreign Agricultural Service, Department of Agriculture.

Bureau of International Programs, Department of Commerce.

Bureau of International Business Operations, Department of Commerce.

Bureau of International Labor Affairs, Department of Labor.

Office of International Affairs, Atomic Energy Commission.

Office of International Programs, National Aeronautics and Space Administration.

U.S. Information Agency.

Export-Import Bank.

U.S. Tariff Commission.

Foreign Claims Settlement Commission.

The first nine are now located inside other agencies; the last four are now independent, reporting to the President.

This suggestion goes further than others and will cause pain in all those agencies that are now outside the State Department but engaged full-time in foreign relations. Arthur Macmahon of Columbia was the first university analyst, so far as I know, to recommend in print a new Department of Foreign Affairs with subdepartments of political, economic, and informational activities.[3] He had in mind the federation of no more than the inde-

[3] Arthur Macmahon, *Administration in Foreign Affairs* (University, Ala.: University of Alabama Press, 1953).

pendent agencies engaged full-time in foreign affairs. I think the
time has come to merge all civil agencies engaged full-time in
foreign affairs whether or not they are independent. All the main,
full-time work of international relations would then be handled in
the Department of State, the Department of Defense, and the Executive Office of the President.

VII

Among the cries of outrage at the idea that Agriculture, Commerce, and the others should lose their international units, earnest
citizens ignore those that come because status and independence
are threatened. These will be disguised in high-flown rationaliza-
tion, but at bottom they come from people who do not want to
become less important. The status of public agents is not truly a
national concern; whether or not they report directly to a department head is not worth weakening the nation's competence in the
world.

Other arguments have to be taken seriously. Foremost is the one
that the State Department as now composed and staffed is inadequate for a bigger job. This is true. One can go further to say
that the State Department is inadequate for its present assignment.
It is crippled by two infirmities.

For one, the Department is so poorly organized that the good
men and women in it are frustrated when they try to accomplish
change. The excessive sprawl of its chart, the excessive time spent
in coordination, the exorbitant use of manpower in the routines
of management are all signs of poor organization.

For the other, the Department is too much dominated by career
Foreign Service Officers; remember that this group is not chosen or
trained to work at foreign policy but only at foreign relations.
More will be said about career men—including how good they
are—in a later chapter on personnel. Here, though, I must justify
the statement that the present kind of career Foreign Service Officers handicap the State Department for its proper larger task.

One of the oldest dogmas of diplomacy is that career diplomats should staff the foreign office except for the handful of some six or eight political executives who decide policy at the top. In reality the overuse of the present kind of career man has helped to cripple the State Department because of an error of definition. The American career Foreign Service Officer is usually not a diplomat in the broad, old meaning of the term. Always with the usual exceptions of certain individuals, he cannot think of world patterns, but only of current events in particular countries. Therefore he cannot plan ahead, cannot see policy in the large, cannot arrange events ahead of time to make them advantageous to us. He did not look ahead in Cuba, Southeast Asia, and Space because he could not. As we shall see later, he is chosen, trained, and promoted for his competence in routine foreign relations and not for his ability as a thinker, analyst, or planner. It is more to his credit that he writes accurate reports, knows laws and regulations, and issues no questionable visas than that he devise a new policy before it is too late.

Foreign relations, not foreign policy, have become almost the only concern of the present State Department. Policy is made in answering the mail but not in writing before the other nation beats us to it. Response, not initiative is the routine. Men who spend at least two-thirds of their careers in other countries learn habits that make response more comfortable than initiative, and they do not experience miraculous changes when they are put at desks in Washington.

Abroad, also, they are official guests of another nation, bound by the courtesy expected. Their success depends upon their good standing with their hosts, both public and private. A young officer soon learns to cultivate "sources" of information and to get acquainted with all those officials who can help him negotiate. He adopts readily the doctrine that the United States should never interfere in the affairs of other nations, that we should deal amiably and equally both with foreign scoundrels and righteous men, that we should not stir up trouble by bold projects. This doctrine is both good etiquette and good tactics for the diplomat stationed abroad. When transplanted to the State Department, it obscures insight and deadens thought.

Finally, the career man stationed abroad knows from four centuries of custom that he is an agent of foreign policy, not its maker. Policy is decided by political chiefs and carried out by diplomats. When the diplomat is seated at a desk and told to make policy, he cannot shed the creed of his profession. Nor should we expect him to.

A new State Department will be needed for the central, single pipe, conduct of diplomacy. Much pain and turmoil will be required to get it. The results will be worth the effort. After deep surgery we could have a system in which simplicity would be provided as much as it could ever be in government. Excessive conference and compromise would be avoided. Responsibility and authority would be clearly located. The new diplomacy of all-in-one could be practiced. Political, economic, and social factors could be used in each decision and each negotiation without the delay, watering-down, and dimness that now attend efforts to get agreement among a half-dozen agencies. Most of all, a new State Department, staffed with a new kind of policy-maker, could look ahead and make policy for what it sees. It could escape from its compulsion that answering the daily mail is diplomacy.

Another serious argument against drastic merger is that foreign policy is too complex to be made by one group. It is true that few decisions can exclude all but one of the political, military, economic, and social elements. The question is not whether any be ignored but how all will be injected without fail. At present each separate agency acts as advocate for its view, and each is confined to its field. A decision is reached in a competition of advocates. Defense opposes Treasury. Agriculture opposes Defense and Treasury. Commerce opposes State and Agriculture. State can't make up its mind so it delays any solution. At last, some sort of common denominator is accepted. It may be the most sensible decision, but it is more likely to be whatever can be accepted by most of the contenders.

If no agreement at all can be reached at the first level, the arguments are sent up to the next level, where superiors negotiate in argument with each other. Only those matters that are heavy enough to get presidential attention are sure to get decided by authority; only the President or one of his aides is in position to make a decision that is based upon the analysis of evidence rather than viewpoints, or a decision that need not please a majority of the agencies represented.

After a merger the head of the new Department of State would stand in authority. He and his subordinates could make the best decisions indicated by analysis of the political, economic, and social considerations. The President and his subordinates could then coordinate the new State Department position with that of the military, represented by the Defense Department, and with the policies of the President. By all the rules of experience, this is better organization than the present. The present dispersion does not work well enough to do what we need as a nation.

A final argument against merger is that domestic interests should be represented in foreign policy by their domestic advocates. Only the Department of Agriculture can protect the American farmer; only the Department of Commerce can represent the businessman, Labor the workers, Treasury the taxpayers. The State Department, in this view, is more responsive to other nations than to homefolks. The proposal to let a new State Department decide foreign policy except for the military portion, subject to presidential supervision, assumes that the total national interest is more important than any particular interests. What happens to all counts more than what happens to farmers, businessmen, or workers. This is hardly a radical doctrine, but in past practice we have so ignored it that now it can be made to look radical. We have served special interests through their special departments until they can now argue that they have some "natural" American right to special service. They don't, really. We can still as a nation say that foreign policy shall be made for the total national interest and this will best serve all the special interests. In any case, the new State Department will be sensitive to domestic pressures because it alone would be plainly responsible for civil foreign policy and thus subject to the special pleas and censures that are now registered in other departments.

CHAPTER 8 RATIONAL ORGANIZATION: THE DEPARTMENTS OF STATE AND DEFENSE

Inside a department too the rules of organization can guide the struggle for coherence.

The gigantic and sudden growth of the executive branch, [the first Hoover Commission said] has produced great confusion within the departments and agencies as well as in their relations to the President and to each other. . . . Within each department, the subsidiary bureaus should be grouped as nearly as possible according to major purposes. . . . The heads of departments must hold full responsibility for the conduct of their departments. There must be a clear line of authority reaching down through every step of the organization. . . .[1]

For the conduct of diplomacy we are faced in the new scheme proposed here with the organization of State and Defense, the only two departments that would be engaged full-time. Their purposes, to agree with the Hoover Commission, should define their internal arrangements. Above all, the definitions of what these departments are expected to do should be kept as simple as possible. In past floundering we have overcomplicated the structure because we have failed to seek the utmost simplicity in a world that encour-

[1] Commission on Organization of the Executive Branch of the Government, *General Management of the Executive Branch* (Washington: Government Printing Office, 1949), pp. 31, 34.

ages men to seek difficult ways to deal with it. This might become a social law: The more difficult the work, the more difficult men will make the work when they set up organization. Much of the present confusion is due to a refusal to fight the wolves of complexity with the dogs of simplicity.

II

A new State Department would have a threefold purpose. (1) It would decide foreign policy so far as political, economic, and social factors are involved. (2) It would advise the Defense Department and the President, or his office, concerning military policy, both for military moves needed to enforce general foreign policy and for the non-military consequences of moves proposed by the military. (3) It would conduct foreign relations in the full sense, serving as the only civilian mission so engaged in Washington and abroad, acting as reporter, negotiator, propagandist, distributor of aid, adviser, and protector of citizens. Over these assignments the new Department would have final authority and would be subordinate only to the President and his staff. For example, when the Post Office, or any other occasional agency, might need foreign policy, it would make its request of the new State Department, send its own experts to give arguments, then submit to the decision of State.

The new State Department, as anyone who has worked in Washington knows, will have to deserve this authority. A mere executive order will not get respect. Respect and subordination will come only when the State Department proves to be more skilled than anyone else at general foreign policy and foreign relations. Since 1940 the present Department has failed to convince anyone of its peculiar excellence. It has tried, instead, to be a little of too many things, a little political analyst, a little economist, a little diplomat. When it has not been superior, and on its record it has been as often a failure as a success at the job of international relations, no wonder other agencies demand equal roles. Only by concise organization will a new State Department do any better. A fat, waddling, ill-kempt diffusion will be no more competent and no more respected than now.

Two of the three purposes of the new Department are to decide policy and can be considered as one for the purpose of organization. To decide non-military foreign policy and to advise on military policy are so connected that one unit should handle them. Only the conduct of foreign relations remains. It is so intimately necessary to the formation of policy that it should be handled as a service to policy. Reports, negotiation, propaganda, aid, and advice all affect policy. At times even such minor activities as the granting of passports and visas become questions of foreign policy.

III

A new department that concentrates on policy is indicated. Its organization can be based on either of two designs.

It can be divided according to the factors that make up policy—political, military, economic, social—and lead to difficulty. These elements are indivisible in any complete, well-prepared decision. When organization sets them up in separate compartments, they have to be collected if the decision is wise, or they are not collected and the decision is unwise.

The other basis for organization is by nations toward which and with which foreign policy is made. Since the end of the Second World War, and the beginning of our postwar tension, the most acute observers have recommended that the heart of the department be the geographical bureaus.[2] They have been heeded

[2] The first official report to bring out the conflict of bases for organization was made by Otto L. Nelson, Jr., assisted by Just Lunning, in 1946. Both men were sophisticated observers of the federal culture. Gen. Nelson was still a career Army man who had also written a landmark book in public administration, *National Security and the General Staff,* and taken a Ph.D. at Harvard. Mr. Lunning had worked as a civil servant and naval officer in economic warfare and intelligence. Gen. Nelson later became vice-president of New York Life Insurance Company; Mr. Lunning, president of Georg Jensen, Inc. The Nelson report was withheld from the public when it was delivered. Later its substance was published in Felix A. Nigro (ed.), *Public Administration Readings and Documents* (New York: Rinehart & Co., 1951), pp. 153–194. Other, more

only in paper orders without effect. No Secretary of State has abolished the units that deal separately with economic and social factors of foreign policy. There is in fact no center of action for all that is done in connection with another country. The geographical units are given central authority only on paper, while they continue to have to coordinate with other units as equals in reality, and coordination takes much time.

The present Department of State is a mixture of geographical and subject-matter, or so-called functional, units that rest upon alternative bases of organization. Naturally there is a conflict when alternatives are placed in inevitable conflict. Naturally there is confusion, delay, and inefficiency. A Secretary of State, wearing toga and head ribbon, rides two horses in tandem when he had better sit down on one horse to win this race.

IV

The heart of the new department, then, would be units that handle all aspects of foreign policy and foreign relations by nations and by regions. These units would decide for their nations the composite political, economic, and social American foreign policy, from the smallest decision to the largest. They would advise the armed forces and the President's staff on military policy as it is involved in foreign policy. They would supervise foreign relations, including consular work. They would do their own economic analysis for their nations, their own policy for propaganda, their own collection and analysis of intelligence. They would unify diplomacy and abolish the incessant compromise that is now required to get political, economic, and social views together.

---

parochial voices killed the main idea of the Nelson report and concocted a pretended reorganization that preserved past disabilities. The next report came in 1949 from the first Hoover Commission. It recommended, as the Nelson report had implied, organization centered on the geographical bureaus, where decisions would be made. Again shortsighted men smothered the main idea under a blanket of pretended reorganization that preserved the status quo. For the Hoover Commission recommendation, see Commission on Organization of the Executive Branch of the Government, *Foreign Affairs* (Washington: Government Printing Office, 1949).

If the present collections of nations are kept in the new department, and they are logical, the Secretary and Under Secretary will deal with Assistant Secretaries for Africa, Latin America, Europe, the Far East, and the Near East and South Asia, or five subordinates who could carry out orders and bring up authoritative recommendations. These five would have subordinates in charge of all the work for sub-regions, and the lines would be clear.

One present bureau is not in the new list. It is the one that handles policy for international organizations. Since its creation when we took to joining international organizations, this unit, paralleling the geographical bureaus, has been a sore and redundant thumb. It mixes theories of organization. When its five companion bureaus deal with nations where they live, the Bureau of International Organization Affairs deals with the same nations when they go to an international meeting, or get ready to go. Under one theory a nation is one thing at home; under the other theory the same nation takes on a new definition when it approaches the international meeting place. Mr. Ogburn's tracing of the telegram, reported earlier, is an example of the double definition at work. A representative of the Bureau of International Organization Affairs was engaged in the replies to Country X; so was the desk officer who deals with X through our mission there, and the responsibility and authority were both clouded.

We might as well accept the sad fact that a nation is first and last a nation, self-interested no matter where encountered. No spirit of special charity or understanding comes with transfer to the bank of the East River. International conferences are meetings of sovereign nations. The new State Department can deal with them on questions to come up at international conferences as it deals with them on other questions.

One must add quickly that coordination will still be needed. It will come laterally, as always, when men confer with each other. It will come more importantly from the top, from the Secretary of State and his immediate staff and from the President and his office. The issues considered at international conferences are among the biggest the nation faces. Korea, the Congo, and Cuba are examples. These issues deserve and demand handling at the top, not handling in just another bureau that has no more than equal stature with other bureaus that handle individual nations in their capitals.

John F. Kennedy made this point when he appointed Adlai E. Stevenson to be ambassador to the United Nations. Mr. Stevenson, the best known and most prestigious defeated candidate in American politics, was too eminent, and too much better at the job, to take orders from minor bureaucrats. He stood before the world as a symbol of the politician who believed in reason, decency, and idealism. He was the first man of his tall stature ever to be appointed as our ambassador to the United Nations. Immediately the United Nations took on stature in American policy because Mr. Stevenson himself commanded a large following. The fact that Mr. Stevenson was at the top, better known than the Secretary of State, as well known in the early days as the President, and the fact that all knew that Mr. Stevenson dealt only with the Secretary of State and the President on any important matter must also have made a difference. Now that precedent is set, it should not be too difficult to keep the coordination of our affairs at international organizations at the top instead of in a fifth wheel bureau.

Staff offices, finally, are standard for any department. The new Secretary of State will still need a director of administration, who will head units that handle budget, accounting, personnel, facilities, and services. Incidentally, the routine mechanics of passports and visas can be grouped with other services while any question of policy is settled in a geographical bureau. A Secretary will also need a legal staff, a public information staff, and a policy-planning, policy coordinating staff.

V

This last office must be explained. Two elements are missing in the proposition so far. They are planning and coordination. Under the new organization there is more likelihood that the geographical bureaus will spend more time than now in foresight, but they cannot be expected to have true vision. They will deal with only parts of the world. They will still have to answer the mail, and the easiest way will continue to be found in reacting and not in dangerous initiative. A staff unit at the top is still needed to see the whole and the future.

Because such a staff loses support the very moment it is labelled "planning," we might avoid the word. Call it a policy corps until some better term is found. Some smart Secretary of State will one day try a small group of close aides who will do planning as no more than the proper work of an executive. Not many are needed. One of them should be the head assistant to keep down the number of people who think they have to see the Secretary every day. A small staff of high caliber thinkers can do the reading, talking, and writing needed to plan. But action would come from the Secretary and his staff.

Authority would coordinate, and plans would lose their stigma if announced as policy from the peak of Olympus. Certainly planning would no longer, as it does now, have to argue with a voice no louder than many others. For years observers have lamented that the Policy Planning Staff was not more influential for longer periods. I wonder now, looking at the chart anew, whether it ever had a chance.

Only a Secretary of State who respected vision would ever have listened to the planners. Perhaps more would have respected vision if they had known that the praise or blame for what came in the future would be laid on the Secretary and not on some group tagged "planning" in the chart. Coordination and planning are the highest duties of an executive. Let this executive handle them in his own name, using his personal aides as he wants but holding himself responsible for all they do.

VI

After reorganization the Secretary would have reporting to him 10 persons: 1 Under Secretary, 5 heads of geographical bureaus, the 3 heads of staff offices to handle administration, legal advice, and public information, and the chief of the small planning and coordinating group in his own inner office. Ten subordinates is less than half as many as the 24 who reported to the Secretary at last count. With ten the top command could have some hope of dealing with the whole department and, with diligence, could have some time left to think.

We Americans, rich and democratic, get too many people involved in most ventures that we undertake. If we form an interest group, our first concern is to build up the membership. If we plan a cocktail party, that weird institution that brings into the living room the ruckus of a bird-house at the zoo, our first thought is for how many people the room will hold, perpendicular. When we try to think of foreign policy in the State Department or the White House, we have too many people present, and the decision is made difficult as well as diluted.

The greatest contrast between the British Foreign Office and our State Department is in numbers. A small group of three or four, including the political chiefs, can make a decision in London. There is no telling how many will get involved in Washington, as shown by the twelve in the U-2 affair or the nine in a White House conference on disarmament already mentioned. "To get the very best foreign policy," a British career diplomat once told me in the Foreign Office, "I would prefer no more than five men, who call each other by first names, who know the broad policy and the background of each big event."

Such a group can talk without explaining and can think quickly to the point. Its members already know each other's minds. The fewer people who report to the Secretary of State, the better decisions of policy. It is a simple law. The more simplicity the better.

VII

Now such drastic change as proposed here leaves several units screaming about their virtue and necessity. For all the years that drastic reorganization has been needed their screams have held off change, and the general welfare has suffered from politeness to these few, and ears beguiled by their arguments. Hearts must be broken in a reorganization; there is no doubt of this.

I have already argued that the Bureau of International Organization Affairs is more confusing than useful. Its work can be done in the geographical bureaus and the Secretary's office. The other units to disappear can be handled in the same way. They deal with parts of foreign policy when the distress call is to deal with foreign policy as a whole. Only the geographical bureaus and the Secretary's Staff in the new department will deal with foreign policy and always in the indivisible whole of political, military, economic, and social. The bureaus of economic affairs and educational and cultural affairs could be distributed among the geographical bureaus or the personnel dropped. (Courage is required.)

Other units perform services. One is the Bureau of Intelligence and Research which already, in its independent status, is subdivided by geographical areas. It can be moved into the geographical bureaus. The sooner we recognize that intelligence and research are routine for every decision, the sooner we can begin to clear up the mess of intelligence in Washington. Another is the Bureau of Security and Consular Affairs. It can be moved into the bureau for administration.

Some others will be scattered like sheep to find new folds, and perhaps to die. An office of the Under Secretary, now filled with 180 employees, will be distributed. Its people who work on mutual security, a military matter, can be used in the President's office since military and civil foreign policy have to be coordinated there. Its Office of Protocol can be assigned to Administration, for in truth the exact and delicate adherence to etiquette is not the essence of diplomacy but only a service to it. Another independent staff that works on disarmament can be sent to the President's Office or dropped. The Counselor and his staff can be dropped or used as the new chief assistant to the Secretary for planning, a move made, in fact, by Secretary Dean Rusk for at least one time when Walt W. Rostow became Counselor and Chairman of the Policy Planning Council.

Congressional relations have become a new, strange specialty. The State Department now has 22 persons devoted to "channeling," as they say in government, relations with Congress. Some question whether the relations between members of Congress and any department should be channeled at all, beyond the routing of mail and phone calls which once was handled by the mail room and information-receptionists—and still can be. While we slash to get a coherent Department, we do not need a special office for Congressional relations. Abolish it. If a Congressman needs guidance into the Department, let him call the Secretary's office. If officials of the Department want to reach members of Congress, let them go direct, in normal coordination with each other. If the Department wants to know about bills in Congress, let the Bureau of the Budget keep it informed as it is charged to do. Finally, the Policy Planning Staff, if retained, would be under the command of the chief assistant to the Secretary for planning, or Counselor if this title survives.

Only by rough treatment, and drastic change, will we ever get a Department of State that can surely do its job.

VIII

A thorough analysis of the Department of Defense is unthinkable short of great expenditure and almost unlimited time. Here are a few of the broad categories the analyst would face.

In size the Department is so much larger than any other public agency that no comparisons can be made. Its some 1,000,000 civilian employees are almost half of all the civilians employed by the federal government. Its some 3,000,000 military employees are almost 5 percent of the total national employed work force. It spends usually about half of all money spent by the federal government. It spends the money for, in descending order of the amount spent, the purchase of aircraft, missiles, ships, and other equipment; the payment of personnel; the operation of equipment and facilities; research and development; construction of facilities; atomic energy; military aid to other nations; and stockpiling and defense production. The telephone directory for the Department in Washington alone is as large as one for a city of 100,000. Its section in which components of organization and their chief officials are listed has an estimated 17,000 entries, including several for a new officer born of large size, the Locator of Personnel.

In form the Department is several departments in confederation, with the strength of the central command varying from year to year and subject to subject.

First the Department of Defense is two large structures, one the military and the other the civilian. Thus from top to bottom the armed forces, in uniform, have their customary form ranging from Chief of Staff at the top to private at the bottom and through all the apparatus of armies, fleets, and air commands, and their descending orders. These military units make up one whole system that can be self-sufficient. Within the system the Army, Navy, Marines, and Air Force exist as institutions in themselves and also as the collective military force. Parallel with this military structure is the civil system of the Office of the Secretary of Defense, the Department of the Army, Department of the Navy, and Department of the Air Force. Civilian control is exercised not only by the President and Secretary of Defense but by subordinates who extend their authority. More complexity is added when military men work in the civil apparatus under command of civilians, as some do, and civilians work in the military under command of the military.

Next the main components are not units but collections of units that compete with each other and tend to break up. The Air Force is not as simple as it sounds. It is the Strategic Air Command, the Air Defense Command, or Research and Development. The Navy is carriers, submarines, escorts, and not just a happy family of everything that floats. The Marines cultivate independence. The Army is artillery, infantry, staff services. All have their own arguments too between field offices and headquarters.

Finally, to make the analysis still more difficult, the defense establishment is changing all the time and has been since it was reorganized in 1947. It changes not so much in the form of its structure as in the location of the centers of power and in emphasis in work. Usually the two go together, center of power and emphasis in work. The long-distance striking arm, Strategic Air Command, becomes the center of power when the emphasis in work is heavy on nuclear counterattack—or massive retaliation as Secretary John Foster Dulles called it. When small wars, fought on the ground by troops supplied from far away, become more probable than massive retaliation, the Army, Navy, and Marines rise again. Within the Army, guerilla fighters become most favored because their ability is most needed for so many of the possible small wars.

Change also comes from circumstances. When the power of the military is divided, as it is when four services compete, the civilian Secretary of Defense and his central Office can step in to take a stronger hand. If military men wonder how it happened that civilians got so much control over such detailed matters, they should look to their own failure to unite.

But when the Secretary of Defense deals most with the Joint Chiefs of Staff, that five-headed commander of the four main branches of the armed forces, he increases the power of this group and decreases the power of each service by itself. He also diminishes the power of the civilian heads of the departments of Army, Navy, and Air Force in favor of his own office. The main purpose of the military is to fight and be ready to fight, and the Joint Chiefs of Staff are specialists in this. With the emphasis on force, more than upon managerial functions; the Joint Chiefs gain power at the expense of the civilian heads of the particular services and departments of Army, Navy, and Air Force.

Men make a difference in the rate of change, here as everywhere. Robert S. McNamara, reportedly the most brilliant, systematic, informed, and impersonal man ever to become Secretary of Defense, gathered to his office more control than anyone before him had thought possible. He did it by the budget, a device that had been available as well to his predecessors but not used by them. His Assistant Secretary of Defense and Comptroller, Charles J. Hitch, was in immediate charge of the new move.

Both men deserve praise in every future book about public administration. They put into practice what every perceptive teacher of public administration has known for years and few public officials have tried: the budget is a versatile instrument and can be used for many ends besides the mere listing of how much money is needed by the units of government. Both men were—and still are—serious students, each with experience as professional academic men, Mr. McNamara as an assistant professor of business administration for three years at Harvard and Mr. Hitch as a fellow of Queen's College, Oxford, for thirteen years with time out for the war. Mr. McNamara had then gone into Ford Motor Company and Mr. Hitch into economic research with the Rand Corporation, which works under contracts with the Air Force. Thinking men question habitual ways and go to the center of a question to start working out the answer.

For years most talk of unifying the armed forces had been in terms of structure and command. The talk went on and on to little conclusion. Men in the Executive Branch and in Congress could hold up any major action by raising a counterproposal or, sometimes, by merely crying alarm, often an alarm that the German General Staff was about to be recreated in America in a unified command over all services. Messrs. McNamara and Hitch went to the center of the question and found that they had certain controls which they were already authorized to use, and need not go to Congress to ask for change. One was the budget, not the amount of money, of course, for Congress decides that, but the form in which the categories would be set up. If Congress wanted to appropriate money by the same categories, so much the better. In any case, the planning of work, coordination, supervision, and all the other aspects of management would be handled internally according to the new categories.

No longer would the Air Force, Army, or Navy each make its claims and handle its own plans in self-protection. During the Kennedy-McNamara-Hitch years all weapons and activities would be placed in these nine categories: (1) central war offensive forces, (2) central war defensive forces, (3) general purpose forces, (4) sea and airlift forces, (5) Reserve and National Guard forces, (6) research and development, including Space, (7) servicewide support, (8) classified projects, and (9) the Department of Defense.

All offensive weapons, regardless of service, were put in the first category; for example, long-range bombers, land based missiles, and sea based missiles, and the command and communications to go with them. Under central war defensive forces all types of defensive weapons and forces (for example, air defense interceptors, surface-to-air missiles, surveillance and warning systems) were grouped regardless of which service managed them.

General purpose forces were those used either for offense or defense, and these grouped more by service, although they were all in the same budget category. Airborne divisions, artillery, carriers, cruisers, submarines, were examples of all purpose weapons. Troop carrier planes, the Military Air Transport Service, and Military Sea Transportation Service made up the sealift and airlift category.

All elements connected with reserve and national guard forces of all services were included in the fifth category, considering the reserve and national guard as true reinforcements.

Research and development was left distributed by projects by service but was coordinated through inclusion in one category for the budget. Servicewide support, the seventh category, included all such activities as recruitment and training, supply, intelligence, and medical care, still divided by services, although coordinated in the budget. Classified projects were unlisted. The Department of Defense category, finally, included some units centered in it, such as the Defense Atomic Support Agency and the Defense Communications Agency.[3]

The overwhelming significance of such budgeting was that by allocating funds for main purposes rather than by Army, Navy, Marines, and Air Force, the Secretary of Defense could control strategy, or grand policy in nonmilitary terms, and everything else that mattered. In the exercise of his new central power, it helped immensely that Mr. McNamara was just plainly more competent

[3] The categories, with listed items, appeared in testimony by Charles J. Hitch, Assistant Secretary of Defense, before the Subcommittee on National Policy Machinery of the U.S. Senate Committee on Government Operations, July 24, 1961. Printed for the committee, "Organizing for National Security: The Budget and the Policy Process" (Washington: Government Printing Office, 1961). The list, in one place, of all the elements of the military effort is itself remarkable.

than anyone else in sight and associates had to respect him for the way he worked.

Analysts would be in much better shape if Mr. McNamara were immortal. Unfortunately, Secretaries of Defense wear out or disappear rather rapidly. The turnover is high. The next man may lose all that Mr. McNamara gained, or he may gain more. None can say.

About the only conclusion an analyst can draw for the long range is that any Secretary of Defense who deals mostly with the Joint Chiefs of Staff, who are specialists in the use of force, will control military policy and administration more than one who deals mostly with the civilian heads of the service departments. The use of force is the main purpose of the military. An analyst might move one step further to conclude that any Secretary of Defense who uses the budget for the purpose of planning and control can enhance his power over the whole establishment and all its work. He might add then that any Secretary who also controls research and development, another tool for planning, can command strategy and administration, when he also uses the budget.

But these are armchair conclusions. The truth is that the Department of Defense is big, bewildering, and mostly unknown both to insiders and outsiders. Millions of dollars and man-hours will be required to analyze it truly and come up with a new organization that is defensible without doubt.

In the meantime some principles can be offered. Those who must some day reorganize will be drowned in compromise if they do not carry some principles as guides into the wilderness.

IX

The six rules of organization listed in the preceding chapter are principles to carry into any analysis of organization. They come from years of study of both private and public administration by a long line of students. If followed, a reorganized defense establishment will do its job better than the present sprawling monster.

Some additional principles can be suggested that apply particularly to Defense.

First, planning is the key to success in warfare, hot or cold. Research and development in weapons and organization, the allotment of money and men to various uses, the use of alliances, the choice of strategy are all planning. No longer can valor and the longbow make enough difference to win. The modern commander must be ready for small war, big war, and armed truce; missiles, bombers, and parachutes; land, oceans, and outer space; propaganda, intrigue, and treachery; sacrifice, bravery, and honor. His instruments and environment change steadily, and what worked last time may not work again. For all history the forces with the smartest planning were the most formidable.

Second, the chief military purpose is to fight. All military activities should contribute to strength in combat, to the slaughter of enemies and protection against them. If, for example, wives and children are sent abroad with the men, it should be done because this improves morale for fighting and not for sentimental reasons. I make this debatable, and perhaps foolish, point because it is so often ignored by both civilians and military men who talk as if the main purpose of the military is to administer to itself, or debate policy, or maintain the local economy that lives off a base. Such reasoning appears whenever an obsolete weapon is preserved because its custodian argues that no one can be sure it will not be useful again. No one has ever calculated the money wasted from this one result of the fallacy. Horses were retained for years after they ceased being useful; so were some types of airplanes and tanks. The poison of forgetting why armed forces exist spreads as well whenever men make routine management the main reason for existence. When papers, regulations, or looseleaf binders become the most important things to military men, we are in danger. No one in all history ever won a battle with a mimeograph machine.

Third, fighting is for professionals. Techniques, strategy, tactics, and the choice of weapons are part of fighting and should be decided by the professionals, subject only to approval by their civilian political chiefs for reasons of national policy. We cloud the responsibility when everyone can be an expert and talk about war as if it were academic. We should worry when political chiefs, and their civilian advisers, decide questions of fighting without knowing what happens in combat.

It is true that the civilians at present cannot trust the technical advice they get from the professionals, the jungle of indecision and competition having grown so thick that too many military men forsake their technical integrity in order to live. Civilian chiefs as a result have pushed themselves more and more into the consideration of technical matters in the hope of finding reliable evidence. As a result of life in the jungle professionals also have used civilians more on technical matters. Perhaps it is true too that professionals in a time of no shooting forget what combat is, and never learn first-hand how men die.

The training of professionals, however, even in peace, is still more likely to produce an awareness of combat than the experience of civilians in natural or social science or mathematics. Combat is a bloody mess. Its whole end is to avoid death and to kill others. All planning, all theorizing about war should be done in the knowledge of combat, and only those experienced or trained in the purpose of death are qualified experts in fighting.

This point is urgent. During the anxiety of threat, when the professionals dispute among themselves, laymen get accepted as experts, although their ideas are no more than hypotheses untested in combat. They speculate about the limited use of nuclear weapons in war when the economy of combat has always moved commanders to use their strength as far as necessary as fast as possible to defeat the enemy. Or they rely upon a theory of victory by retaliation to reverse the old doctrine that victory goes to the side that gets there first with the most.

Now is a time to grasp for straws, when the prospect of combat is so frightening, but a nation can be ruined if it plans strategy in an ivory tower. Professional fighters, if properly trained, will not lose sight of killing as the central fact of war. (I have yet to meet a thoughtful, sensitive, professional military man who was not a pacifist at heart, provided he understood the central purpose of combat. His sincere inner hope is to avoid war. Trigger-happy officers are the fools and knaves of their profession and are tolerated but not respected by the responsible.)

Fourth, one armed force under single-headed command is essential. We can no longer afford the waste, the indecision, the weakness that comes from four separate competing branches. Fighting is the main activity. Some fighting is on land, some on sea, some in the air, but most fighting is in all elements at once. Ships, planes, and trucks transport the men who fight on land. Planes reconnoitre, bomb, and strafe, and go home to bases on land and sea. Missiles can be launched from the ground or from planes and ships and submarines.

The present separation began when the Army and Navy truly had different jobs and seldom had to deal with each other. It spread when the Air Force, feeling its muscle after the Second World War and aided by its own propaganda, persuaded the powers that it had to be independent. The Marine Corps followed cue. While it did not separate from the Navy, it did win a seat on the Joint Chiefs of Staff.

We have learned from the separation that it will not work. Long ago conditions changed to the present interdependence. Only fictions, myths, and memories justify any continued separation. The President and Congress can start to make sense for the present when they abolish the Joint Chiefs of Staff for a single Commander of the Armed Forces. Then they can put under his command all those who fight, no matter how—with guns, rockets, on land or sea, in the air, or in all the elements. The easiest unification will come in the field, as it already has come to a small degree. Thus the powers can already put all the armed forces under one commander in Alaska, in the Atlantic, the Caribbean, the Eastern Atlantic and Mediterranean, the European, the Pacific, or in Continental defense, or world strategic attack commands. Area commanders could under complete unification be in charge of unified armed forces, including those who fight in ships, in planes, and on the ground. Equipment, facilities, manpower could be used for all kinds of fighting whenever possible. General functions, such as intelligence, communications, and supply can be handled for all in the field and in Washington. In fact steps to do this have been taken. It is hard to imagine how much money might be saved and, more important, how much stronger the nation would be.

Fifth, civilian control of military policy is necessary in our system and should be maintained, but not civilian interference in the technical matters that are better handled by professionals. Control is wanted over policy, not over techniques. Civilian political chiefs want to decide, for example, whether to prepare for nuclear war, not how to use nuclear weapons with the greatest effect in combat.

Such control over policy can be managed through the budget and through planning. Mr. McNamara proved this for the form of the budget. If the Secretary of Defense, the President, and Congress keep close to them the units that recommend budget and planning, they need not fear loss of control. Money decides all plans. The military professionals will have to submit their technical ideas to a civilian decision of policy whenever they ask for money or seek a change in plans. Beyond these two control points, civilians should not pass. If the professional military men are to be held responsible for fighting, give them authority once the policy has been settled at the top.

These five principles of military administration are hard to enforce. Each one is fought over bitterly. Human nature is in its most non-rational mood when it argues against change. The last fight to be settled will be over uniforms. Shall the unified service wear one or several colors? But such questions have to be answered. Civilian chiefs will have to be firm and will, incidentally, have to chastise those professionals who make unauthorized runs to Congress and the press in pursuit of their own jealousies. Unless a firm hand insists on deep reorganization, we face only more years of waste in time and money, weakness from failure to use all the strength we could have, and confusion about the blending of military strength into foreign policy.

CHAPTER 9 THE PRESIDENCY

A MOST URGENT QUESTION FOR AMERICA IS HOW to make the Presidency work. The President, John F. Kennedy told the National Press Club in January 1960, must be "the vital center of action in our whole scheme of government." He was correct. In a time of executive power, the chief executive must be the center of power.

Mr. Kennedy then got nominated and elected and found himself in the same predicament that his two predecessors had known. He was smothered by events that he did not make. His time was absorbed by business that was brought to him from the enormous apparatus of the federal executive. He had no time to think of events that he would like to cause to happen. As the vital center of action he was more the decider than the leader. The quality of his decisions depended upon the quality of the issues and the advice that was brought to him. At his high level, decision-making (a social scientists' word), was mostly saying yes, no, or maybe to proposals that were the outcome of competition in the lower ranks. There was no assurance that a disinterested and sagacious third party would test the proposals to make sure they were the soundest possible.

Sometimes Mr. Kennedy stood large, as in his personal popularity—and his wife's popularity—and sometimes he took the blame for failures of his subordinates, as when the Central Intelligence Agency left a plain trail of incompetence in the saddening failure of Cuban rebels to overthrow Castro. At no time was the President certain to be on top of his job. He could never be sure that the matters brought to him were all the ones he ought to decide, and he could never get free to decide what were the biggest issues in the world and how he wanted to handle them from his own conscience and ambition.

Mr. Kennedy turned out to be one of the remarkable presidents in American history. He knew many facts, grasped new ideas quickly, was intellectually and socially sophisticated, and he liked this job more than any other he could desire, so that he worked very fast and very hard. He was among his associates, as Secretary McNamara was in the Defense Department, the smartest, ablest man present, respected by all as their leader in talent as well as title. This President believed in the use of executive power and responsibility. He was willing to make decisions and did not willingly serve as chairman of a team, as his predecessor described the job. Mr. Kennedy collected the most energetic, best educated, and all-round ablest subordinates since Franklin Roosevelt had started the New Deal. He gave them clear general orders and left them free to handle details. He had, in sum, all the personal attributes that a manual would prescribe for the job. If the Presidency was ever to work, now was the time.

No improvement showed beyond the change brought by the extraordinary personal ability of Mr. Kennedy himself. The Presidency continued as if the one man could make all the decisions that needed to be made at the center. No reorganization occurred to create at the center an institutional source of authority that was clearly identified to all subordinates who had to deal with it. Several presidential aides might work on the same subject, sometimes in disagreement with each other and always without authority themselves to make decisions, although they used their influence freely with officials outside the White House. Really close control over the most important issues, such as Cuba before the Russian offensive missiles appeared, was lacking too often, when it was very dangerous for the President to lose sight of the most important issues. Mr. Kennedy showed very early that he would get a high rating in history for his personal skill. He did not improve the Presidency, however, at least not in the short time allowed before he was assassinated and the world lost the skill and the promise of this extraordinary man.

Dwight D. Eisenhower wanted to depend upon subordinates and did. His army days had taught him that authority should be used below the top and a top commander should keep himself free to see the whole. The confused, competitive machinery upon which the President depended was not, however, the same as an army's pigeonholes, plainly marked so that a commander could assign his questions. A President had no single sources of intelligence, plans, personnel, supply, or operations. He had many sources in conflict. Mr. Eisenhower tried the obvious next best. He told subordinates to work out their differences and give him a joint recommendation. He appointed study groups to report on broad subjects. He talked of teamwork. Over eight years he received compromise solutions of immediate questions. He could do nothing that was bold and new save rescue and promote the peaceful use of atomic energy. And to do this Mr. Eisenhower had to fight the apparatus, in which habits were firmly set to stress military uses. His one significant change of course, toward a new plan for more peaceful use of atoms, was also his one time of firm leadership with initiative from the top. (Once in eight years is not often, certainly not when the man who was President was a good man who wanted to use his power to make the world a better place in many ways.)

Harry S Truman changed course twice after the war—and its staggering decision to use the Thing—once when he began economic and military aid in peacetime, and once when he proclaimed the containment of Soviet Communism and backed up the policy with guns in Korea. For both these changes the apparatus worked. It raised proposals for which a yes or no decision was appropriate and sound. Either we gave aid to Greece and Turkey or not; either we saved South Korea or not; the President could decide in clarity and fullness.

Still, the administration of foreign aid after the policy was adopted was hardly a model of government at its best. This is true mainly because the conflicts and compromises within the Executive Branch still produced compromise in operation. As the best known example, the conflict over how much military and how much economic aid is not yet settled after twelve years, nor is the question of how far aid should be decided by politics. Instead of a policy, we continue a compromise. We give military aid when economic aid might get more desirable results, or vice versa, and we give aid to knaves as well as honorable men without knowing for sure that the knaves can be useful to us when we need them. In more than a decade, for more than $75 billion, no coherent policy of foreign aid was developed. Presidents relied upon organization that could not produce coherence but could only work out compromise.

The apparatus did not work in these two cases as well as it should have. The President needed a good horse and received a camel, which is, the joke says, a horse designed by a committee. Also the apparatus was slow. At the third session of the United Nations Economic and Social Council, the need for foreign aid for the reconstruction of Europe was plain. This was in 1946. Parts of the American apparatus, at least those representatives at the session, were agreed on an American position to support aid through the United Nations. They were not allowed, however, to promise that America would pay the cost. It took more than a year for the international plan to get redesigned as the Marshall Plan, an American enterprise. A year is a long, long time in the lives of people who are hungry.

But the most depressing evidence that the Presidency is not working is in unhappy review of all the results of government since the Second World War. The President was responsible for such accomplishments as containment, foreign aid, more stress on the peaceful use of atomic energy, and the refusal to allow Russian offensive weapons in Cuba. He was also responsible for such results as the isolation of West Berlin, the failure to see that North Korea would invade South Korea, the failure to do enough of the right things in Africa and Latin America soon enough to make them strong and friendly in their strength (if this was ever possible as we assumed), and the President was responsible for such crashing events as the U-2 flight just before the Paris summit and the incompetent effort to invade Cuba.

Messrs. Truman, Eisenhower, and Kennedy are equally represented in the record. A President's party politics or personality cannot make the difference between good and bad results. No President will succeed most of the time in foreign affairs until the apparatus is reorganized.

II

Reorganization of the Presidency will not be easy to design. We lack the experience in dealing with the Presidency that we have in the Executive Branch as a whole and inside each of the departments. The Presidency exists to perform the duties of the President without losing the credit or the attention that he wants as a man who is almost certain to be running for re-election in four of his allotted eight years. On the job, at the heart of the institution, "a President is many men," as Merriman Smith once said in the title of a book. Seldom is the President one and only one man at a time. He is, at any moment a blend of politician, philosopher of the national purpose, legislator, lobbyist, judge, military strategist, diplomat, leader in foreign policy, economist, signing machine, administrator, and ceremonial symbol. Any member of his staff has to be broad enough in sensibility to see all these roles and to think as the President thinks on all fronts at once, knowing that one button can ring more than one bell and a President has nowhere to run after he pushes a button.

The President is also an individual with his own way of doing things. Franklin Roosevelt and John Kennedy allowed many cooks to mill around the same cauldron; Harry Truman and Dwight Eisenhower liked more order even though they often failed to get it from the disordered spread around them. Members of the staffs of all Presidents had to learn the bosses' ways and conform to them. Presidential style discouraged some observers from reaching any conclusions for change in the Presidency. "Each man will make the office to suit himself," they said. They failed to see that, no matter what a President's style, he kept the same organization, in general, and expressed his personal style through the persons he chose to fill the positions on the same chart his predecessor had used. He could make the organization less confused without losing his personal expression. A President could, indeed, be more efficient in a well designed house than in a series of caves, and he could still be himself.

One role of the President is superior to the others in its importance to the nation. It is the function of politician, in the broadest definition of that misunderstood word. As politician the President decides national policy. He also leads the nation to accept the policy that he decides is needed. And he represents the nation whenever he decides policy, with his mind aware of how far the people will follow and when they will stop, or in the calculation of whether he and his party will lose or gain votes or cause no change at all.

Politics is the decision of public policy. Sometimes it is expressed in the choice of men to hold office, and other times it is expressed in laws or executive decisions. The range of politics is total. It runs from the choice of a coroner to the choice of a President and from the choice of which chug holes to fill in a back-country lane to the choice of international friends and foes.

In all public decisions forces work from various sides. The politician deals with forces when he decides public policy. He may find the most acceptable agreement, or he may, if he has ideas of his own, choose a position that pleases few but does not stir up serious hostility. One great strength of politicians in any country is the widespread acquiescence of citizens. Whether organized as interest groups or only present in the salt of earth mass, people accept nearly any decision their politicians make. This is made easier because politicians avoid decisions that they know people will not accept.

I go into this because in the semantic chaos of our time politics is a dirty word. In a first college course in political science a good many students respond in conditioned reflex when asked about the ethics of politics. From somewhere, from crunchy breakfast food and peanut butter, from parents or teachers, from each other in that great assurance of the formative years, they get the conviction that politics is dirty and politicians crooked.

It is not politics when vestrymen choose a rich man who can be generous to the church. It is not politics when fathers scheme for positions in the office and seek the help of friends. When the scoutmaster purrs over honorary awards to the hardest working and most influential committee members, good scouts do not see politics. Let public office be mentioned, however, and these young, righteous, ignorant, unthinking, lovable citizens draw away from the taint.

In fairness, when pinned against well-known politicians, the clichéd freshmen will begin to trim. They do not mean that Thomas Jefferson, Abraham Lincoln, Harry Truman, Dwight Eisenhower, or John Kennedy were crooks. Just politicians in general are crooks. So it becomes necessary to justify the term politics in its noble meaning.

The President is supreme in politics. He is the Politician in Chief for the nation. If he fails, the nation fails. In recent years, to repeat, men of undoubted merit have failed badly in some episodes. They have lacked organization for success.

A successful organization can be built around the President as politician. His role as policy-maker and seeker of support—or at least acquiescence—is dominant over his other roles.

The successful organization must also be built around the President as a person. He is not an abstraction but a man of ambition and likes and dislikes, whose goose is the first cooked when anything goes wrong. We have lived so long under image-makers, the hypnotists who create sports and film personalities, that we tend, dangerously, to allow Presidents to work as images. A President has to be judged as a man, if freedom lives. Men fail as well as succeed. Images almost never fail. The hypnotists make failures look like successes. Any organization of the Presidency, to insure responsibility in a free society, must reflect the President as a man, in weakness and strength.

It must, in other words, be under one man's control, subject to one man's personality. The Messrs. Truman, Eisenhower, and Kennedy were the postwar Presidents, not the Executive Office of the President. Their successors will be Presidents, and their aides will remain obscure because people will continue to look to the one man they elected.

III

As now organized, the Executive Office of the President fails on two points. First, it does not guarantee that the President will or can take the initiative in the formation of major policy. Second, it does not enable him to control policy decisions for which he may have to answer.

Only rarely has a recent President been free of the mountains brought to him long enough to think of a mountain he would like to create. The present machinery is designed to move mountains toward him. It will neat them up as much as possible, but it will still move them onto his desk in such number that he cannot find time for anything else. Only rarely has a recent President been able to control the policies that either blew up in his face or came to him in such advanced stages that his best course was to accept and not fight them.

Of course any President under these two handicaps is fair game for department heads who scheme to get his approval. Common questions asked in top departmental councils are: How far will the President go? When is the best time to hit him? Through whom are we most likely to get his sympathy, a member of his family, an aide, a party man who helped him get elected? Will he overlook the claims of other departments which have been kept in the dark?

When initiative and control are kept from the President, they are seized by the departments. But this weakens the President as the man responsible for policy. Mr. Eisenhower could have or-dered the U-2 flights stopped after Camp David only if he had thought about them in the multitude of events that took place hourly within his jurisdiction. Alone he could never think of everything. As an institution his staff could have thought of a category: "things to do after Camp David," and a quick review of what the departments were doing should have raised the U-2 flights for question. The institution of the Presidency failed to work. A department—in this case it is not clear which, State, Central Intelligence, Space Administration, or Defense—retained the decision and the President lost it through inattention.

The Executive Office of the President fails to give the President initiative and control because of two defects of organization.

First, it is itself too diffuse in organization and so adds to the federal sprawl in general. Second, its officials below the President in person have no stated authority of command yet they exert power and cloud the responsibility of those who do have the stated authority of command.

In 1962 the Presidency consisted of the man himself plus a conglomeration of bureaus, individuals, and committees. The segments and number of employees were:

BUREAUS
The White House
  Office   439
Mansion and Grounds
  Staff   73
Office of Emergency
  Planning   538
Central Intelligence
  Agency   ?[1]
Bureau of the Budget 456

INDIVIDUALS (These are
  counted in the White
  House Office above.)
Press Secretary and deputy
Special Counsel and three
  deputies
Special Assistants (10)
Deputy Special Assistant
Administrative Assistants
  (3)
Special Assistants in the
  White House Office (2)

Staff Assistants in the
  White House office (2)
Physician to the President
Special Consultant to the
  President
Special Consultant on
  Youth Fitness
Special Assistant and Director Food for Peace
Military Aide
Naval Aide
Air Force Aide
Personal Secretary
Social Secretary
Assistant Social Secretary
  for Press Relations

COMMITTEES
Council of Economic
  Advisers   45
National Security
  Council   43
National Aeronautics
  and Space Council   14

[1] This figure is kept secret but is publicly estimated by journalists at 10,000 or more in Washington and overseas.

The total number of reported employees was 1,609. This was fewer than a year earlier because Civil Defense had been moved out to the Department of Defense. On the whole, though, the shape of the Executive Office has not changed much under three postwar Presidents. All three have used much the same number of personal aides, the same bureaus and committees, always allowing for some variation. Each man has had his own method of working with the Office, of course—Mr. Eisenhower more as a chairman and Mr. Kennedy more as an executive, as discussed earlier.

IV

Again the question boils down to who is in charge? We have seen the sprawl in foreign affairs outside the White House. A sprawl exists also inside the White House. No one is in charge save the President, and he cannot begin to control all the steps taken in his Executive Office.

Both Presidents Eisenhower and Kennedy allowed their aides to duplicate each other in the handling of foreign affairs. Both failed to make clear to heads of departments how far they depended upon their aides and how far upon department heads. Even John Foster Dulles, the strongest Secretary of State in recent times because President Eisenhower trusted him so firmly, had to worry over what the President's assistants for foreign affairs were doing. There was a Presidential assistant for disarmament, another for psychological cold warfare, another for foreign economic policy, another for food for peace, another for national security affairs. Sherman Adams, who was the number one Presidential assistant, recalls in *Firsthand Report:*

The President made none of these appointments without Dulles' full approval. Still, Dulles watched these specialists intently and, at the first sign of what he suspected to be a possible threat to the tight and straight line-of-command between himself and the President, he straightened out the difficulty quickly. If he thought he couldn't straighten it out himself, he did not hesitate to take it to me and finally to Eisenhower.

The significant point is that a strong Secretary of State, under a trusting President, had to deal with several Presidential assistants, all working in foreign affairs.

President Kennedy continued to assign foreign affairs to his assistants. At one time or another, an assistant dealt with State and Defense Departments, another with monitoring our activities in intelligence, another with disarmament, another with the Peace Corps, another with military policy and general intelligence, another with food for peace. At one time three dealt with Latin American policy. In the case of the Peace Corps the President created the job of director in his office, then moved it nominally into the Department of State. In the cases of then Vice-President Lyndon Johnson and the American Ambassador to the United Nations, Adlai Stevenson, both men would deal with the President whenever they wanted, and he with them, and the Secretary of State could hope that he would be kept informed.

It all added up in the first year of the Kennedy Administration to more diffusion than Eisenhower had allowed. Hostile editorial writers deplored. This was usual. More serious, officials in the ranks found uncertainty in the White House instead of leadership. The uncertainty came from debate among the President's assistants. Decisions were delayed while the staff debated. It seemed truer than ever that no President could be a great success unless he reorganized the Executive Branch including his own Office.

V

The second defect in the Presidency that keeps the President from having initiative and control is that his assistants have no stated authority.

This statement is heresy. Orthodox doctrine says that staff aides should listen to others, analyze proposals to the executive, give him their own ideas, transmit his ideas to others, but they never, never give orders. Only the executive is supposed to give orders. He may have received the draft of an order, already in final form, from a member of his staff, and may sign it without reading it, but in theory a staff assistant is a looker and thinker while only the men in the line of command are doers.

We have taught this theory to the young until its orthodoxy makes it seem true. And men on the line, believing the theory, resent what they call meddling by staff, while men in the staff call it, not meddling, but coordination. In most organizations the fight between line and staff is inevitable. The executive simply does not have time to make all the decisions that have to be made in his name. His staff aides make them in fact though not in theory. Direction and supervision fall into the hands of staff people because someone must direct and supervise even though the executive does not have the time. All who respect the executive agree that trouble should be kept off his desk as much as possible. The staff aides find that he expects them to handle problems for him and they fail in their jobs if too much trouble reaches the boss.

Theory and custom still forbid the aides to be open about direction and supervision. An "assistant to the executive" must still suggest, cajole, and persuade line officers to do what the boss would tell them to do if he had the time. The aide must genuflect daily before the creed that his only role is to help the executive and to stay out of the way of men on the line. But no matter how strong the myth, staff aides in the federal executive have power, and they use it.

The myth is more vulnerable in the White House than in a department. For one reason, the volume of decision piles higher here than elsewhere and the staff aides have more to handle because the executive cannot handle more than any other mortal man. For another, the aura of the President is stronger than that of a department head. Nothing else in our culture equals his magic. He is our foremost celebrity, our defender, our decider, our advocate, our hero or villain, and in the deep unspoken psyche of each citizen, he is a member of the family who can be liked or disliked but who is often present on radio and television whenever, as Fred Allen said, the furniture talks. An aide who works within this aura can make others heed him without half trying.

Most of all, the White House aides are powerful because the President has no deputies in his top command. A department head can when he chooses spread his responsibility to his Under Secretary and Assistant Secretaries and diminish the role of his personal aides. A President cannot share that part of his authority that is peculiar to the Presidency.

The Vice-President is unavailable. He has no constitutional role save to preside over the Senate and to take over when the President dies or becomes disabled. Because he is nominated to complement the candidate for President, he may or may not agree with the policies and personal ambitions of the boss. Few Presidents can be sure that the man who was chosen because he came from a different region and different faction of the party will be the most loyal and dedicated deputy.

If these handicaps were not enough, there is a final one that bars the Vice-President from being more than an odd-job man in the Presidency. He is elected, the only member of the Executive Branch besides the President who is chosen by the voters. A President cannot dismiss the Vice-President if he disapproves his views. If he gives him an assignment, he may not relieve him of it without a scandal. Both Presidents Eisenhower and Kennedy used their Vice-Presidents, as Roosevelt had used Henry A. Wallace, to carry out short-term diplomatic missions or to be chairmen of interagency committees. No President would be wise if he made the Vice-President a permanent deputy president.

Heads of departments cannot perform as deputies of the President. Under any sensible President they will already have as much delegated authority as he can give them, for only a foolish executive tries to do anything he is not required to do. But authority given to heads of departments is quite a different thing from the central authority of the President. It should be confined to the jurisdiction of one department, while the President has to deal with all departments. It will be used in nine cases out of ten, as a President knows well, to promote the interests of the one department.

Heads of departments are not personally to blame. They will be loyal to the President but only in their fashion. Each department head has his own mission cut out. His first duty is to perform that mission. He will be surrounded by his own subordinates who persuade him and use him to accomplish their missions and to defend parochial interests. A head of department is a servant of that department. He must serve its purpose; he has a responsibility to his subordinates as well as to his President. He will be in conflict with other heads of departments because government in truth does resemble the animal kingdom where dogs just don't like cats and there is not much the law can do about it.

The President's job is unique. He sits in the center of conflicting claims and decides in the light of the whole. His office can never listen to one advocate alone nor rely upon the heads of departments to weigh the whole more than their particular claims.

To do his job the President needs aides who do as he does— smart people who think in larger perspective than the heads of departments, who can keep their heads in the bombardment of particular segments from the departments, and who are fast and tough in discussions with heads of departments. It is no surprise that newsmen have found good feature stories in the personalities close to the President from Franklin D. Roosevelt's brain trust to John F. Kennedy's new frontiersmen. For a group that was supposed at birth to have a passion for anonymity, the White House aides have been most publicized federal officials. In some cases books have been written by them.[2] Power concentrates in the White House and this makes news, but, more interesting, the White House aides are freer to be different and to talk of innovation in broad terms without being confined to a department.

Men who are free to think in broader terms than department heads, yet without formal authority, have become as much a part of the Presidency as the President himself. And oftener than not these men are more competent with ideas than the run-of-the-mine top officials in government. Their type will conform to the President. Eisenhower's men were not as bent to reform as Kennedy's men. No matter the views, the intellectual qualities have been good. A President can get the best for his own office and does.

Able, imaginative men full of ideas and the desire for change

[2] Robert E. Sherwood, *Roosevelt and Hopkins, an Intimate History* (New York: Harper & Brothers, 1948); Admiral William D. Leahy, *I Was There* (New York: McGraw-Hill Book Company, 1950); Sherman Adams, *First Hand Report* (New York: Harper & Row, 1961).

inevitably prod department heads. They also initiate changes. When after ritualistic committee thinking departments fail to agree on the large view, the President's aides will state the view. If departments do not act as the President would have them act, his aides will see that they do. Should a department head resent the pressure, he can, of course, go to the President. There he finds that the President's aide was closer to the President's thinking than any department head could be. Chances are good that if the President did not respect his aide's judgment he would not keep him at hand.

Presidential aides do in fact direct and supervise by persuasion, superior knowledge, not a little unspoken threat, and the power of magic aura. They are dominant in many decisions that the President knows nothing about.

CHAPTER 10 RATIONAL
ORGANIZATION: EXECUTIVE
OFFICE OF THE PRESIDENT

THE POSITION OF PRESIDENTIAL AIDES WOULD be clearer, and the President's job more feasible, if the aides were given authority to direct and supervise.

Some other good results would follow too. For one, aides would be less annoying to line officials. As the theory now makes them operate, staff aides bring pressure but do not hold public responsibility, and line officials resent this. For another gain, staff aides, if given authority, will have to be organized within the Executive Office of the President more systematically than now. Jurisdictions will have to be assigned when men are given authority. The confusion that now comes from float and miscellany, and the chance of corridor coordination, will diminish.

To give the aides authority will mean that we have to discard a theory. But is the theory an accurate statement of reality? Is the hypothesis proved in practice? It is certainly not in the Executive Office of the President. It can be discarded with no foul results. More light will shine.

II

A President who decides to give his aides open authority to give orders will have to adopt some new theory for this topmost work.

First, he must choose deputies who will be fiercely loyal to him as a person. No President has yet been discovered who did not make mistakes in his job and reveal personal traits that never appear in the rules for success. The human President's deputies have to understand their boss. They can warn him against his foibles, but if he insists on being himself they must carry out his mistakes as well as his wisdom. The Presidency is truly, as so many have said, whatever the President makes it.

Any President will want deputies who handle the work the way he wants it handled, without argument or incompetence. It needn't be said that the President should pick his deputies himself, without Senate confirmation or any other pressure to choose those who will be acceptable to others than himself. Equally, he should dismiss them when it suits his needs. No deputy should ever be allowed to build up such fame in public that he cannot be dismissed without embarrassment. The President in person must be the boss. Only he was elected to the office. Only he is responsible to the electorate for success or failure in his work. Only he can run for re-election or help his party win. At best a President has enough conflict with the department heads, who defend and expand their parishes. He would be foolish to allow his presidential deputies to show the slightest insubordination.

Second, a wise President will make clear that he will not depend solely upon his immediate deputies for all advice. He will support them, yes, for all the decisions they make on their own authorities, and certainly for those made with his own foreknowledge. But he will make many decisions of his own. The main purpose of reorganization is to give the President time and freedom to be a leader more than a decider of debatable propositions brought to him from compromise. As leader the President will consult as many kinds of people as his temperament decides. One kind of President— Eisenhower was an example—will depend largely upon the top officials with whom he deals. Another, like Franklin Roosevelt, will get advice from officials in the lower ranks and from people outside the government. All Presidents, if they are smart, will keep themselves free of too much dependence upon their deputies. A President can be kept so busy by his deputies that he does not have time for his larger mission, even as he is now confined by the diffusion and confusion within the whole apparatus.

Third, the President should have as few deputies as possible. Otherwise, he can get too involved with his own immediate staff to be free to initiate action or to be a leader. No matter how hard he tries to simplify his staff, the President will still have the most difficult job in the world. He has to use every possibility to free himself from work that can be done by someone else. No one can be sure how many deputies will be ideal. Firm conclusions come from deep analysis and questioning.

Still anyone can say flatly that the present twenty or more is too many and can propose a number as a hypothesis. In this tentative way I suggest that a President should have no more than five immediate subordinates in the White House. We will discuss them more in detail in the next section. Here I should say that one deputy would supervise all aspects of foreign affairs; another would supervise domestic programs; another would be in charge of all management; and the fourth would be responsible for press relations, congressional relations, and party politics. A fifth would head a general planning staff.

III

Each of the five deputies will be in charge for the President of work now handled by various assistants or none. To illustrate—

The deputy for foreign affairs will coordinate the military and civil sides of foreign policy and will supervise both policy and operations. He will displace or absorb all the various individuals who now work on foreign affairs in the White House. When executive coordination is established, the National Security Council, an inter-agency committee, will not be needed and will wither away. (Remember that all constant civil programs in foreign affairs will have been unified, by the proposal of an earlier chapter, under one department and one Secretary; the presidential task will be easier than now.)

Intelligence will come under the deputy for foreign affairs

but not in a literal transfer of the Central Intelligence Agency. The President and his deputy for foreign affairs at their level of top decision need their own evaluation of what the facts mean. Their own staff can be divorced from the biases that so often ruin evaluation within a single department where real, and sometimes unconscious, commitments make people blind to the meaning of facts. If the Strategic Air Command has a doctrine devotedly held, its evaluation of intelligence must be discounted to allow for the doctrine. The same can be said of any other unit of government when considered alone, for the sad truth is that men tend to see facts in the shadows of desire and faith. Intelligence should be the most scientific product of government. Its history is full of error due to childlike and very human disregard of the scientific attitude.

But to say that the President needs his own staff to decide what the facts mean is not to say that he should be the conspicuous spymaster that he will be so long as the spooks who collect secret information are in the Executive Office of the President. In the U-2 affair the President could not escape responsibility when the chart showed that the Director of the Central Intelligence Agency reported to the President.

Collection of intelligence, both open and secret, is performed by several agencies. Some of the earliest collection of secret intelligence in our history was handled by consuls, as it still is, although today the man labelled a consul may be working for the Central Intelligence Agency, and one never knows. There is no good reason why the collection of secret information should be directed from the President's office. All the military services also collect secret intelligence. Not all military men wear uniforms when on duty; not all foreign informants by any means report to the agents of Central Intelligence. After the failure of its effort in 1961 to manage a counterrevolution in Cuba, a good many critics questioned whether the Central Intelligence Agency should continue to be in charge of sabotage, subversion, and related dark arts in other lands. They were dubious for the old human reason that the agency's dream might distort its view of the intelligence it collected, as seemed to happen in Cuba when the agency so overestimated the support for revolution as to be criminally negligent of the invaders' lives.

The decision of foreign policy is a noble enterprise for a President. It rests upon the evaluation of intelligence, not first upon the immediate direction of the agency that collects secret intelligence and arranges skulduggery.

Secret intelligence has stronger reasons for being than subversion and sabotage, of course. So long as nations keep secrets, other nations will try to get them. Most intelligence is obtained, as all practitioners agree, from open sources, but the collection of secrets adds that last and sometimes most revealing portion. We will continue to collect secrets, as we have always done. But we should keep the President out of the business. Espionage should be removed from his immediate supervision, even as sabotage and subversion should be removed. Let the President's deputy for foreign affairs supervise the central evaluation of intelligence from all sources—but not subversion and espionage.

The deputy for domestic affairs will act for the President in all that remains after foreign affairs are covered. This includes agriculture, commerce, labor, welfare, finance, and justice, all the services and regulations administered by all the agencies save the new departments of Defense and State.

The deputy for management will supervise budget, personnel, and services. He will command the present Bureau of the Budget, the Civil Service Commission, if a single director of personnel cannot be obtained, and the General Services Administration.

When the Council of Economic Advisers was created after the War, some wise political scientists said that its work belonged more properly to the Bureau of the Budget. The Federal Budget has never been used as it could be to make federal spending complement economic needs in the nation. Despite noble intentions, the budget always turns out to be not so much a plan for controlling inflation or counteracting the business cycle by changes in taxes or expenditure as it is a listing of the minimum needs to carry on the activities of government. To serve its greater purpose the budget needs to be based more upon analysis of the nation's economic health and solutions through action by the federal government. The Council of Economic Advisers has this job, to analyze the nation's economic health and propose government action to keep the nation healthy. It can well be moved into the Bureau of the Budget.

The deputy for press relations, congressional relations, and party politics already exists in segments of the White House staff. One, the press secretary, is in these times of insatiable media better known outside government than most other officials. A lesser known assistant deals with Congress, and another handles matters of concern to the party, including patronage.

Any President is always onstage, poor man. His every mood would be reported if newsmen could learn it. In India, Arthur Koestler reported in *The Lotus and the Robot,* the devotees of one self-centered Swami were allowed to sit in the next room to hear in adoration the bathroom noises of his morning toilet. As a climax to this ceremony the Swami emerged into the front room and gargled three times. A misfortuned President would have such an audience equipped for sound and camera if he did not fight for privacy. Further, he would be asked questions and petitioned while he gargled. Press and public seem to have no limit to their interest in the President. News coverage went into intimate detail of Mr. Eisenhower's physiology when he was in the hospital seriously ill.

Such prominence is the man's best gift as well as his burden. Because he is the most celebrated, he is also the most influential person in our society. A good part of the work of his office is spent on the use of his influence. It shows in the calculated news release, the people he sees, the statements in press conference, his speeches, his dealings with Congress and, perhaps more significant, with single members of Congress. All this is one whole; we cannot snatch one moment and say that in it the President was dealing with party, or Congress, or press; he uses his influence with all to operate on any, and his influence comes from his popularity. In the new organization one deputy will be in charge of the protection, development, and use of presidential influence. (I have avoided that overused term public relations. It is much too limited to describe the intricate and unique condition of presidential influence.)

IV

The fifth deputy will head a planning staff, for want of a better term. "I have always thought," says Sherman Adams, "that Eisenhower went to the roots of his biggest problem when he said with some exasperation at a staff meeting in his first year in office, 'when does anybody get any time to think around here?' "

All Presidents have asked it since the whirlwind started, and done almost nothing about it. As a person the President can get more time to think if he gets fewer subordinates to deal with and gives them authority to make decisions in his name. The more routine he can get off his own desk, the more time he will have for ideas.

But thinking at this high level of national policy is more than a one-man job. It involves now all those who work day-to-day and who see policy come from their work. These are the people who make policy while answering the mail. They keep the President so swamped with issues that he seldom does get any time to think. A presidential planning staff will broaden the issues and see things that do not occur in the mail. Only a few people are needed, but this must be their only job and their chief must be recognized in the organization as having a firm, authoritative voice.

What would the members of this staff do when they go to work in the morning? It is easier to say what they would not do, for the Policy Planning Staff of the State Department set the sad example of failure due to suffocation in routine. They would not attend staff meetings or read house organs to keep up with what happened in the last few hours. Instead they would, each man in his own office and in conference with others, study and write papers on fundamental questions that government policy will have to meet.

In foreign affairs some such questions are: How much really (not idealistically) can standards of living be raised in the low-income nations without a great inflow of investment for industrial plant? If not by advanced industrialization, can standards be raised through changes in the controls over international trade?

What happens to the political attitudes of people in the various cultures when their standards rise? Do they really become pro-democratic, as we hope, or do they still think authoritarianism makes more sense? What new elites will appear? How will the changes vary from one nation to another?

So far American foreign aid since 1947 has been based on assumptions, not analysis. We have assumed that better sanitation, education, public administration, and economic development within the existing economy will raise levels enough to make a difference in political attitudes. (An equally sensible hypothesis is that they only show deprived people what else they are missing and make them resentful of rich Americans.) A poultice, however, will not cure anemia. Sanitation and the other benefits of the good life under technology are manifestations, not causes, of high production per man-hour. No real gain in standards of living will come from sticking on a few manifestations. Blood transfusion is indicated, and probably major surgery. In some countries an old-fashioned democratic revolution may be necessary before the economic change can begin.

At present no one in the whole blessed government is thinking about these questions, at least not at the level where he can be heard. Rarely a President combines just the right elements of education, intellectual curiosity, and experience to do his own long thinking. On top of this combination he must have the rare ambition and rarer skill that enable him among all the millions to win the post.

Obviously we cannot depend upon such a phenomenon to appear very often. Only Jefferson, Lincoln, and Wilson have been it so far. Kennedy had the extraordinary combination of talents but still had to show by deeds how he would enter history. He might have been so tangled in chaotic organization that his personal talents could not get the results that he knew were needed.

An institution for thinking is indicated. Besides studying and writing, the members of the thinking staff will talk with others who can help them and with each other. They must take care to avoid mere hot air conferences, and they will have to fight off special advocates. Members of the staff will be ruined if they begin to work on current policies, just as they will be ruined if they begin to initial telegrams to show that they have been informed. Their job is to see patterns, not to worry about the day's events or answer the daily mail.

Their only client is the President. Probably the deputy in charge of planning will deliver a report to the President and his four other deputies only when he has something worth saying. He will not be in on everything; his phone will not ring as much as the others'; he will not get stacks of mail to sign or initial. Unless he is a strong and stable man who knows what his job is and is happy with it, he will feel left out. Prestige inside bureaucracy so often goes with swimming in the right circles. It is the lonely swimmer who sets records, though, and a planning staff may in the end make more history than those who handle events.

One unit of the present Executive Office can be transformed into the planning staff. The Office of Emergency Planning has planning as its mission. The kind of planning it does has little relation to the large, far policy planning that is needed. It is devoted to stockpiles, transport, manpower, and other such necessary elements of cold war that might become hot. All such work can be transferred to agencies outside the White House; stockpiles and transport, for example, to the Department of Commerce, manpower to Labor, as civil defense, once here, was transferred to Defense. All departments have to plan the down-to-earth future moves in their fields of work. The President needs a larger vision.

V

Given five deputies, loyal to him personally, able to give directions to department heads, acting only as extensions of his authority, the President can be the supreme politician, or policy leader. He will be freed from the tyranny of miscellaneous causes poured into his schedule from an apparatus that is poorly designed to select only those causes on which a President should act.

The President will still be in command. It will be *his* administration. The right kind of deputies will make sure that he gets credit for good news, and no matter what the organization he gets blamed for bad news.

As supreme executive the President will still consult anyone he chooses, either from the departments or from the considerable world outside government. He will still be able to bring into his own hands any matter that he wants to handle personally. If precedent holds, as it will, the deputies will try to take more issues to the President than he will want to handle. Every top executive of good sense and sophistication urges his deputies to handle more decisions than they prefer. A good and loyal deputy wants to be sure he is doing what the boss would do and wants too the comfort to morale that comes from talks between men who respect each other.

The President will also talk with heads of departments together and alone. Certainly no President will make the life and death decisions of foreign policy without talking with anyone he finds instructive. This point needs to be clear. Always when deputies to the President are discussed, there are cries of alarm. The heads of departments will be layered, a bureaucratic term which means that a layer of supervisors is placed between an official and the boss. Secretaries of Defense, State, and the other departments, not to mention the Federal Tariff Commission, do not like to be layered. They prefer direct access even though it burdens the President unendurably.

Under the new scheme all such executives will still deal with the President when they and a President's deputy decide that the cause is serious enough to take to the top. But the President will not be compelled by the structure of the federal executive branch to deal with eighty different people. He can control his own time and work.

Layering is a steady trend, it should be pointed out to those who are threatened with it. John Quincy Adams used to write in his own hand instructions to his ambassadors. Abraham Lincoln walked to the telegraph room of the War Department where he read the day's messages from the field. His door was open to department heads and job-seekers alike. But for years now a department head has seen the President only by appointment. And for years department heads have found it wise to stand well with the aide in charge of appointments by not overdoing their visits to the overworked boss. In the top circle of federal bureaucracy the aide for appointments is better known and more cultivated than any other presidential aide save the chief assistant, when one exists, in contrast to the press secretary, whom the public knows best. Department heads are already layered in fact by presidential aides. Until now the layering is unspoken and both sides hold the fiction that the President's staff does not intervene. To give authority openly to presidential deputies would make the layer plain and true.

One great gain from reorganization will be easier selective consultation. The President will no longer be burdened by the National Security Council which was established by law to advise him on foreign policy. Presidents Truman and Eisenhower held meetings, though both of them found that they wanted the advice of other men than the legal members and invited them to the meetings. President Kennedy early disbanded a subsidiary group called the Operations Coordinating Board, a kind of servant committee to the Council. He still met with the Council for some purposes, but he soon showed that he was not the type to appreciate administration by committee.

His most serious problems in foreign affairs were discussed with handpicked groups not tainted with the committee label. He took with him for a weekend on the chronic Berlin crisis no more than the Secretaries of State and Defense and his personal adviser on military affairs. Those left behind deplored such selectivity and missed the large, wasteful conference to which they were accustomed. When Mr. Kennedy settled his course on one subject, he turned to another group for the next subject, as any competent executive does.

Nothing in the theory of a strong executive denies that he should get advice. Only the noxious dogma of group-think holds that he must decide after getting advice from everyone who wants to give it, preferably organized in a standing committee.

A President can have deputies and still be himself.

This is perhaps the most important virtue to retain. Voters can hold truly responsible only a man they can judge in their own image. They cannot judge a head of machinery, an executive over so many employees and such varied affairs that no ordinary citizen can grasp the nature of the President's work. A citizen can judge only the man who shows through that work. The citizen can detect courage, sound judgment, the high mind and heart and the motives not so high.

Then a President is entitled to be himself both for his record with voters and for his own personality. He can be himself if he picks the right deputies and fires any who show the least sign of deviation from the spirit of the office. Once the President looks outside his own office, he begins to negotiate; he tempers his decisions to the people who carry them out. Considerations of politics and the kind of men who will accept the posts limit the President when he appoints heads of departments, members of commissions, and the other top men who make up his administration. He inherits the much larger group of permanent civil and military officials. His personal advocates who will do what he wants just because he wants it are to be found for certain only in his personal staff.

The President indeed can be most competent as himself in a competent organization. So long as his own office is filled with wandering aides who sometimes cross each other he cannot reach his best. It is time to make the Chief Executive able to command his own forces in his own way.

VI

Two other questions should be raised, beyond the one of any threat to the President's personal authority, whenever this concept of the Presidency is suggested. They are serious. No one can be sure of the answers except to say that practice is what counts. Structure and theory only set the frame. What people do is practice.

The first question is whether the top command won't be top-heavy. Won't so many decisions have to be made by the President and his subordinates that the work will be jammed in a bottleneck? The second is: Won't more authority in the White House be taken as license to interfere more in matters that can best be handled in the line?

Practice will certainly determine the answer to the first. If a President and his deputies want to haul details in for decision, they will do so under the present scheme. They will waste their time and soon discover that their assignment is much larger than doing those things that can be handled by a bureau. We have to assume that the President will be a man of good sense and a great desire to make a good record. The man was not elected as a ninny. He will get deputies who can soon learn their jobs.

When a bottleneck develops in the White House now, it is due to too many aides who cannot make decisions but only persuade, suggest, hold interdepartmental conferences, try to agree among themselves, and try as long as possible to keep the President from being bothered by an unsettled fight. Deputies with authority can make decisions and give orders. They should cause less delay than the present group of floating questioners. If they want to insist upon too much central handling, they will do so now.

We are not likely, however, to get men in the White House who take control blindly. The best men will want strategic control, and they should have it. Strategic control means that only those issues will be chosen for presidential control that make a difference to his purpose and performance. There is no way under heaven to define such issues ahead of time. One day the closing of a single air base may be taken to the President because it is a hot political question in the district of the chairman of the House Committee for the Armed Services. The next day the Air Force may close ten other bases and the President need never pass judgment. Subordinates, executives in the departments and aides to the President, decide when an issue is strategic. And a President who so desires can always reach into the swirl of lesser issues and take charge of one that interests him. John F. Kennedy did so frequently from his omnivorous concern and competence. Such action should be the President's choice, though, and not his inescapable fate.

Of course to some men in the line a man at the center seems to be creating a bottleneck by his mere existence. Such men argue against the need for any central executive at all. They contend that the departments should be autonomous and that efficiency will come only from the grassroots, by the grassroots, for the grassroots. They deny the need for a strong President. I confess that I do not try to reason with anachronistic Jeffersonians. They live in a make-believe world, in which their theory is so remote from reality that it becomes more a mystical faith than a serious proposition. The President is the nation's chief policy leader and executive. Our system cannot work without a strong President. To do his duty, he needs a strong central staff. If this state of affairs angers the decentralists, I can pity them, caught as they are in centralization, but I cannot join them for I cannot understand them.

As for the second question of central license to interfere, there is a difference between interference and command. The same line officials who see a bottleneck at the center when they fail to see waste of time in their own locale tend to call any question from the center an intereference. We should pay no attention to them, except to start looking for better men.

A chief executive is supposed to direct, organize, assign jurisdictions, coordinate, make decisions, and set goals. Because he cannot do all this by himself in large organization, he will get staff help. If this help follows the customary doctrine for staff work, it will advise, question, persuade, and guide the chief executive by drafting the decision which he will sign. If it holds authority to give orders, it will do an executive's work for him, taking to him only those issues that require his personal decision.

In neither case is action at the center an interference with the line. Better say that the line exists to carry out the will of the chief executive, but this is not true either. The only truth is that federal executive organization is too complicated to describe in easy clichés. We can say only that policies and action come from both the line and the central staff and neither can interfere with the other since they are both engaged in the same enterprise. Talk of the threat of interference has to be confined, then, to particular episodes in which one side or the other errs. Good sense and good will should prevent error, but not all government men, alas, are filled with both, so the talk of interference continues as it must while men are imperfect. Practice again decides how structure works.

VII

The President more than anyone else will decide practice in a new Presidency organized as I suggest here. Any good student of public administration can tell him to watch first three most delicate and difficult parts of his job.

The first is the definition of his own personal role. No other job on earth is identical with his so the man cannot read a handbook on how to be President. He can detect a few guides from his predecessors. The strong Presidents have been strong personalities who made decisions on their own after listening to varied advice. They gave subordinates authority without fretting over its use so long as things went all right, but they noticed small issues as well as large whenever small issues concerned them. They knew that their job was not that of an executive alone, comparable to the presidency of a private corporation, but rather a post of awful responsibility to lead in policy and to move the people forward in ideas. No strong President can be either a chief clerk or the chairman of interagency conferences in which consensus rules. Strong Presidents welcome responsibility and the power to answer.

The second delicate zone is the role of administrative management, defined to mean the handling of budget, accounting, personnel, and the so-called housekeeping services of purchases, space, communication, and transportation. These offices can serve policy or control it depending upon how the President defines their role. If they serve policy, they give advice during its formation on what it will cost and how it can best be carried out. If they control policy, they argue that a policy should not be adopted because it costs too much or is too difficult to administer.

A quiet, almost unnoticed reversal in the American approach to foreign policy occurred in the 1950s. It began when President Truman invited the Secretary of the Treasury to sit in meetings of the National Security Council, and it reached its peak when President Eisenhower invited both the Secretary of the Treasury and the Director of the Bureau of the Budget to take part in the decisions of general foreign policy.

Before the change, policy was decided and then the budget and accounting men were told to find the money or say why it could not be found. Wiser executives took them into planning a policy so that they could estimate costs and suggest the most efficient execution. After the change, the fiscal agents argued the policy for the sake of saving money. A policy of spend as little as possible was their goal. Others from the State and Defense Departments, who had the goal of the most security, were forced to compete with moneysavers. The change was Presidents' choice. Mr. Kennedy seemed to return to the pre-Truman custom of deciding what he wanted to do before asking the price, although his Director of the Budget still held great power in the interpretation of the President's desires for many issues that never reached the President.

Administrative staffs can also control policy by loading its execution with overburdensome accounting, petty inspection, and too anxious scrutiny of busy people. Next to the President, the people in the most strategic positions to help or hurt any program are those in charge of budget, accounting, personnel, and services, from the Executive Office of the President to the most remote mission in the field.

The poison of overmanagement spreads once it starts and is hard to cure. It has now included a full third of the employees of the Department of State, as we saw earlier. That one in three who handles budget, accounting, personnel, and services (for two other employees) is not a loafer. He thinks up all kinds of controls and checks over hiring, spending, allocation of funds, and the use of facilities. For years the Department of State has been notorious among federal departments for restrictive management. The whole government will be as inefficient if a President fails to choose the right kind of managers and fails to make them see their job as helpers and not restrainers.

The third delicate spot is planning. A President should listen to his deputy for planning with open mind and a willingness to do something about the ideas that are good. This deputy alone of the five will have nothing to direct save his own staff. Some day there may be long-range planning staffs in all departments whose work would be directed from the White House by the deputy for planning, but for the present the first need is for a thinking staff for the President alone, and for the State Department, a point to be discussed later. Without real authority of his own, the deputy for planning must rely upon the President to put any plans to use. The President owes it to himself and his country to listen to the planners and then give orders that will prepare the nation for the future.

Above all a new President must remember that he was not elected to be an administrator but a leader. He has to be everybody's battle axe in a time of trouble, to borrow from a chant heard long ago when gospel singers sang only in church. The people want him to decide policies. Organization exists only to enable the President to do his job most efficiently in his own way. It still holds that no President can do his best work, and express himself best as a person, until the Presidency is reorganized out of its present confusion.

PART THREE PERSONNEL

CHAPTER 11   THE NEW
DIPLOMACY

THE PEOPLE WHO HANDLE FOREIGN AFFAIRS FOR
the United States can be discussed only in relation to the work to
be done. Negotiation among nations and all the skills that attend it
are diplomacy. Once, when princes in person made all their own
decisions and their diplomats dealt directly with their princes as
reporters, advisers, and negotiators, the term diplomacy was confined to the art of the diplomat. Now, when nearly all the work in
the home government is done by professional diplomats and most
policy is decided as well as carried out by them, the term can be
used for the whole process of foreign affairs, from policy decisions
through execution. It is so used here.

Diplomacy has changed greatly in its practice by the United
States since our entrance into the Second World War. The change
during war was to be expected; indeed we used to refer to the wartime measures as ways to cope with emergency. When the wartime
changes were carried into the postwar years, something very significant had happened, a change so deep that we have not yet ad-
justed to it with a theory of personnel management that fits the
startling circumstance.

Without much notice the United States in a few years after 1945
displaced 500 years of the practice of diplomacy. From the time the
Duke of Milan established at Genoa in 1455 the first recorded
mission sent from one state to reside in another, diplomats knew

pretty well what was expected of them. They represented at royal courts and capitals their sovereign lords and governments in manner befitting. They negotiated with their hosts and with other ambassadors any matters that came up either locally or from home. They reported to their own governments on any subjects of interest, with the greatest attention to developing alliances and enmities.

Always they watched and reported opportunities for their own states to gain advantages. Whenever possible, they intervened to turn a development to their own countries' interests, for only the dolts confined their work to reports and requests for instructions. Their most quoted mentor, Francois de Callieres in *On the Manner of Negotiating with Princes* (1716) described as well as anyone after him the diplomat's role in the strategy of international relations:

Now, the enlightened and assiduous negotiator serves not only to discover all projects and cabals by which coalitions may arise against his prince in the country where he is sent to negotiate, but also to dissipate their very beginnings by giving timely advice. . . . The able negotiator will know how to profit by the various dispositions and changes which arise in the country where he lives, not merely in order to frustrate designs hostile to the interest of his master, but also for the positive and fruitful purpose of bringing to an apt result those other designs which may work to his advantage. By his industry and application he may himself produce changes of opinion favorable to the office which he has to discharge; indeed, if he do but once in an apt moment catch the tide at the flood he may confer a benefit on his prince a hundredfold greater than any expense in treasure or personal effort which he may have put forth.

Other agents, more plebeian than ambassadors, were needed to take care of the protection of citizens, especially as democracy spread and common people gained the right to be protected. Consuls took on the work of dealing with seamen and other travellers. Because consuls could enter the market place and ask prices, they were also the only official help for exporters and importers of their own and their host countries. They developed trade reporting to a system. Consuls told businessmen where they might find markets and goods and gave advice on the reputations of firms in other countries.

Broader economic reporting then developed as both a consular and, very recently, a diplomatic function. It includes facts and interpretation about production, wages, trade, and any other elements of a country's economy that might be significant. The separation of diplomats and consuls in different corps continued in American organization until 1924.

Economics and politics in reality have always been indivisible, and history is full of dukes and kings who made alliances because they needed money, but, because the diplomatic corps was born aristocratic, the snobbish attitude toward economic work was still held as late as 1945. When truth is spoken in the shop talk of the service, the men who work in political affairs still think they are more important than men who work on economic and consular matters, and the inside prestige goes most to them.

The diplomatic assignment was clear and unchanging during those 500 years. First attention was given always to political affairs, such as changing alliances. A diplomat reported shifts in position at court or told of angling by other nations for power. He suggested moves to his own government. If time was too short to get the word from home, the good diplomat acted on his own to get an advantage for his country. At home, in the Ministry of Foreign Affairs, men of the same stripe thought of all nations at once and saw relations with any one in a pattern of relations with all. These men, schemers if you please, advised their prince, whether king or president, on the moves he should make to gain strength. Abroad and at home the good diplomat looked ahead. He went below appearances to analyze any event in its context of the past, the present, and the future, for to a diplomat the event was never taken alone.

Note that I have said the *good* diplomat did this. The diplomatic service has always had its share of inadequate chatterboxes and dull, slow men without insight, more in the days before selection by examination than now, always remembering that giants too walked in those days.

During the Second World War and afterward America added new work to foreign affairs until the old comfortable diplomacy was smothered.

Fast changes occurred simultaneously. Some, it is true, were changes in degree only, but all added up to make a brand new kind of job both at home and abroad. We grew so accustomed to upheaval that we took it as normal. The conduct of foreign affairs had forever left the course it had followed since the Renaissance.

II

For the first time in our history two major powers, Germany and Japan, were taken over in defeat to be governed by the United States Army, in Germany with Britain, France, and Russia as allies, in Japan with a nominal alliance but in fact alone. Commanding Generals of the United States thus became governors of prostrate nations, under orders to make them live on their own again but peacefully, with democratic governments. Here was a new diplomacy most drastic in change. The doctrine that a diplomat visited another country was scarcely an echo when generals ruled conquered nations. Only remote doctrines of conquest from Greece, Rome, and the Middle Ages were precedents at large. The United States could cite in its own history only some small experience in the defeated South, the Phillipine Islands, and the Rhineland.

Some very serious foreign policies were decided for the occupations. For one, both Japan and West Germany were made strong again. For another, both were remade as capitalist, competitive, forms of economy so that alliance with other private enterprise nations was arranged by the very policy of recovery. Political power, reflecting economic power, was pro-capitalistic from the start. Two strong allies in the Cold War against communism were created from the ruins of the hot war. Communists did not particularly like this, although they certainly would have built communist countries in Japan and West Germany if they had occupied them. As foreign policy the significant central decision was to use our occupied nations in the Cold War by making them strong and free. We did not leave them to work out their own destinies.

Other decisions made the strategy clearer. American troops remained in Japan, partly because the new Japanese Constitution, written in American headquarters, contained by special desire of General Douglas MacArthur a provision that the new Japan would not engage in war again. Germany was divided into four zones, and Berlin in the Russian zone was divided, for the purpose of occupation. This division was the cause of crises in later years. The capitalistic powers rebuilt and united their zones; the communist power bled its zone, then found it could not simply absorb Berlin when its western zones were happily, belligerently capitalistic and supported by powerful friends. The lines for economic and psychological warfare were drawn early in the occupations.

Generals had a strong voice in the occupation policies. In Washington the State Department was only an equal of the old War and Navy Departments, and State sent only a political adviser to each Commanding General. By long tradition the commander in the field had almost as much authority as he himself established by use, provided he did not grossly violate the rules and custom by open defiance of his commanders in Washington, as MacArthur did before he was removed. The political advisers were only as strong as the generals allowed them to be. As civilians in a military theater, they were under command of the generals. General Lucius Clay in the memoir of his command in postwar Germany tells how he demanded, and made stick, that the State Department should not send its messages directly to his political adviser, Robert Murphy, but to the Office of Military Government, the military command.

From the first days of occupation, the military forces and departments were strong partners in making foreign policy toward Germany and Japan, both during occupation and after recognition of new governments. They made a new atmosphere for older diplomats, most of whom had never got closer to military men than the ceremonies when a warship put into a foreign port.

Two other military activities in foreign affairs grew beyond any size we had ever known before, one the foreign relations of troops stationed abroad, the other military aid and advice.

III

Americans with the armed forces abroad were men and women in uniform, wives and children, and civilians who worked for the services. They lived in bases that were so self-sufficient that a little bit of Shopping Center fell to earth wherever Americans gathered. Everywhere the Americans had more and better goods than the local people. No matter how loud the local conservatives denounced gadgetry and vulgar display, the local masses admired American ways. Housewives saw merit in automatic washing machines; their children liked blue jeans and phonograph records; their husbands coveted the big automobiles with lavish grills and jukebox behinds. The mere presence of all those Americans, well paid and well supplied, created both enmities and friendships, in either case a new kind of face-to-face relation between foreigners and Americans who worked for government under military jurisdiction, far from the usual responsibility of the ambassador.

On the whole the relations between Americans and local residents were made easy by kindness. Most Americans, as most foreigners, are kind. Being kind, they are considerate, therefore courteous and generous in spirit. Only the exceptions are mean and vulgar, as in other nationalities. When the armed forces command urged their people to get acquainted with foreigners, in what was called the people-to-people program, their first asset was this wide existence of good feeling. Arrangements for its expression were needed and were suggested.

The presence of troops also required more formal arrangements. Traffic accidents occurred. Crimes were committed. Actions over debts and property were taken to law. Agreements with the host government provided for legal rights, and jurisdictions, country by country where our troops were stationed.

Usually the press at home ignored the routine flow of cases

under these agreements. Once, a sergeant shot a Japanese woman and was tried in a Japanese court under our arrangement with Japan. For the first time many Americans became aware that the nations where our troops were stationed had something to say about legal control over their behavior. After the usual extreme demands from the irresponsible right, which in America always seems oddly close to advocating anarchism, the case came to its end. Most cases still go little noticed at home or in the nations that are hosts to thousands of Americans.

Other relations are less legal and less predictable but just as intense. Some are social; some are economic. Americans' casual dress and decorum offend more formal people. The American man's bold, frank, and overt interest in women violates convention in some countries. Higher pay for the American does not help smooth understanding among men. Average Americans can spend more money than any other average men in the world for the entertainment of their ladies. They are also clean, brave, generous, courteous, kind, and as true as any courting male can be. Women all over the world want to marry American men, and many do. This does not make international relations easier, but it can hardly be prevented by law. When a big crisis develops, as when Iceland officially threatens to ask our troops to leave, the best we can do is to restrict our men to their base, with a high fence and numerous guards to enforce the restriction. Such action does not make the Americans feel very friendly toward Iceland, and, while it pleases Icelandic males, it deprives the ladies.

To turn to economic relations caused by troops abroad, the sensitivity of local purses can never be overanticipated. Purse anger is as common abroad as at home, where trade associations are always alert to demand profit from any action by government. National defense stands or falls, we are told at home, by whether real estate promoters provide the only housing for families in the armed forces or whether the clubs on post are allowed to sell drinks at prices below those charged by dismal taverns in the town. Overseas the greed of small merchants is just as prevalent if not as well organized. A post exchange may run into trouble whenever it prices local articles lower than the private stores. Once the exchange in Paris created a ticklish few days of excited negotiation between the governments of France and the United States because it sold perfume at a lower price than the Paris shops.

Wages can cause as much trouble as prices. If the armed forces should pay American scale wages to local employees, every worker of good sense would (a) rush to the American jobs or (b) demand higher pay from his local employer. Such recklessness would upset the whole local economy, the local employers say, loudest in those countries where a few are rich and many are half-starved on low wages. So the Americans agree to pay no more than limited amounts.

Next comes the unhappiness of the local employee of an American establishment who is paid less than the American who does the same work. If not this, perhaps local workers discover that, while their friends who work at the American base get the same wages, they get some quiet additions such as a high-calorie meal at work and a free shower bath, and the rich Americans rush medical aid to a man who is hurt on the job, without deducting from his pay.

To move a cross section of America into another nation is not easy. Oldtime diplomats never dreamed of these involvements.

IV

Military aid and advice is more confined and less noticed than the intrusion of thousands of Americans into a country, but it is more a threat to the tranquility of governments. All programs for supply reduce to haggling over needs and uses. The donor nation insists that whatever it gives should get the most results; the receiving nation asks for more than it will ever get and wants items that suit its own definition of what will get the most results. All governments are self-interested first and international second.

A minister of defense will decide that an airplane for his own use is more strategic than mortars. His prime minister, who already has an airplane, will want those things that give his government most prestige at home, most strength against possible assaults, from within or without, and least dependence upon the United States for spare parts. Ambitious and earnest young army officers want the most up-to-date weapons so that if war comes they will not be outdated. American negotiators have to hammer out a program for equipment and training that will keep the ally on our side and at the same time truly mean more strength for the West.

All have unspoken thoughts, so often no more than fears that cannot be mentioned because at the moment they are unsupported by evidence. Nations with arms are more dangerous to their neighbors than nations without arms. Rulers think of what they might conquer, and of how they might be conquered. Members of the Military Assistance Advisory Group, our men, think of the possible end when supplies given to a friendly nation are captured if that nation is defeated. Captured equipment, even when spare parts come from America, can be used until it breaks down, until all possible cannibal repairs are exhausted, until all other improvisation fails. Food, drugs, and clothing can be used until the stores are gone. Communist China's capture of American equipment from Nationalist China is a bad memory to the managers of military supply.

Then the men who hold office in new and unstable nations never forget that armies can seize power at home. The better equipped an army is, the stronger it is to take over and run the country. Armies are truly the most feasible revolutionary instruments left, perhaps the only ones, since no civil party is ever likely again to get advanced weapons for a successful revolt and a palace cabal has no hope without the support of the army. Pistols and gasoline bombs cannot beat tanks. The brave men of Budapest learned this. Civilian heads in the dissatisfied lands know the threat of armies. Officers know it too. So do the Americans who work with them.

What could be closer to the heart of another nation's politics than these unspoken thoughts? Military activities brought a depth of intervention in the life of another nation that was never dreamed of in the first 500 years of modern diplomacy. We began to deal with the most sensitive matters, such as social relations, trade, and the strength of rulers.

V

American economic operations in other countries, different from economic reporting, became permanent after the war, having begun during the war in lend-lease and the purchase of strategic materials for import. The reporting of economic matters was already established, although disdained by older diplomats who still dreamed of the seventeenth century and tried to preserve traditions. Economic operations are new. They mean that agents of the United States government on the soil of another nation buy and sell, lend money, and provide help to the other government and its citizens. Again, as in military aid, the donor nation, following its self-interest, wants the most results for the lowest amounts. The receiving government wants those grants that will give it the most prestige and give strength and benefit to the groups that control the country and its government.

Seldom do the two interests agree. The American wants efficiency. If steel can be bought cheaper in a third country than it can be produced in a new industry, he will argue for purchase. His opposite sees national pride as more important than economics and so argues for capital and equipment to build his nation's own steel plant. Nothing seems to serve a new nation's pride quite like a steel plant. It is proof to nationalists that they are free of colonial status.

Anxieties over homemade steel are not the only cause of argument. Everything about the other nation's economy gets involved with American aid. Our purpose is to create at once a stronger ally and a less favorable prospect for communist recruiters. We try first to win governments and second to win the masses. Some Americans have never understood this fact of life. In certain countries, whether we like it or not, governments are composed of men very different from the masses. We deal with these in hope that we also do something for the masses. Only the advanced nations have the literate, interested masses that provide popular influence as we know it.

Governments want to get American aid on their terms, both

noble and base. We want to give it on our terms. Capital will be lost if sensible industries are not built with it. Industries cannot succeed without skilled workers. To get skills, workers need new school systems. In the bedrock of any plan, taxation, public health, and public administration determine what can and cannot be done with either production or the pursuit of happiness. Taxation decides the distribution of benefits. Public health decides the efficiency and quality of the people. Public administration decides the competence and honesty of government. Americans who intervene in these internal affairs cut very near the bone in any nation's way of doing things. To do their duty to America, they must intervene in everything from nuts and bolts to the standards of civil servants.

Economic operations can be divided into three types.

One is development, the use of capital and physical resources to raise the nation's strength and welfare. American help goes to improve transportation, clear land, dig irrigation ditches, build industries, schools, hospitals.

The second is technical assistance. American specialists go to the other country to show its people how to do things they want to learn to do. For some reason, Americans of good heart seem to talk more about technical assistance than any other part of foreign affairs. They have more experience with it, despite the fact that most of us think it is a new idea. Missionaries began technical assistance with the first schools and clinics in poor lands, then reached many Americans at home with requests for money to continue the good work. All of us saw too at home the miracle of what could be done with technical knowledge. Technical training in America was deliberate. Vocational courses and schools were commonplace, from woodworking in the seventh grade to architecture in the colleges. County agents took technical knowledge to farmers at home. Industries and unions provided training for apprentices. If it worked so well at home, it should help pre-industrial people.

Now the variety of technical assistance is stopped only by the variety of requests. It includes help with, to list a few, the preservation of food, public budgeting, police administration, school administration, the use of chemical fertilizers, community planning, water supply, nursing, engineering, epidemiology, taxation. The work is often handled under contract by an American university or other non-profit institution. Government agents decide which services to provide. They also work abroad with other governments and contractors.

The third type of economic operation is buying and selling. A surprising amount of this goes on in our mixture of public and private enterprise. At any given time somewhere in the world an American official or a private citizen acting within a government plan is buying strategic materials for a stockpile to be used if we mobilize for war. Strategic material can be nearly anything, animal, vegetable, or mineral. Sometimes the American official will sell some farm surplus.

Since 1954 he has been able to accept foreign money when the nations that buy food lack dollars to pay for it.

Another American official spends the local money, known as counterpart funds, now held by the United States after the sale of the surplus food. He buys supplies and services for American operations in the country; for example, building material for the embassy and the services of local employees.

In a large transaction such spending for our own needs uses only a portion of the total. The remainder is used for purposes agreed to by both nations. It can be used for economic development, reducing the need for dollars. It can be used to pay the expense of American students and artists who come to the country. It can be used for education, health, village welfare, or any other part of technical assistance. Whatever the use, the United States as a party to the agreement has helped decide what goods and services to buy in the country which paid its own money for the American surplus farm goods. If this sounds involved, it is. International trade for the United States, with its surpluses, long ago left the serene logic of economics as taught in the older books.

Americans also buy abroad in more conventional manner whenever they spend dollars abroad. The armed forces need everything known to man. When stationed abroad, do they order everything from the United States or buy some things locally? Weapons and equipment come from home. Most of the rest can be bought on the spot in Western Europe and much can be bought in Japan. Decisions have to be made for each category, each country, and each time; for food, coal, and medicine, or petrol, lubricant, and laundry. In 1960 when America's gold supply had dwindled too far, clamps were put on the spill of dollars spent abroad but we still buy some goods abroad.

An old-time diplomat never dreamed that diplomacy would enter the market place as buyer and seller.

VI

While the new jobs were being added, the old jobs grew larger.

Economic reporting broke into specialties, most prominently into labor and agriculture. The whole of economic work grew at the same time. Each move in economic operations required reporting and decisions of policy before it was made. Conferences in Washington and abroad multiplied like rabbits. Economic foreign relations became a full member of the ancient club and the dominant member for those nations that received American aid. Political affairs officers among themselves on Saturday night might still boast that they alone carried the true faith of diplomacy, but on Monday they faced another conference in which the political relations with a country depended upon the economic relations.

Scientific relations appeared, but without final definition. Government seemed to be as baffled by what to do with science in foreign affairs as in domestic. It was not easy. Science as one whole does not exist and cannot be represented. In its components science is much too varied to be represented. Yet, certainly if we include social science as we should, science has become central to all foreign policy. Nations must consult the natural and social scientists on such subjects as the growth of population, the prospects for food supply, the effects of nuclear testing, or the way to get peace in a troubled new nation.

As a tentative answer the State Department sends science attachés to some countries, representing only the natural sciences.

They report any news they think worthy, meet with natural scientists in the country, arrange visits of American scientists. The permanent answer will be found only when science, broadly defined, is accepted as part of all that government does and the experts are kept at hand all the time for all the subjects involved. We are baffled now because we treat science as something new and separate from other human affairs when it cannot be separate in fact.

Three old jobs sent off shoots that became bigger than the parents. Representation, as old as diplomacy, produced extensive propaganda. Reporting, equally old, produced secret intelligence on a large scale. Old-fashioned diplomatic intrigue, once a matter of supporting factions in schemes to gain power, produced modern large-scale organized armed efforts to upset governments or to protect them.

VII

Old-fashioned representation meant doing the right thing socially in the right way. A diplomat entertained his hosts and colleagues. He appeared at the ceremonies where he was expected to be, properly dressed and following the rules of protocol. Occasionally he made a speech. He was ready to act in any proper way to make his country better liked abroad. The diplomat and his prince had never thought much about representation as promotion. Gentlemen did not praise their own virtues. They only did the proper thing and answered questions. The Cold War upset this quietness as it did most pleasant old ways.

Three developments coincided to turn diplomats into propagandists. For one, the two strongest nations and their followers began a secular religious war. Under the labels of communism and democracy, neither of which was defined any more exactly than ideologies ever are, Russia and the United States began to hold friends who agreed with their ideas and seek new allies. To evangelize is to propagandize, as the Catholic church knew when it first began to use the word propaganda. Nations became propagandists.

A second development came in the techniques of propaganda. As part of the whole burst of technology, messages were delivered faster, to larger audiences, in more persuasive form. Rapid color printing, hand motion picture cameras, fast film and fast lenses for still photography, radio, television, tape recording, loud speakers, all became standard equipment during the years just before the Second War and in the early stages of the Cold War.

Thirdly, with the glorious, golden new techniques came a faith that propaganda could do anything its users wanted. Mr. Lincoln's adage that you can't fool all the people all the time fell before Mr. Barnum's practice that you can fool enough people to get what you want. The one born every minute makes quite a crowd. Communists, fascists, and nazis all showed that propaganda was a central tool of totalitarianism. Advertisers in the capitalist and pluralist world proved that they could change the culture to make profits. By the time the Cold War began nations had accepted faith in propaganda and turned to use of the new techniques.

When the international contest became one between systems of political economy, diplomacy became a contest of propagandas as much as it was anything else. The battle for men's minds, as orators liked to call it, was fought with words; the words came from propaganda breaks, as we called the gain or loss of advantage to Russia and America in each event. When America was caught spying with the U-2 plane just before the Paris conference, she lost the propaganda break. When Russia began nuclear testing again just as the unaligned nations began a conference in Belgrade, she lost it. In both cases, as in all others, the nation that won the break took all possible advantage of it.

Americans in government service for foreign affairs wrote news and articles, radio and television scripts, speeches and pamphlets. Others produced motion pictures and still photographs, exhibits and tours. Others made speeches, ran information centers and libraries abroad. Our officials used all sensible means of spreading the word. They worked in the armed forces, the Information Agency and its overseas service, the State Department, and the other agencies that dealt with foreign affairs.

Two aspects of propaganda are never called by that still dirty word. Partly we feel that they are nobler stuff, and partly we gain in propaganda if we are vague about some purposes. One is cultural exchange, the other the Peace Corps. Cultural exchange in broad definition includes anything from the exchange of students to tours of large orchestras. The purpose is to show what America, as a democracy, has produced in that broad, usually absurd, usage of the word culture with a capital "C."

We too read books, paint, write plays, and make music. All kinds of music. The board of the Metropolitan Opera Company would never recognize as Culture the kind of music that is most popular abroad, but we are more interested in what the natives think. They like most, for the early teens, the current fad music, such as rock-and-roll in its time; for the young intellectuals, honest jazz; for the serious Culturists, American ballet (not American performance of European classical ballet), American drama, and the American musical which combines drama, light music, and dance. No matter the form of the art or the level of Culture, as preserved by Culturists, the result is propaganda.

The Peace Corps is composed of Americans who go by invitation to backward lands and work in the simplest stages of economic development. They may teach in a rural school, for example, or help the local people dig wells or build roads. Only a few are chosen from the many applicants. Those who go abroad are selected for good health, good brains, good spirit, right attitude. They are paid only enough to live on, for they are supposed to show that not all Americans are rich. If they live up to the noblest dream, they will eat what the natives eat and no doubt become the most heroic of all government employees, considering the messes that most poor people eat, not to mention the disease that rides the food.

All sorts of good reasons can be argued for the Peace Corps. It gives Americans that personal opportunity to serve people that is hard to find in urban life. It gives Americans an education in the hard side of poverty. It may spread technical aid farther than otherwise and may start village programs that will continue.

Most of all, though, it will show other people that Americans are not greedy materialists but healthy, cheerful souls who want to work for the less fortunate. And in some cases it will show by example that rarest creature in the pre-industrial world, a college graduate who does hard physical labor without feeling disgraced. The biggest gain for the United States will be in propaganda. We will demonstrate through the Corps how genuine is our interest in others and how our system turns out good neighbors.

VIII

Secret intelligence and intrigue are certainly nothing new under the sun. Diplomats have always listened for inside bits and relayed them home. They have always been ready to take sides with one party or another in a revolution, if by no more than a gesture that said their governments would be pleased by change or would recognize a new regime as the new government in fact. Always factions in the other country have tried to use diplomats in their schemes. They tell them information they want to get to other nations; they ask for secret aid; they seek understandings about asylum if they fail and international support if they win.

In his own country a revolutionist is a traitor unless he wins. Diplomats have always walked cautiously with traitors in subterranean passages, but they have travelled with them all through history, and it gets us nowhere to pretend that secret operations are brand new, born with the Cold War and so mysterious that only the Central Intelligence Agency ever learned how to work at them.

The character and volume of secret intelligence and intrigue, however, have changed enormously in the conduct of diplomacy since the war. This is the difference. In the most extreme definition, but with much truth too, secret operations have become a separate, independent system of diplomacy that competes with the open system. Secrecy almost always requires its own system. When the lives of informants are risked by discovery, agents, who can also die or go to jail, will tell no one of their work, not even each other.

A secret agent arrives in a foreign country identified openly as a member of the embassy or consular staff or as a businessman, journalist, or student. His true identity, if all works as the book says, will be known only to the chief of mission and perhaps not to him when the agent is not covered in a government job. This agent for his true work becomes a code name in a network of code names who persuade local citizens to give or sell information, nearly always in violation of local law. All the agents send reports to someone who sends reports to Washington.

Only the ambassador, consul, or, in the case of military intelligence, the commanding officer is permitted to see these reports. A separate channel hidden in secrecy is the beginning of a separate diplomacy. Reports necessarily mean interpretation. When the secret agents interpret in contradiction to the open diplomats, one or the other has to be upheld in Washington. Rivalry blooms again. Each faction, the open and the secret, promotes the policy that comes from its own interpretation.

Sinister acts begin to be rumored because the temptation to play dirty is present in the rivalry. Whether verified or not, open diplomats talk about false reports and frame-ups committed against them by secret agents, and secret agents talk about the dangerous innocence of open Foreign Service Officers. The young vice-consul hears tales of a fellow whose career was hurt because a Central Intelligence agent claimed in his secret report that he was no good. A new secret agent is told to beware all career Foreign Service Officers because they talk too much and are without sympathy for the noble fraternity of spies.

When a code clerk defected from the Russian embassy in Ottawa in 1946, he revealed among other matters that no less than three secret intelligence networks existed in the mission; one for the Red Army, another, in addition, for the military, and one for the secret police. Each one could report on the others. Five different ciphers were used, one for the military, one for the Party, one for the secret police, one for the commercial section, and one for the Embassy. Each cipher was known only to those who used it. No single Russian who worked in the embassy could breathe without feeling that he was subject to malicious reports filed by rivals in one of the systems. Russians are not so different from the rest of mankind that we can say it could never happen here. Not the national traits or form of government but the practice of secrecy prepares the ground for sinister uses in rivalry.

Add secret operations to secret intelligence and the existence of a separate diplomacy is assured. Since the Second World War the Central Intelligence Agency by open report of reliable journalists has helped rebellion when it was feasible and enough in the interest of the United States to make the risk worthwhile. It helped get Mossadegh out of office as Premier of Iran, and power returned to the Shah. It supported a revolutionary invasion of Guatemala to overthrow a regime too friendly with communism. It arranged commando raids on Communist China and helped Nasser seize power from King Farouk in Egypt.

The agency's subversive (to the other governments) activities were revealed to the world loudly, nakedly when it sponsored an invasion of Cuba by anti-Castro rebels who were defeated. Now, at last, the troubled President and others began to ask whether decisions of foreign policy should be made by the same agency that collects secret intelligence. They had discovered in tragedy that the combination of secret intelligence and secret operations meant an added diplomatic service and, further, one that, because it was secret, escaped scrutiny unless it made such a horrible mistake as the Central Intelligence Agency did in Cuba. Granted that a secret agency can never deny or explain in public, this one appeared at least to be so compromised by name and details of the Cuban plan that its future in secret operations was dim.

It was a good time for the President, if he wanted to go beyond casting the Central Intelligence Agency out of his immediate office, to cancel the secret system of diplomacy and to stop the duplication and rivalry. He could depend upon orthodox means to collect secret as well as open intelligence and, if he wanted to incite rebellion, he could do so less conspicuously than the Central Intelligence Agency had managed to do. The less he said about whatever he did the better diplomat he was. To outward appearance not much changed after the Cuban failure. The nation's best hope was that changes were made unannounced. We were in danger of more error so long as secret intelligence and operations were as important as open diplomacy and inevitably separate.

IX

Diplomacy by international conference was still another departure from conventional diplomacy. Like secret intelligence, it was not new, and Elmer Plischke in *Summit Diplomacy* shows that even this form of negotiation at international conference is old. But also like secret intelligence, diplomacy by international conference has expanded in variety and dimension since 1945.

We have entered more international organizations than most Americans of the past generation ever dreamed possible. Our officials from many different agencies attend hundreds of meetings a year with delegates from other nations to negotiate agreements on matters upon which each nation has a position. The variety of such meetings is as great as the number. Accomplishment varies. A General Assembly of the United Nations, holding in trust the hope of mankind, can end with little more than a record of angry words. One of the technical organizations, says the International Civil Aviation Organization, meets unnoticed but reaches agreements that make life among nations much easier. The world may die from the failure of one international body to live up to its mission, but the world could not live as it does without the success of many others. World or regional, economic, social, or technical, some international organizations succeed and some do not.

The one conclusion that can be made about all international organizations is that for the United States they have grown much more common in more fields since 1945, and much of our foreign policy is now negotiated at international conferences. An ambassador to a nation, working in his embassy, may miss most of the important dealing with that nation. If he wants to handle the big jobs, he has to get to Geneva, New York, or Paris where men settle things offstage before revealing their understandings in the conference room.

Sometimes the ambassador is called upon for this negotiation in corridor and lounge with the country to which he is assigned. Oftener he is not. He sits in his embassy handling routine while someone else is assigned to liaison with the delegates from his host country at the meeing of the General Assembly, the World Health Organization, the Economic and Social Council, the Food and Agriculture Organization, or dozens of others.

Relations of all the nations together are still one sovereign nation to another, but they happen at one place at an international conference. Old-style diplomacy as known in a mission resident in another country has been crimped.

X

The expansion of diplomacy has had deep effect in the kinds of people we hire to work in foreign affairs, but our theory of personnel management has failed to change. We still act as if the new functions are the business of people who are not truly engaged in diplomacy. True careers in foreign affairs, the present theory goes, belong only to Foreign Service Officers who are chosen for their general ability and poise and who learn on the job to be specialists in diplomatic and consular relations.

For the development of a new theory, some pointed new assumptions can be drawn from the new facts.

1. The new work is permanent, not temporary. It is at least as permanent as other government programs for which new appropriations have to be voted each year. Foreign aid is by now as stable as, say, price supports in agriculture which also began in a crisis. The nature of the present world dictates certain policies: military aid and advice to allies, standing forces abroad, economic aid, secret intelligence, attendance at international conferences. Each accommodation to the demands of new development creates a new kind of work and lasts as long as the demands continue. Present demands show no letup.

2. Professional Foreign Service Officers lost their exclusive claim to be the only specialists in foreign relations when the new work became permanent. A variety of both generalists and specialists do the new work in the same places in the same environment as the career consuls and diplomats do their work.

3. A single foreign service is needed to replace the present

system. All men and women in the new service would have the same social status, the same chances of promotion to the top, the same perquisites of duty-free imports, the same services in travel and moving, the same scales of pay and allowances, the same use of our government's communications. Until now such conditions of employment have varied from agency to agency, sometimes to the advantage of the older career service and sometimes not. Above all, the new service would have one agency in Washington to which its members look for direction. It would be the new Department of State proposed earlier.

4. Because the Constitution and long practice separate military from civil activities and place the President in command of the armed forces the military will have to remain separate abroad and report to the Defense Department. Various degrees of separateness will continue. The military attaché will be the closest to subordination to the civilian ambassador; the military aid mission will be more detached; the standing force will be independent except that its commander, like the ambassador, is responsible at the top to the President. When the Presidency is reorganized—or organized, as the view may be—a deputy president in charge of foreign affairs can settle arguments that rise to the top.

CHAPTER 12 THE NATURE
OF THE WORK

ONE OF THE EASY ANSWERS IN AMERICAN DIS-
course is that all would be well with foreign policy if we only
turned it over to professional diplomats of the old model. This
instant wisdom is often given by people who loom with assorted
clichés at cocktail parties. It isn't this easy. The nature of the
work, the kind of people we have, the kind we need, how to get
them, and how to treat them, all are relevant to a true answer to
those who promote the easy answer.

The talkers are correct to this extent, though. Craftsmen do make
a lot of difference in the results of government. They cannot
overcome poor organization, but neither can good organization
overcome poor people. For the rest of the cliché, those who do the
work and those who study the subject know that there is no simple
answer. Professional diplomats are undefined. Political appointees
are not always amateurs and may be more qualified than career
men. The job of foreign affairs is about as mixed as the job of
government at home. It needs new definition and reorganization
just as much.

II

Any easy answer that one kind of person should be in charge is
pricked by the variety of work to be done. For example, the one

answer for the model cannot be simply that he know the language or be congenial with the common man, desirable as these qualities may be. Nor can the traditional argument stand firm that the diplomat is a general practitioner able to handle any matter that arises in the great variety of work to be done.

Work overseas shows the variety of foreign affairs more than work in Washington because it is more concentrated and conspicuous. An official representative of the United States overseas can be anything from a vice-consul to a specialist in solid fuel for rockets. He may be, to name only a few, a political analyst, radio-television writer, librarian, agricultural economist, budgeter, accountant, enlisted man of bad manners and no sense, enlisted man of good manners and good sense, officer mean and stupid, officer gracious and wise, labor expert who was formerly a union organizer, money lender who formerly worked as a bond salesman, a vice-consul assigned to visas, another who reports on such exotic commodities as goat skins, engineer civil, mechanical, electrical, industrial, or mining, military engineer, jute man, pulp man, cotton man, news man, good will man, scientist, philosopher, teacher, and nearly any others you can think of except beggars and thieves.

Included in this welter of specialities is the job of ambassador. "All our ambassadors should be men who know what it is to have the barnyard on their shoes," an agricultural man once told me. Ambassadors should speak the language and all will be well, others say, or mix more with the people, or go to fewer parties, or come only from business where men are said to be practical, or come only from the foreign service career where men are said to be expert in foreign policy.

To make the easy answer still more difficult, about two aliens for every one American civilian represent the United States overseas. The figures on January 1, 1962, were 62,160 American citizens and 113,139 nationals of other countries, counting civilians only and as usual omitting the Central Intelligence Agency's spooks because their number is secret. Aliens do as great a variety of work as Americans. Some are laborers, janitors, and chauffeurs; others work on economic and political reports, translations, or administrative chores. A firm line is draw against the alien in state secrets and the kind of work, such as the issuance of visas, that is reserved to Foreign Service Officers. Otherwise the alien employees may be found in nearly any American enterprise. We cannot even say that if all Americans who work overseas had certain qualities all would be well. Those two aliens for one American, employed in their own country, make it harder to prescribe exactly the kind of people who should represent us abroad.

The special talents needed in work overseas are as varied as the agencies that send men. Table 3 shows the list and the numbers of overseas employees on January 1, 1962. This list and total are typical of the postwar years.

We are faced then with facts. The government in many agencies employs many civilians overseas. Seven percent of all civilians employed by the Executive Branch work abroad. Sixty-five percent of those abroad are aliens who do much the same kind of work as American citizens except for handling secrets, diplomatic and consular work reserved for Foreign Service Officers, and negotiation at the higher level with officials of another country.

Add to these civilians the thousands of military men and women who work abroad. These Americans in uniform (who wear civilian clothes whenever they can) are in three main types of mission, by, to repeat, the nature of the new diplomacy. One is the fighting force stationed abroad either by itself or as part of an alliance, such as the North Atlantic Treaty Organization in Europe. Another is the military advisory group, which administers military aid. The third is the usual military staff attached to the ambassador to report, negotiate, and represent in military affairs.

We should add to be accurate, though irreverent, an unknown number of American and alien employees who spy abroad and sometimes abet subversion. They are joined and crossed by American military spies and psychological warriors. This dark side of representation is just as routine as any other civil and military function.

All the government employees, civil and military, open and secret, citizen and alien, perform such a variety of work, and do it with such a variety of skills, that no easy generalization can be made about the kind of person we should employ.

TABLE 3. CIVILIANS EMPLOYED OVERSEAS BY U.S. GOVERNMENT JANUARY 1, 1962

	U.S. Citizens	Nationals of Other Countries
State	6,656	9,822
Agency for International Development	4,624	8,481
Treasury	540	36
Health, Education, Welfare	418	85
Post Office	1,403	———
Agriculture	685	370
Secretary of Defense[a]	(65)	———
Army[a]	(14,558)	(37,177)
Navy[a]	(7,056)	(16,361)
Air Force[a]	(14,054)	(18,846)
Total Department of Defense[a]	35,733	72,384
Commerce	601	114
Interior	511	5
Justice	491	28
Labor	80	16
Veterans Administration	702	336
Federal Aviation Agency	3,608	13
Small Business Administration	62	———
Atomic Energy Commission	31	———
General Services Administration	85	1
Tennessee Valley Authority	6	———
Civil Service Commission	2	———
Housing and Home Finance Agency	214	———
Panama Canal Company	3,783	14,248
Federal Communications Commission	24	———
Federal Deposit Insurance Corporation	2	———
American Battle Monuments Commission	43	364
National Aeronautics and Space Administration	13	———
Virgin Islands Corporation	465	66
Smithsonian Institution	3	8
National Science Foundation	5	2
U.S. Information Agency	1,173	6,760
National Labor Relations Board	36	———
Selective Service System	161	———
Total	62,160	113,139

[a] Civilians only.

Source: Extracted from chart, "Organization of Federal Executive Departments and Agencies," to accompany Committee Report No. 22, U.S. Senate Committee on Government Operations (Washington: Government Printing Office, 1962).

III

Variety also exists in the publics with which American representatives deal. This is a point too little understood by those Americans who worry that we are not liked. They want everybody to like us, the coolies and the moguls, the worker and royalty, the conservative, the liberal, and the Russians because, as everyone says, if we can only get through to the Russian people, there will be no rumors of war.

Certain novelists who should know better encourage the simple faith that American prestige can be raised if we send abroad only people who speak the language and get their hands dirty from work alongside villagers. People of good will earnestly think our ambassadors should live as the common people, and would have found nothing incongruous in former Ambassador John Kenneth Galbraith, who rises more than six and one half bony feet, dressed in dhoti, riding a bicycle through the streets of New Delhi, brief case flapping as befits an educated man on a bicycle.

Such easy generalization fails because the United States does not deal with one amiable blob that is the people of another country. It deals with a variety of groups through a variety of Americans. No single American official ever sees all groups. (For that matter, how many Americans at home ever see an official from the embassy of another country?)

An ambassador and his top men spend most of their time in the embassy where they handle mountains of reports and other papers and where they deal with a flow of American visitors, some private citizens on business, some students, some professors under contract, officials from Washington, and members of Congress. Outside the embassy, an ambassador and his top men see the top men in other embassies and in the government. They try to achieve personal rapport so that they can get information and help when they need it.

Much of the meeting and talking is done at luncheons, cocktail parties, dinners, and receptions. From this, ambassadors get labelled party-goers, though many of them deplore the custom.

Protocol in the sense of who calls on whom and how to dress is also part of ambassadorial custom but easier to take. Without rules each occasion could cause trouble if a nation's official representative felt aggrieved. Protocol is the great convenience of international relations. It treats each person impersonally, according to the rank of his position or the length of his tenure. It will continue to be used. So will the custom of parties as ways to get together with the right people.

That term, right people, is the answer to those who argue that the ambassador ought to invite all types and classes to his parties. An ambassador seldom needs to know anyone outside his public of other top officials. If he cultivated working men, he would do so for public relations, and nothing is so easily detected by the people who are being cultivated as the big shot engaged at public relations. Of course, if an ambassador wants genuinely to meet working men, farmers, small merchants, or students, and can talk with them without cultivating them, he can do so. But he should not invite them to the same parties with top officials. Good sense requires that people who are invited to a party should have some hope of being congenial. Americans at home are probably the least class-conscious people on earth, but they select guests for compatibility and the easy feeling of common manners. Whenever a member of Congress back from a tour of embassies says that he never saw a labor man or farmer at any of the parties, someone should ask him how often he sees union men, dirt farmers, and high officials at the same party anywhere in the United States. Not many hosts would risk the stiffness.

Other Americans deal with people in the same line of work and at the same rank in hundreds of groups that form and reform in every society. An army colonel deals with army colonels. The air force major sees other air force majors. A chemical engineer sees people in industry, most likely in the chemical industry. The labor reporter knows labor leaders. The agricultural engineer knows farm demonstration agents and may possibly, if the rural class lines are not too tight, get to know a few farmers.

None of this says that Americans should not meet as many different types as possible if they are sincere about wanting to meet people. It is not easy to do, as anyone who has worked abroad knows. Two main barriers exist.

The first is already mentioned. Any sign of public relations may raise hostility. Humanity has suffered too long from manipulators for its alert members not to smell the intention.

The second barrier is that very few foreigners anywhere ever get invited to know local people outside their work. A peasant in the Ukraine is not inclined to invite an economic specialist from the American Embassy to Sunday dinner. A merchant in Delhi will hardly think of an American consul as the man with whom he most wants to discuss trade. Rarely an American will make a friend in the country. It can begin in work together at the office, or it can happen through common interests in orphans, archaeology, chess, and any number of things. Getting acquainted deliberately on a large scale is almost impossible unless one is a celebrated entertainer, and no permanent staff member ever sold a million records.

Once in a long while a natural mixer will appear who can break the barriers and still be recognized as genuine. During the Second World War I was on a plane that was held by weather in the Azores. The late Maury Maverick was another passenger. For one morning he led two English manufacturers and me on a tour of friendship and good feeling.

Speaking only English with gruff friendliness he got all of us into jail to visit a dumfounded American sailor who needed solace. Then we saw city hall with the mayor as guide, once he got the idea that Mr. Maverick had been mayor of San Antonio, a city known in many a port for the Alamo, western movies, and a well-sung rose. Next we went to the church. A priest was more than cordial. He took us behind the railing to show us the treasure chest. I looked toward the nave and saw a wedding party coming down the aisle. We left by the side steps just as the bride and groom reached the altar.

By now it was 11 A.M., a good time to visit a farm. We told our taxi driver to go to a hillside cottage that we saw in the distance. Maverick hailed the cottage, knocked on a door, and with his smile and expansive manner explained that we had come to visit. A puzzled farm wife and daughter invited us in. So one expansive

American and his three reserved companions, all cold sober, passed the morning time of day with two Portuguese housewives and discussed in two languages with lots of gestures the artifacts of their kitchen.

Only a Maury Maverick could have done it. Not many like him ever appear in government service. If either of the Englishmen or I had tried the same tour, the result would have been sad. We would have been too embarrassed and phony, and a phony is the same in any language. The overseas service will always be filled by the self-conscious, which is only to say that all but the rarest human being is self-conscious. When a Maverick comes along, he can be given free rein. It would be monstrous stupidity to restrain him in a world that needs him so badly. But he won't come along often enough to plan a corps in his image.

Lacking a corps of natural mixers, the government encourages all American employees to mix as nicely as possible with their hosts. The armed forces tell every member, officer or enlisted man, that he is an unofficial ambassador. Information for the troops for twenty years has included handbooks on the country and the people to be visited and enough vocabulary to ask directions and order a meal politely. These handbooks cover manners, religion, government, politics, and recommend behavior for Americans in the other country.

Be courteous [says the book for Okinawa]. A highly developed social code governs personal relationships among Ryukyuans. You can't hope to learn the intricate details of the code of manners, but good manners by American standards will be adequate.

Be patient. . . . Raising your voice or waving your arms won't help a bit.

Be helpful. You will have many opportunities to cooperate with Ryukyuan individuals or organizations on a person to person basis and through the efforts of your organization, clubs, or religious group. Don't fail to do so when the opportunity presents itself.

Be fair. Boasting and sneering are trademarks of ignorance. . . . It is not our purpose to Americanize Asians, and any Ryukyuan will understandably become annoyed at hearing his way of doing things compared unfavorably with the American way. A lavish display of money can be annoying, too, to a Ryukyuan wage earner who considers $40 a month extremely good pay.

The armed forces try to persuade all members to be good ambassadors. The fools, the knaves, the churls, and the boors will remain no matter how much instruction is applied. But they appear everywhere else as well, in all cultures, and they will make the headlines while all decent folk go unnoticed. It is true as well in the corner tavern, the country club, and high school prom at home.

Civil agencies too offer advice to employees and wives and tell them how to behave amongst strangers. Civilian and military Americans are urged to make friends of the locals. It remains as difficult as ever to do because of the barriers discussed above.

While making personal friends of individuals is difficult, organized relations are booming. All over the world American men and women work in local welfare, education, and art. Military units adopt whole orphanages. Civilians and their wives collect books for children, organize clubs for the young, volunteer for charitable work. American generosity holds abroad as at home, whether the gift be food to the children who gather about a field mess or a fund to build a hospital. The woe-singers never mention such expressions of good feeling.

And we should count too the occasional Americans who visit for cultural relations. These are musicians, who draw different publics according to the kind of music they play, painters, writers, teachers, labor leaders, journalists, merchants, manufacturers, all of whom have an aura of official status because their trips are sponsored by the government. These have spread friendly feeling, how much no one knows because no one ever checks results here any more than in the program for foreign students in the United States. We can guess that American artists, entertainers, and others, when chosen for their manners, do more good than harm when they go abroad.

IV

If variety in the work to be done appears overseas, it also is true between Washington and overseas.

We decided in 1954, following the recommendations of a committee named for its chairman, Henry M. Wriston, that the same person should be eligible and expected to work in the Foreign Service as in the Department of State. Soon all good jobs concerned with policy at home or abroad were filled by career Foreign Service Officers. The exceptions were some posts that required special skills, as in research and intelligence, and certain posts that were filled politically. Many positions in lower levels of management and other spots not considered to be in the mainstream of foreign policy were filled at home and abroad by more ordinary civil servants.

The Foreign Service Officer is now the only recognized craftsman of policy in the geographical bureaus and the secretariat of the Department of State as well as in a diplomatic or consular mission. He arrived at this strength before changes were also made (a) in the kind of skills sought for the service and (b) in the definition of the work to be done in Washington and abroad. Confusion has plagued us ever since Wristonization occurred. It has usually been unrecognized confusion, and always defended by its creators, but it is there and it is troublesome.

I think the main cause of confusion is our failure to recognize that work in a mission is different from work in the Department.

The environment is different. A man abroad is surrounded by foreigners with whom he usually dares not talk intimately about his work, for reasons of security and discretion. When he turns to fellow Americans in the mission, he is limited by the smaller number and fewer types, skills, ideas, and knowledge. Then superiors mean more in a mission than in Washington. They are able to supervise more thoroughly. Their opinion can make the future of a subordinate and make life pleasanter for the present. The way officers abroad must depend upon each other, whether in all of a small mission or in one division of a large mission, is reality. It occurs on the island that is an American mission, a small place all on its own whose inhabitants at work must try to please each other and after work mix socially to please each other some more.

Wives double all factors. They have to get along with other wives. While husbands work, wives cope. They make sure that safe food and water reach the children, a big job when no raw food or unboiled water is safe outside Europe, the United States, and the white dominions of the Commonwealth. Native cooks often do not agree with germ theory and have to be watched like carriers of the plague. Wives also have to nurse children through the going local diseases and pray that a small child won't be exposed to rabies without reporting it. And then education is necessary. Some wives teach at home with the help of a correspondence school; others find local schools that are adequate. Most of all, wives get ready to move. The packing cases are never far away, and transfer comes to Foreign Service Officers as surely as to Army officers.

Wives in Washington argue that their sisters overseas get more space in houses for the same money and, due to the grace of underdevelopment, can still hire domestic servants. India is not a bad assignment when you can live in eight rooms and have four servants. It should be said that eight rooms look strange with only four rooms worth of furniture, the family will have to sleep under mosquito nets, and four Indian servants create a domestic problem in labor-management that can make a housewife long to do her own work.

Work abroad takes place in a different environment from Washington, and it is naive to argue against the fact. For one result the Foreign Service overseas has its own threats to morale. Too much drinking is one. It is an occupational hazard, liquor being a tool of the trade. Marital trouble is another. Loss of interest in work is another. All these occur in Washington as well, but there they are not so clearly due to the isolation of a few Americans in the midst of a foreign culture.

Another difference between Washington and a mission is in the type of responsibility. By custom that began in the aristocratic origin of modern diplomacy an ambassador reports to his home government with always an emphasis on his own nation's interest. He negotiates with the host government only within the limits of decisions made at home. And he represents his country in a manner that maintains its dignity and rights. By now the same duties—and limits—are true for all other officials in the field, with the exception in degree of military commanders, who have more authority within their command than civilians have. Even the most celebrated chief of an overseas mission finds, to his surprise if he is new, that he may not do what he wants to do until he has approval from Washington.

A special kind of resignation is required for work abroad. Without fail in the judgment of field men, the offices of Washington will be slow, ignorant, and unwise. They are not as close to the subtle realities; they have to see a region and a world as well as one country; and they accept the best decision they can get from the competition of views that forms an agreement. A man overseas sees what is in front of him and can understand Washington only with patience if at all. The merger of foreign and domestic personnel presumably will in time diminish the gap, after enough men have worked in both places. Always there will be a difference in responsibility, however, and different skills will be needed.

At best the man overseas will be more confused by the discussion at home of his role than by the plain, simple difference from Washington in his work. He knows his role as the work defines it. He is to report, negotiate, represent, and under subheadings he makes loans, gives military advice, propagandizes, or does any of a great many things, all under policies decided in Washington. No one else seems to know what his job is. His professional colleagues in Washington who do know make no effort to clear up the matter. Some of the fuzzier thinkers among professionals fall for easy answers and add to the confusion.

Is the man overseas supposed to keep his host happy? His human nature will incline this way. Work and association is easier when the host government is pleased. Then a visiting Congressman cries appeasement. To him our representatives should be nasty to all governments that do not get the Congressman's approval. A policy man in Washington next sends a curt reminder that the job overseas is to represent the national interest of the United States and not to please any other nation. Next day a columnist deplores the loss of American prestige in the country where our man labors.

The office in Washington orders him to report on why we have lost prestige. We lost prestige because our man got the host government angry and it slammed back through its own press and radio. The American columnist knew his American readers; they wanted to be liked and at the same time liked to keep a morbid catalog of all the places where they were not liked. Their representative overseas could make America liked if he never did anything to offend foreigners, and if he could guarantee that no one in Washington would do anything. He would then be denounced as a mollycoddle, appeaser, no better than a neutralist. Voices now swell to say that we want not to be liked so much as to be respected. What do we want?

Is the man overseas supposed to understand the people of another culture, as so many say? How much? Most people who argue for understanding clearly mean sympathy. They want our representatives to deal with foreigners within the foreign culture and not try to apply American standards. There are practical arguments for this position. If any effort thwarts culture too much, it will fail.

No American official of good sense should fail to think of culture as the frame in which he must work. He will see culture expressed through his opposites with whom he deals, and he had better know how their reactions differ from his. How formal are they? Are they formal or pompous? What are the ingrained ritual ways of communicating? How much do compliments really mean and how much are they ceremonial? Is delay customary or a sign of denial? Are bribes expected? In what amount and what disguise? How important is face?

Any realist learns to understand the culture of another people in this sense. An occasional fool makes a bad mistake and gets in the news. Thousands who are not fools get no notice.

Realists will not subscribe, however, to the theory that Americans overseas should sympathize with other cultures. Sadly they know that many cultural traits have to change before many nations can reach the dignity and well-being that Americans want for them.

When, as a teacher, I face foreign officials who appear alongside American students of public administration, I wish I could tell whoever sent them to call it off. Teaching the subject in the American culture, I can assume that public corruption will be unusual and not the foremost topic. I can assume that money will be available for reasonable causes and that the rights of citizens will be respected. I can assume that appointments to the civil service will be made for merit to a great extent in the federal government and to some extent in all the states. When merit is not the standard, patronage will be more political than familial. I can assume that religion will support good government and that education will produce helpful attitudes as well as competence.

None of these American traits is necessarily true in the backward nations from which my foreign students come. We cannot talk on the same wave length. What they need is not a course in American public administration in an American university but a course at home in how to break their cultural barriers that deny honest, democratic government. American officials need to help change other cultures if they are to succeed.

The American representative, coming from his own culture, will already be biased toward tolerance and has to fight the tendency. He will want to like his host and be liked. When a sheik entertains him at that party, hovered over lamb and accessories, the American may forget that a redistribution of income is required for economic development to help the masses of Araby. A few urbane, gracious, and rich Latin American hosts can dim an American's eyes to the appalling poverty that is the major way of life below the Rio Grande. Soon he babbles of the way the poor have happy lives though short and deprived. He becomes *sympatico,* the country club men tell him, but he will do little toward economic development.

An American who keeps his balance in India is to be praised. He has escaped both the danger of incurable shock and the other extreme of blind approval of the whole buzzing hive, from old sculpture to present yoga. If he works approvingly with the culture, he will not see that India needs a scientific revolution before it can enter the good life, twentieth-century definition. Indians to be modern, as they and all other people on earth want to be, need to debate philosophy less and public sanitation more. They should develop a hatred of bed bugs. An American who says this, and recommends policies to encourage change, will understand Indian culture but will not sympathize with it.

All our men abroad now must wonder what is expected of them. They get from home a confusion of tongues. Be nice to the host, but don't concede to him; be firm, but don't lose prestige; be tough, but popular. Work with another culture, but work for a better life for the masses; understand people, but don't try to change them even though you know that the American hope for democracy cannot be reached until science is practiced, religions that encourage apathy decline, and income is redistributed.

V

Learn the language is another easy answer for all that is wrong with overseas representation, and language does offer some help, though it is by no means a simple solution.

There are strong reasons for every American employee to know a foreign language well whether he works at home or abroad. The strongest reason has nothing to do with use. It is simply that a liberal education includes an awareness of people outside the native land, and the study of language gives many students the only sure exposure to other kinds of people. When so many of us say that we never use the language we studied in school, we miss this point. In the study of the language we learned about Frenchmen, Germans, and Spaniards. In future years our children may learn about Russians and Chinese.

A second reason is good manners. If an American goes to another country, he should speak the language from courtesy. If he cannot speak it well, he should learn and begin to speak in short takes as soon as possible. An American who learns enough to read a simple greeting in the host's language is more courteous and more welcome than one who makes no effort at all.

A third good reason is morale. No loneliness quite equals that of the alien who cannot speak to fellow beings nor understand in passing what they say to each other. He is cut off from all the usual ties of belonging. He gets a shoe shine but cannot question the urchin; he buys a paper by pointing; he looks in shop windows but cannot go inside with assurance. So for human company he is confined to fellow aliens. He learns about the place only from what these aliens tell him. His information is muffled through a blanket, his appreciation cut to a fraction.

If the country has no interesting art, architecture, ruins, or scenery, things that can be seen without speech, there is not much a mute visitor can learn firsthand. Some very unhappy Americans stationed in physically uninteresting places would be happier if they could converse with the local people and find in them the stuff of universal interest. After all, it is only an interest in other people and the routine things of life that keep up the morale of most humans who live in cities, for not many cities have interest in themselves. For each Manhattan, there are miles of Bronx; for Paris, London, or Rome there are hundreds of drab cities where life has to be made interesting without help from the place itself.

Living can be an awful bore for the majority of Americans who live abroad without a language. Sadly, not many of them realize this. They stay closer to each other than they ever would at home and may soon begin to despise the natives in the standard but unconscious way of people who are insecure.

Knowledge of a language is good for all who work abroad, as, for that matter, it is good for all who stay at home. This much is easy to say.

How to prepare Americans in languages is quite a different matter. Here are some of the questions for which we have no answers yet. Who should be required, without question, to learn a language? Which language? Where learn it? And how do we make sure anyone has the ability to handle a language with the subtle shades that make such a difference?

To get over the biggest hurdle first, we can agree with Harlan Cleveland and his associates who conclude in *The Overseas Americans:*

The sober fact is that we have neither the time nor the manpower necessary to prepare all our overseas representatives with high language skills. . . . The ability to use and understand the local language of a foreign country is of unquestionable value to the overseas American. But, like other skills, its value for any given individual is not absolute, it is relative to other types of skill and understanding required for the particular assignment.

This conclusion deflates the easy answer that all would be well if every American who works abroad would speak the language. There are among talkative men, Mario Pei reported in the *Saturday Review,* September 9, 1961, almost 3,000 languages in spoken use. More than 100 languages are spoken by more than 1,000,000 persons each, thirteen by more than 50,000,000. The Foreign Service Institute now gives intensive training in some 45 languages in Washington and at schools in Lebanon, Taiwan, and Japan, or by arrangement with universities. It provides part-time instruction in any language known to man, whenever needed, in Washington, New York, and missions abroad. The Armed Forces train in the main languages, either in their own schools or by contract with universities. These efforts are small in the total. All employees cannot be trained. All languages cannot be taught.

Nor do all need even one language to do their work. Stenographers and clerks need to speak the local language only for their own morale and for good manners. They will not use it in their work. (Reception desks and switchboards will likely be manned by local aliens who speak English.) At the other end of the ladder, an ambassador needs the local language for the same reasons of morale and good manners. He does not have to have it for negotiation because he and his opposite will both want interpreters to handle any serious talk where words must be chosen carefully.

Those who need the language in their work are in the middle ranks. They might be called the outside men; such faithful servants as the vice-consul who interviews applicants for visas, military men who instruct local military men in the use of martial tools, engineers who deal with local builders and workmen (or work-women), agricultural agents who instruct their local counterparts, medical men of the armed forces who treat local civilians, the rare economic analysts who get out of the office and into markets, plants, and union halls where economics happens, and the rarer political analysts who mix with the people who make politics.

Language is still not the first requisite for these specialists. A man who knows how can reach considerable rapport through an interpreter. He takes time to say the amenities expected in the culture, looks in the eyes of the principal as if the interpreter were not there, and pauses frequently so that the interpreter can keep up easier and so the conversation will avoid long speeches.

Other skills than language come first. To agree again with Mr. Cleveland and associates, "A third-rate engineer sent to India with fluent Hindi will not build as good bridges or as durable social institutions as a first-rate engineer with no Hindi." A first-rate American of any skill but no language, and perhaps no aptitude for language because of his shyness, is always preferable over the linguist who lacks skill, judgment, or warmth.

Anyway which language does an American learn to be equipped for foreign service? Does the engineer who builds a dam and social relations in India learn Hindi-Urdu, the language of literature and public life in the central and western regions, or does he learn Bengali because he will have headquarters in Calcutta? Or Telegu or Tamil for the deep South of India? Or Marathi for Bombay? Or even within the regions where Hindi-Urdu is the language of literature and public service would an engineer do better to learn Bihari for Benares, Punjabi for Lahore, Rajasthani for Jodhpur, Eastern Hindi for Lucknow, or Western Hindi for Delhi if he is to be working in one of these places and needs to talk to those who speak only the local language?

What language an American representative learns will have to depend upon what kind of work he does and the publics he meets. If he works with the educated locals, he should study whatever language they speak. If he works with farmers, the young, laborers, or whatever group from the mass, he should learn the dialect they use among themselves.

To accept this principle also opens the answer to how and where Americans should learn languages. Everyone, to repeat, should have studied a foreign language in school. The purpose of this is education, not utility. Americans who work abroad need language for use.

When use, not liberal education, is the purpose, the teaching must be rapid, pruned to the needs of use and speeded by all available devices, whether traditional and dignified or not. Instruction must be given on the site, as it is now, so that a man can learn the language while he works. To send men to language centers, where they are useless for any other service, is too expensive to allow many of them to learn languages. And the instruction must be available in many languages and dialects, as it is now. Because Americans are mobile overseas, each man who meets natives face to face may learn several languages and dialects during a career. He will probably be under constant instruction, learning as he works in each new assignment. Inside workers can be taught on the spot too, although, since they need the language only for manners and morale, speed is not so urgent for them.

I do not think that we have found the method of teaching language for use, perhaps because we think first of centers and adaptation of the old-style methods that began when Greek and Latin were taught, not for use, but for structure, precision, and discipline. The aural-oral method, preferably based on a sound study of grammar and vocabulary, is still costly in time. Then when centers are created, either at universities or by themselves, colonies of refugees gather. Only the strongest, most balanced refugee can overcome the persistent fear that comes from violent displacement, deaths of friends and family, and the loss of status in a strange land. From fear come the pretensions of past glory and complaints about the low culture of America, so common among refugees and so untrue. I doubt that frightened people are the best teachers of their own language and culture. A refugee from Russia is hardly the best man to discuss in a language class communist successes, especially if he left there ten years ago. Certainly displaced persons are not the ones to plan new methods of instruction in their languages. They are too constrained by fear and pretension.

Nor can college teachers plan new methods of instruction. They are bound to their own training in language as literature and to their esteem as members of a faculty that as a whole values education above utility. Those who teach only the use of a language and never do research in linguistics or literature lack merit in the eyes of their colleagues and may remain in the lowest ranks and salaries all their years. Justice is at work. The proper job of a liberal arts college is to educate in humanities, natural science, and social science, not to train students in the use of languages, test tubes, and adding machines.

The most obvious specialists to devise new methods are psychologists, assisted perhaps by engineers who know electronics. The most obvious place for them to study the needs for language, for example the minimums of grammar and vocabulary required to be clear, is overseas where the work is done. There they can study comparative results from such alternative methods as instruction by tutors in set-aside hours, or instruction by tutors who accompany an employee all day to correct his mistakes, or instruction that uses machines. The psychologists can also analyze the way adults learn —and don't learn—a language. They can study too how children learn, for to all who have heard travelled children switch from one language to another without falter, it is clear that children have some secret that adults need to know.

A last unanswered question concerns facility in a language. It is just as important to show an American how well or poorly he speaks and writes another language as to teach him the language. If he speaks the equivalent of baby talk; he should not pose as able to speak the language. If he speaks well but with a certain accent, he should know in which circles the accent is a barrier. If he misuses the language of status and intimacy, as in addressing judges the same as servants, he may do more harm than if he does not try to speak the language at all. Mixing with foreigners is full of pitfalls, many of them outside the experience of Americans at home, many connected with the use of language.

Some tests of social facility are needed. They would ascertain not just ability in grammar, vocabulary, and pronunciation but the kind of impression an American will leave in various kinds of groups when he uses the language. When he knows how well he can talk to villagers, tradesmen, professional men, or workingmen, he can begin to act accordingly. He need not change his speech, but he can change his manner in the use of it, and he will know what to expect. A man with Oxbridge speech can still talk to dock-workers but he has to recognize their first impression that he comes from a different class.

VI

The most obvious generalization about the nature of work in foreign affairs is that there is no easy generalization. Tasks vary here as much as in the government as a whole. Only degrees are different; we do not have as large a post office staff in the foreign as in the domestic field, but we do have a staff. In different degree the problems of the conduct of foreign affairs are the problems of American public administration, and few subjects are less subject to easy answers. Nonetheless a few points stand out that may help in planning change.

First, because of its very extent and variety, the American effort abroad calls for organization and all the consequent interplay of persons that work in Washington requires. Therefore no solution that applies only to individuals is very pertinent. To say, for example, that only men who know the language and culture should be employed is beside the point. Individuals will be chosen for any number of reasons, among them knowledge of language and culture. They become part of an organization. Each, equipped inevitably with his own traits, remains both an individual and a member of the American group. Our concern has to be for the institutions as well as the men.

Second, while, from our own viewpoint, we may see all our people as individuals caught in complex organization, to the local residents abroad all Americans look alike and are conspicuous. An army officer, a vice-consul, and their wives, are taken as the same. Their hosts have no interest in the jurisdictional lines of Washington and the field, unless they are officials who try to play one American agency against another. All agencies should require their employees overseas, and their wives, to follow uniform rules of decorum. A few rules, strictly enforced by the chiefs of each mission in a country, could prevent some of the horror stories so familiar to sophisticated travellers: adults who still act as adolescents, wives who talk about "these people" in their presence, men who boast of the way Americans do things, men and women who let their incomes show, the rude, the vulgar, and the proud. Work with foreigners is delicate at any level. We need not burden it by failure to enforce a little discipline over employees and their dependents.

More serious is the disunity of Americans at work. It has two consequences. In one, the American simply looks foolish when he tries to explain that his agency has no connection with the work of that other agency and then sees foreign officials scheme to use him against another unit of his own government. In the other, the foreigner will reveal to our man from one agency information of interest to another agency but it will never get delivered. A military adviser in some unstable land is the American closest to the local army officers who will win a revolution and become the next government. But our military man has been told to stay out of politics—that's State Department business—so he never reports on the politics of his military friends. The Treasury man may learn the key to who controls whom in the government with what mortgages, but since this is not relevant to exchange rates or the price of bonds, he does not tell anyone. To do otherwise invites a rebuff. Our men learn quickly that to relay information to another agency rouses defenses. "We know that already, and we will always know such things before and better than you because it is our special field." Compartments have high psychological fences. Those inside resist anyone outside who pretends to a knowledge of their business, and they suspect outsiders of plans to invade.

Outsiders seldom try to cross the walls. Most of the time they fail to see the significance of what they encounter if it is outside their specialty. "So you're going to seize the palace," the military American is likely to say. "What kind of artillery do you plan to use?" Not, "My God! I must get this news to the Ambassador and the men in political affairs." Unless executives insist, workers in our system feel no obligation to the whole but only to the part for which they work. They are never drilled in the duty to be aware of total foreign affairs. They are discouraged by their fellows from crossing lines to report in other fields.

Third, we have never decided how to use alien employees, or local nationals; locals, as they are called in the trade. Usually we act as if they do not exist except as furniture. Yet some top qualified people are alien. Local employees in those nations where education is advancing can do much of the routine work now done by Foreign Service Officers. They can write political and economic reports, gather all the information before a visa is issued, negotiate with local authorities on that wide range of troubles that American citizens encounter abroad, from a Saturday night drunk and disorderly charge to a fatal auto smash. Aliens can do, and already do, much of the work in American propaganda. And they can do more in management. By now in most nations educated aliens are available.

In most of the underdeveloped world, the educated but unemployed or underpaid are a sad group. Some of them were educated in the United States. (One of the rankling worries of a professor who deals with foreign students is his knowledge of what happens to them when they go home; few get jobs comparable to those their American classmates get.) American missions abroad can help themselves and the other nation by giving jobs to the educated unemployed or underpaid, especially to those educated in the United States.

Of course, all locals should be examined for character and discretion and should be supervised by Americans to see that they do not abuse their position. Then they should be given more kinds of work, and more responsible work, than now.

Fourth, the assignment in foreign affairs is so unclear that only confusion can be expected until we decide what we want to do and what kind of people we want to do it. When we tell our men to act tough but don't lose friends, be generous but penurious, smart but not original, we tend to paralyze them. Their safest way is to do nothing much because the press, Congressmen, the White House, and others in authority are unpredictable. No man is wise enough to make only the right moves when his bosses are unclear as to what they want him to do. This says again that American foreign policy is made up of uncoordinated bits and pieces. The people who work with it can do no more than reflect its incoherence, and play safe by doing as little as possible that is new.

VII

The reasons for incoherence in Washington are reflected in the nature of work. Policy is decided, to go back to the earlier point, by answering the mail, allowing each event to shape its own answer. About the only large policy is the containment of communism, and it is so large that the interpretation of each event anywhere in the world by this creed alone can still be wide open.

Too few take the time to think. While men in Washington answer the mail, men in the missions write more mail. An ambassador and his staff report what they see, make recommendations, negotiate whatever deals the government sends them, and leave a good impression by the way they represent their country. Today this means by and large that our valuable men abroad go to work each morning to handle routine that adds to the routine in Washington.

No one is encouraged to think. A career Foreign Service Officer assigned to political affairs is the closest to general, total foreign policy of anyone we employ, just as the men in the geographical bureaus in the State Department are theoretically concerned with total policy. But even these men do not spend their time at strategy. A political affairs officer stationed abroad files reports on views expressed in conversations, press, and speeches by eminences. He keeps up with shifting power, with alliances and enmities, with the views of the influential. He will treat as hot news any statement that may indicate what leaders in the government think of the United States. Sometimes Washington will want to know what a minister thinks or plans to do. Such a request goes to the highest level, as they say in government, and the Ambassador or Counsellor goes to ask, later writing a careful report of everything said on both sides.

Such is work in political affairs. It is counted as the most important work in a mission, especially by those who do it. The men who get ahead in it write clear reports and, if they are exceptions, sometimes anticipate what will happen next in their country. They are kept busy reporting, asking questions. As they advance, they become executives over others who write reports. At the top, they become ambassadors. Political affairs, despite their prestige and label, are far from policy-making, and the officers who work in them get ahead surest by doing what is put before them. Only the audacious man would volunteer to suggest policy to Washington, and not even he would tell Washington it was wrong.

We make no provision in staffs abroad for analysis of our total policy as it affects a country. While we carry on diplomatic, consular, military, and cultural relations, and manage economic aid and propaganda, we never look at ourselves in the whole. We have no one assigned to relate economic aid to cultural relations and to propose general policy toward the nation in which all sorts of official Americans are busy at carrying out lots of different policies.

The President needs a planning staff in Washington. So does each ambassador in the field. We might then get coherence in foreign policy. We might decide what we want our employees to do.

CHAPTER 13   TESTS FOR
ADMISSION TO THE WORK

If it is impossible to dash off an easy description of the work, it is also impossible to say that any one kind of person is wanted for the work.

Recruiters can state platitudes, and do. The career Foreign Service wants recruits of breadth, attractive personality, quickness to understand people of different backgrounds, eagerness to learn, sense of humor, ability to concentrate, ability to use the English language, integrity, steadiness, sincerity, and modesty. The United States Information Agency for its general representatives adds to these virtues a good background in American history, politics, economics, customs and cultural achievements; an understanding of international relations and current events; and the ability to communicate this knowledge successfully to others. The Armed Forces, Agency for International Development, or Department of Agriculture want all these traits plus technical skill.

So does everyone. The church, commerce, industry, finance, the professions, and all other agencies of government want this perfect man who knows a lot and is always nice to all kinds of people.

He seldom turns up. One so favored can start nearly any career he wants. Not all of his kind by any measure want to work for government, probably no more than the one in six employed persons in the whole population who works for federal, state, or local government, civil or military. Not all those who want to work for government will choose foreign affairs and the assignments over-seas that are recommended for this career. The recruiters for for-eign affairs, as in all human enterprises, are forced to accept some imperfect men.

Once found, even the perfect young recruit still has to face many hazards on that sea of life so well known to commencement speakers. His chances of marrying the right girl for this career, out of the millions of girls available, are so slim they had best be im-proved by prayer. Always he will live with temptations to eat too much, drink, play, work, talk too much, and even a perfect man will perceive temptation and be interested. By middle age the perfect recruit will show whether he is still among the rarities. If he has fallen to the ranks of imperfection, he is still the best we can get, and so are all his imperfect associates. Let this be the motto of every executive: "Do the best you can with the best you can get." And add in parentheses: "You'll never get all you want."

Instead of dreaming, as Americans do, about the kind of perfect person we would prefer to have work in foreign affairs, we can better think about the kind of people we get and what can be done to improve their competence. Our society being competitive in recruitment, the most talented are always by definition in short supply. Foreign affairs will get some of the most talented, but never only the most talented.

We can at best hope that foreign affairs gets its share of the best. And we can hope that it gets no more than its share of the unfit. There will be some fools, as in nature, and there will be some misfits who never learned to be comfortable members of the human race. Some wives will wear tight slacks long after their anatomies have decided against them; some daughters will wear shorts in public, on the street, after the age of twelve; some sons will have the wrong haircuts and fail to bathe often enough. The worst types will gripe because another country is not the same as back home and foreigners don't think the way Americans do. Such warts occur on society at home. We should expect some overseas. Supervisors overseas should try to correct them, and, if this fails, send them home. Then we can try not to repeat but never with total assurance.

Our public service reflects our society. That society is formed of a few geniuses, a few more extratalented persons, a bulk of competent and tolerant people, and a few stupid and mean. Recruitment for foreign affairs tries to get only the best. It succeeds on the whole more than it fails.

II

Present examinations and other methods of selection surely get the best persons from those who compete for work in foreign relations as now defined. They do not try to get persons to work with foreign policy in its broad definition of planning large strategy.

Taking the whole variety of jobs to be done, in all the agencies, the skills needed in foreign relations group into categories for which different methods of recruitment work.

For one, the technical skills are first for all employees who are to do technical work. This simple rule, so obvious as to look foolish when written, is violated whenever a man is hired first because he knows a language or is a good mixer and secondly because he is good in artillery, seeds, soils, budgets, police, or any other specialty. Nothing conceivable can make America look worse overseas than an American who claims to be a specialist but who is full of good will and no ability.

Sometimes the required ability is so elementary that colleges do not offer courses in it, so that degrees are meaningless. When a mechanical engineer faces a dead Jeep, he had better know how to start it. He does no good to display his college transcript. When an agricultural agent faces a problem of mildew in grain storage that farmers of the west solved so long ago that no record was kept, he needs the common knowledge of experience. When he was director of the Food and Agriculture Organization Ed Dodd found farmers in India who lost grain to mildew. He showed them how to build a platform and ventilate their stacks. He could visualize this commonplace solution not because he learned it in school but because he had been a farmer and had learned from work the common sense of the Western world.

The test for technical skill and common sense is mainly experience plus the judgment of persons who have watched the candidate at work. Nearly all the civil service announcements for engineers, farm experts, sanitarians, librarians, and other specialists tell candidates they must have had experience in their fields before they apply to the government. College degrees are also required. Sometimes degrees and experience may be interchanged, and sometimes an escape phrase "or the equivalent" is added.

Wise employers in any case look first to experience and to recommendations. As often as not they spot a man already at work in the government, or someone tells them of a good man for a certain job, and they hire him after proving that he is qualified. They fix up the civil service papers to get the person they want, not for reasons of patronage but for the reason that they trust experience and the judgment of peers.

Military specialists too are chosen for foreign affairs mainly on the basis of their performance. They have proved out in antiaircraft, small boats, helicopters, fighters, rifles, tanks, supply, plans, personnel, command, or other specialties. Their records show other traits that recommend them; perhaps a language, personable ease with strangers, a desire to live in foreign lands, a family that causes no pain. The wheels of assignment are slow and often strange in the armed forces, but they reflect a faith in performance as the best evidence of ability.

III

A second category of skills includes all those needed for certain types of consular work. No work is comparable hence no experience can be measured. A consul has one set of duties connected with ships and sailors. He checks the papers of American merchant ships when they arrive in a foreign port and stands as a combination of friend and judge to the men and masters. He arbitrates disputes, supervises the signing of work contracts to protect the seaman, intervenes to collect wages if they have not been paid, takes care of stranded seamen by finding them another ship or sending them home, and helps them, as he helps any other American, get a fair trial if they get in trouble with the law.

A consul also has the sole authority to issue a visa on an alien's passport and so permit him to approach the portal of the United States. (An officer of the Immigration and Naturalization Service of the Department of Justice decides at the portal whether the alien may step inside.) The consul is limited by law; he may not give a visa to one who is subversive and a possible threat to American security, nor to one who has a dangerous communicable disease, nor to one who is immoral, destitute, insane, or feeble minded. Quotas have to be guarded, for only a certain number of permanent immigrants may be admitted from another nation in a year. With administrative interpretations added to the law and regulations, the rules are now more numerous and more difficult than those for a major religion and more rigid. Young consuls usually handle visas. The work is dull, tense, and, if emotions are allowed to enter, heartbreaking. All day in a busy office the young men listen to truth and lies and try to know the difference, and they lean twice over to avoid making a mistake that will blot their record.

Next a consul may issue, extend, renew, or amend passports for American citizens abroad subject to the usual regulations that require some types of requests to be sent to Washington. Since a passport is evidence of citizenship, the consul has control over something of enormous value both spiritual and, in those places where hard cash will be paid for a passport, material. Not counting those who work for the government, more American citizens live permanently abroad than most Americans at home ever realize. They got there by marriage to aliens, by moving home after they were born on American soil, and by moving to pleasant climates and lower prices. The nearest consul keeps their passports up to date, witnesses their marriages, registers the births of their children, and reports their loss of American citizenship when they take part in elections or serve in the armed forces of the other country.

Last in this category the consul serves American citizens in his vicinity, both resident and tourist, in a variety of ways. He will try to find charity for the poor, through local welfare societies and relatives at home. He makes sure that those accused get fair trials. He will arrange for care of the dead and take custody of estates. He looks for lost relatives and friends. He runs a small post office and information center. And for a procession of Americans with introductions he arranges interviews, entertains, and acts as travel agent without fee. His visitors come from government and from private work; their only common trait is their tie to the consul. Consuls are seldom surprised by the variety of service requested or the variety of visiting Americans.

Officers who do all kinds of consular work must know laws and their interpretation, how to apply both, how to be generous and how to be firm when an applicant is not eligible. They should be able to size up people, for both aliens and American citizens will come in degrees of sin as well as blessedness. Then consuls can leave a good or bad impression of the United States and its whole foreign service by their manners when they deal with aliens and Americans. Above all, they need to be stable, able to keep their heads when all about them is temptation to take drastic action.

The most routine Saturday night American drunk can become an international incident in many sovereign nations if the consul loses his poise. The drunk may have insulted color, or nationalism, the king, the flag, woman's virtue, the dictator, the party in power, or any number of heroes and ideas that will be defended by lives and sacred honor. Before the rise of Fidel Castro's anti-American campaign, one preceding bitter tension between Cubans and Americans came when American sailors fouled the statue of José Martí in Havana. Consuls who failed to realize the gravity or who defended the sailors' offense could have brought on hatred with destruction of the embassy.

No experience in these categories of consular work can be got in the United States. The young man in Norwalk, Ohio, can't possibly learn first hand how to patch up international relations after drunks in foreign lands. Nor can he learn in college the details of how to handle ships and seamen, visas, citizenship, or service to Americans. Lacking experience and schooling, he can hardly be examined in such specialities before admission to the service.

Instead an applicant for the Foreign Service, from which all consuls come, is examined for general ability in a written test and for personal bent in an interview.

In the written part he is tested for 90 minutes about prose, tables, maps, and graphs that he has before him. No outside information is needed; the data is all in the paper and all questions can be answered from it. Sample questions are available in a booklet to anyone who wants it. Under "General Ability" is this introduction: "This test is designed to measure mastery of the general learning skills, that is, ability to read, to analyze, and to interpret data."

A fairly dense passage of history about Madison's advocacy of congressional veto over state laws in the Constitutional Convention is followed by seven questions based upon the passage. Next is a most difficult exposition of a theory of wages and prices complicated by protective tariffs, with questions. Next comes a census map that shows farmers growing corn for grain, as a percentage of all farmers, for each state, for each of three years. Questions are based on the map. A triangular graph compares for five countries the percentages of deaths due to cancer, other natural causes, and violence. "Each vertex represents 100% of deaths due to the given cause, and the base opposite represents 0% due to that cause." Seven questions must be answered.

The test is difficult. Only a bright person can pass it. Only a person who can learn will pass it, and here is the main value. If the person of intellectual strength combined with ability to learn is found in the examination for General Ability, he can learn to do the special consular jobs.

IV

But a candidate can be bright and still be unsuitable. To get into the Foreign Service he must also be able to mix agreeably with his own kind without losing his own dignity, and he must be well mannered enough to do the social chores. He cannot be a lump, neither can he be a lollipop. Critics who repeat old canards that Foreign Service Officers are dull and dilettante are ignorant.

An officer is chosen today because among those who proved to be bright in the written examination he is most like the successful officers who have preceded him. His typicality is shown in the interview. He is examined by three Foreign Service Officers who know their own duties well and who seek recruits to do the same kind of work that they do. Their instructions say, "In essence, the purpose of the oral examination is to determine whether a candidate is the kind of person who can reasonably be expected to become a useful member of the Foreign Service."

Usually the interview is relaxed, the interviewers being gentlemen older than the candidate and therefore tolerant of any nervousness. Once they sat where he sits now.

For a time the board asks questions designed to bring out intellectual traits. Does the man know much in depth about a subject he professes to know? If he has majored in political science, he may get questions that go into detail; if he has travelled, he may get questions on the places he has seen; if he is a fly fisherman, he may be quizzed (by another fisherman naturally) on what they strike where in what month, day, and hour. No matter the subject, the board tries to see whether the young man knows much about one thing he should know well. Then come some questions to find whether he appreciates and understands the United States. From here the board tests his curiosity about the world around him and the places he has seen. All the time his appearance, poise, manners, and the use of English have been on display.

Questions to give some clue of success in the peculiar life of the foreign service will also be asked. The panel will try to guess whether he will work well under pressure. Why does he want the job? Is he mature enough for his age? How will he get along with associates and foreigners? Does he have "good, normal habits"? Will he have interests outside his work that will allow wholesome relaxation? Many a candidate has been surprised when asked if he likes to play bridge. If not bridge what does he like to play? The panel is after his ability to stay occupied after hours with some feasible interest. It is not seeking only bridge players for the foreign service, as some think.

The interview aims to probe personality in the broad sense. Not so much weight is put upon a knowledge of facts as upon the attitude toward facts. A pretender to knowledge is doomed, rightly, while a modest man will be accepted in spite of ignorance. The key question is: Will he learn? Soon the young recruit will be abroad faced with new work that can be learned only from doing. His capacity has been tested in the written test called General Ability and in the interview, not certainly, for the tests can be improved, but as well as allowed by present time and money. In the crucial interview, where the final decision is made, each candidate is judged by older men who know the kind of work he will have to learn.

Usually one in five succeeds in the written examination and one in two or three is approved at the interview. The tests get the best qualified of all those who want this career enough to apply for examination.

V

The third category of skills consists of reporting and representation, activities shared by all except those who do strictly technical or managerial work.

Reporting can cover nearly any subject. A consul may report on the market for bicycles. A labor specialist will analyze the political alliances of union leaders. The agricultural attaché will count sources of food and say where American exports might fit, including the sale of surplus food. The military attaché measures guns and men and could, if allowed, tell much about the political feelings of officers and men. Political affairs officers report the shifts of strength in a country, when they can find them, and tell Washington how various officials feel about American moves. All reporters, from the newest young man of the Information Service to the Ambassador in Moscow, should be able to know how to pull the significant points out of a tangle, then write clearly, in the least possible space, for readers already harassed, all that needs to be said, day after day.

Representation means making a good impression for the United

States. In its narrowest sense it is official entertaining, and in official jargon a representation allowance is a sum that may be spent to entertain. In the broad sense, representation means any action by Americans abroad which reflects their country and culture, in this case, of course, by Americans who work for government. For this broad definition no test is possible beyond the common effort to keep fools and boors out of the service and to send them home when discovered. The dignity of a man is estimated in the interview before admission. So is poise and ability to converse. A scared man or a bumbler will show. The man who has never learned much about his own country, or worse who despises it and is trying to escape, will be found out if the interviewer has any gumption.

Appearance is easiest of all to judge. Most impassioned democrats resent the fact that it is judged at all, forgetting that all have used it as a measure since puberty. Nothing under heaven concerns an adolescent male more than the way his hair is cut and combed and whether his pants conform. He worries less when he is adult, but he still wears what other men wear because this is expected. Only a "character" chooses his own way through conventional society. Characters seldom go to work for government. Everywhere in the society of higher officials careful grooming is conventional and dress is conservative. Shaggy hair is simply not expected. Loud checks are reserved for Sunday in the country. Dark greys and dark blues are the weekday work clothes for all who deal with outsiders in offices and clubs. An official dresses for his day in a way to be ready for whatever comes up, including a summons from the prime minister. (Technicians who work outside dress as their job indicates, as in military functionalism.)

Not long ago diplomats were much more formal in dress, giving the origin to such a lingering epithet as the striped pants boys. Now they work too fast to pay as much attention as they once did to formality. When an ambassador makes an appointment to deliver a note within the hour he hasn't time to change into striped pants. His subordinates can go for years without changing to anything more formal than black tie and dinner jacket. All that matters today is that officials know how to dress in good taste within the convention of their trade. This is what interviewers note. It is what employers note in any comparable trade, for the foreign service is by no means unique when advertising and finance, to mention only two, are also filled with men who dress alike.

Tests for ability to report are plainer. In purest form, as in the examination for Foreign Service Officers, they measure ability to write, including ability to organize ideas and choose words. A poorly written passage must be edited. Faults of diction and grammar must be detected in a series of sentences. Choices must be made among various ways of writing a passage. The relation of particular statements to a theme must be recognized. Sentences have to be analyzed for precise meaning. Some test of mood and force must also be passed. If all freshmen in college had to succeed in the ninety minutes of trial in which Foreign Service Officers have succeeded, enrollment would be a tenth of what it is.

VI

One large, enveloping trait is relevant to all kinds of work, to the technical skills, to consular duties, and to reporting and representation. It is called by various names but the one term that comes closest to defining it is breadth of knowledge. In the written examinations, half of the grade is given for this trait by both the State Department for the Foreign Service and the U.S. Information Agency for its non-technical staffs abroad.

Breadth of knowledge is evidence of curiosity and alertness, both desirable virtues of the fast learner. Such virtues are the best forecast of performance. They give some assurance of adaptability and elevation through the ranks.

Breadth is tested in the written examination for Foreign Service Officers by questions about many different things. First in the book of samples is a question from American history, requiring identity of the Monroe Doctrine. The next requires precise definition of a cloister. Next is one that asks for the best way to hold down the incidence of intestinal diseases. For two hours the candidate is tested in variety. For each question he has five possible answers and must choose the most correct.

To be perfect he would know some history, economics, political science, geography, science, art, music, and literature. He would have answered questions about the Bible as well as the Monroe Doctrine and about the musical forms most used by four composers. He would know that William James, not Henry, was associated with philosophical pragmatism, and he would also know the difference between a presidential and cabinet system of government. He would know what makes a solar battery work and which nation's drama and novels are realistic, fatalistic, and introspective.

If all this sounds as superficial, and as irrelevant, as a television quiz game, remember that the purpose is not possession of any particular item but of a wide range. The candidate who knows something about a variety of subjects has more curiosity than one who knows only one subject and is a better bet for the future. He will learn consular work quicker and be better at reporting and representation. He will be more the generalist and therefore a prospective executive. And he will be better company for himself and for others.

A novice in the foreign service who has passed such a test of breadth is so exceptional among American college graduates of the same age that one shudders to think of the illiterates who might represent us without the test of breadth.

One small, appalling sign of the ignorance of young Americans who go to Europe, not as employees of government, was published by the Maxwell School of Syracuse University, January 1958, as a research paper. "The sample consisted of university-level Americans with a median age of twenty-two years. Their parents were mainly in the professional or the upper-business class of American society. No less than 80 per cent came from families with incomes above the United States average."

Only 30 percent could translate well into any foreign language a simple, elementary paragraph. Only 37 percent were classed as well informed about Europe's geography, politics, economics, social customs, and arts. Half of the well nurtured young Americans could not name a single Italian or German writer of the last

150 years. Half thought that divorce was not allowed by the law of France. Seventy percent knew of no nation in which the state church was Lutheran. Ninety percent did not know where the Berbers lived.

These young people, if they ever met any foreigners besides guides, might possibly be expected to answer questions about the United States. Only 36 percent were rated reasonably informed. Sixteen percent thought the average family income in America was more than $7,000 a year instead of the $5,000 a year that it was at the time. More than two-thirds had very little knowledge of the proportions of Catholics and Jews in the population. Sixty percent had no idea of the number of Negroes. Eighty percent knew nothing about the number of immigrants admitted currently each year to the United States.

Not many Americans know answers to questions of this kind that foreigners ask, yet upper income, college trained Americans might be expected to know more of the answers when they are going to Europe. Anyone who has served with the armed forces abroad or travelled in the same ship with students knows that not much can be expected, no matter the income and education. He knows the jokes about American student tours and, more, how the students themselves take pride in their darkness. Mont-Saint-Michel? Way the hell away from Paris and no way to have fun. Chartres? Another cathedral. The Louvre? The race goes like this. You time yourself from the main entrance. You must not get stopped by a guard for walking too fast or running. O.K. You have to stand thirty seconds each in front of Venus, Winged Victory, and Mona Lisa, then get back to the main entrance. They say the record is four minutes. It was made by the first guy ever to say Winged Victory would never fly.

Student tourists, fortunately, seldom come in touch with many people where they visit. Only bus drivers, guides, and waiters constantly hear them, and these international types are used to anything. When by chance an American student does speak to a local student, cultural relations are limited to the narrow band of the typical American's limited interest.

College graduates who pass the written examination for the foreign service are far above the average for breadth. They can be expected to converse with their kind in other countries.

VII

The examinations now used are not perfect. More original writing and less editing would make them better. So would a much longer and more intensive interview. Forty-five to ninety minutes of questions and answers, conducted by men with their eyes on the clock, knowing that another candidate is waiting in the outer room, is hardly the recommended way to decide fates or get the best men. This interview is the climax of selection. From it comes a beginner in the career of foreign relations. If the door is closed, the candidate finds another career. He may fail the written examination and take it again, to pass the second or even the third time. The decision of the board that gives the oral examination is final, and it makes its decision after one brief session.

Despite faults, however, the examinations for admission to the Foreign Service of the State Department can be recommended for other agencies after comparison with other types of civil service examinations. Other agencies that send staffs abroad will especially benefit by the use of such examinations, as the United States Information Agency has already decided to do for its general foreign service representatives. If we ever get a unified foreign service, its members who are hired for the skills mentioned in this chapter can be selected by such examinations. They will be the best qualified of all those who apply.

CHAPTER 14 THE OFFICIALS
WHO WORK IN FOREIGN AFFAIRS

HOWEVER THEY ARE CHOSEN, BY EXAMINATION or by previous experience, the permanent people (to differentiate them from political chiefs) who rise to higher positions in the government in foreign affairs are an impressive lot. They come from all parts of the country, are educated in a variety of colleges and graduate schools, and have had experience in other lines of work. At least this much is shown by the statistics that are available about them.

The easiest way to summarize the kind of Americans who work for the government in foreign affairs is to count their traits in *The Biographic Register,* a book published at intervals by the State Department. Only the bare facts of origin, education, and career can be counted. The deeper, more important facts of personality are still to be found by someone who will go into attitudes, habits, and behavior. Still, to know as much as skeleton biographies tell is better than nothing.

Eight categories of government employees were studied in *The Biographic Register, 1960.* They were the career Foreign Service which provides most key officials for embassies, consulates and the State Department; the Foreign Service Reserve, composed of temporary employees attached to the career Foreign Service; General Schedule employees of Grades 14 and higher who hold posts in the Department of State but who are not members of the Foreign Service; and those in similar grades in the International

Cooperation Administration, U.S. Information Agency, the Development Loan Fund, the Foreign Agricultural Service, and the U.S. Mission to the United Nations. Since the *Register, 1960* was published, the International Cooperation Administration has merged with the Development Loan Fund to form the Agency for International Development, whose name may change again by the time this gets into print. At this time we will use the latest name, the Agency for International Development, and hope that it will continue for a few more months. If anyone thinks this is a trivial matter, let him recall that historians some day will have to trace this agency through at least six different names in the twenty years after 1941, when the policy was born as Lend-Lease.

Robert Thiele, Research Assistant in Political Science at the University of Wisconsin, made the count. Facing more than 12,000 biographies in the *Register,* he took every fourth name as a sample. Some exceptions were made. Members of the Foreign Service Staff, in the main clerical workers and specialists in the embassies and consulates, were skipped. So were non-career ambassadors at this point because they were analyzed separately and will be reported later. General Schedule employees were analyzed only if they held Grade 14 or higher, on the assumption that one who had reached Grade 14, when Grade 18 is the top, had reached a position of influence and should be called an official. When a biography was so slight as to be useless, it was discarded. There were very few of these. So few biographies turned up for the Development Loan Fund, the Foreign Agricultural Service, and the U.S. Mission to the United Nations that all were used, regardless of other sampling, whenever one was found.

In all, 3,101 biographies were analyzed. They were divided 965 in the Foreign Service, 287 in the Foreign Service Reserve, 99 General Schedule employees of the State Department of Grade 14 and above, 464 in the U.S. Information Agency, 1,217 in the Agency for International Development (25 in the Development Loan Fund), 60 in the Foreign Agricultural Service, and 9 in the U.S. Mission to the United Nations.

All the facts available about each person were cast into categories and added. Then percentages were taken. The result is a rough indication of the kind of people hired for this work in the career Foreign Service and in the influential positions of the other services. American citizens who work in Washington and overseas for the agencies listed, in posts of influence, are this way in the mass. That is all that is shown. We still do not know about American civilians who work for the military establishment at home and abroad. Nor do we know about aliens who work for both civil and military agencies of government overseas. The data for these are not available, so far as we know, except in the oceanic files of government. The cost of analyzing it is beyond the reach of cloistered scholars. Much can be learned about America's professional military leaders in Morris Janowitz, *The Professional Soldier, A Social and Political Portrait,* published in 1960. Mr. Janowitz did a thorough job, much too thorough for it to be summarized here. Since all military leaders are in some degree engaged in the conduct of foreign affairs, his whole study is relevant and recommended.

Data is available in the biographies of civilians to show region of birth, age, sex, college attended, degrees, experience outside of government, experience inside of government other than in foreign affairs, experience in government foreign affairs, and, overseas, experience in world regions.

It will be summarized for all American citizens working for government in all the agencies whose higher employees are listed in the *Register.* When the employees of any agency differ considerably from the whole, this will be mentioned. So will any significant change from the employees of 1952, for whom some comparable data exists.[1]

II

Region of birth means little for interest or competence in foreign affairs. Americans move around so much that birthplace is no

[1] In an article, James L. McCamy and Allesandro Corridini, "The People of the State Department and Foreign Service," *The American Political Science Review,* Vol. XLVIII, No. 4, December, 1954.

more than a record, and successful men are apt to be from any part of the nation. But Congress is organized by states and districts. A good many of its members, and their constituents, are as parochial as cracker barrels. Executive agencies, living by grace of Congress, pay attention to the regional origins of their employees, and sometimes have to report these to Congress.

Figures on regions of birth mean little unless they are related to the same fact for the whole population. Two types of discrimination must be entered at this point to make the relation more accurate. One is against women; the other against Negroes. Because the people employed by government to handle foreign affairs at this high level are in great majority white males, the only significant comparable figures for place of birth of the total population are those for white males. The latest available figures are for 1950, not the most satisfactory year because Alaska and Hawaii were not yet states.[2] At the time of this counting, the 1960 census report on place of birth was not yet published.

A slightly higher proportion of people who go into this work are born in the Northeast, West, and abroad than white males in the total population. A slightly lower proportion are born in the North Central States. The largest disparity between percentage of total white male births and births of people who go into foreign affairs is in the South. There considerably fewer officials are born, relative to total white males.

For whatever it means in local pride, all regions of the nation seem to be represented evenly enough to hold off all but the most rustic members of Congress. All the agencies conformed to this distribution with the exception of the Development Loan Fund which in this year, 1960, had 52.0 percent of its officials born in the North Central region. Numerically these concentrated Midwesterners were only 13 of a total of 25 so the nation was not shaken to its roots.

---

[2] The figures used are from Census Bureau, *U.S. Census of Population: 1950*, Vol. IV, Special Reports, Part 4, Chapter A (Government Printing Office, 1953), p. 24; Part 3, Chapter A, p. 130. The "Foreign Born" include those white males born in U.S. territories and possessions, born to American parents abroad, and naturalized foreign born.

TABLE 4. REGION OF BIRTH OF GOVERNMENT OFFICIALS IN FOREIGN AFFAIRS

	Percent White Males Born in Region	Percent Foreign Affairs Officials
Northeastern States	25.2	30.5
North Central States	32.0	28.5
South	28.4	20.0
West	7.9	11.5
Foreign Born	6.4	9.5

III

Few women ever rise high enough in this work to be listed in the *Register*. For all the agencies, men are 90.5 percent of all officials. Maiden ladies make up 7.5 percent, and married women 2.0 percent of the total.

One considerable change has occurred since 1952. Though still small, the percentage of women career Foreign Service Officers has increased from 1.3 in 1952 to 10.0 percent in 1960. This may be a temporary figure due to a merger of State Department officials into the Foreign Service between 1954 and 1957.

For good reasons examining boards for the Foreign Service normally hesitate to take women. They cannot work as freely as men in Latin and Moslem countries. The chivalry of men, and their erroneous opinion that women are weaker and due protection, means that men think women cannot be sent on dangerous missions as can men.

More accurately, women are handicapped by the custom of courtship and marriage. A woman who is smart enough and attractive enough to pass the examining board will also know how to find a husband if she wants to get married. Personnel directors shudder at the amount to be spent in training a young woman who will marry and leave the service after a year or two. The boards therefore try to choose smart, attractive women who do not plan to get married, at least not at the time they are interviewed. There is small assurance that what a girl says at twenty-two about plans for marriage is what she will still say at twenty-three if she has met the right man.

IV

In age these people are in majority between 30 and 50, as they were in 1952. Two-thirds in 1960 were in this middle area.

TABLE 5. PERCENTAGES OF FOREIGN AFFAIRS OFFICIALS BY AGE GROUPS, 1960

Under 31	6.3
31–40 years	28.0
41–50	37.9
51–60	22.2
Over 60	5.7

Within the middle range, however, significant changes had occurred in the career Foreign Service, the Foreign Service Reserve, and the General Schedule higher officials of the State Department between 1952 and 1960. The Foreign Service added weight in the middle years. The percentage of its officers 41–50 years old rose from 24.1 in 1952 to 36.5 in 1960. The increase came out of the group 31–40 years old, where the percentage dropped from 42.0 to 32.1, and to a smaller degree from the group under 31. During this time the Foreign Service grew in size by the entrance to higher levels of officials who had been in the domestic service in the State Department and apparently became older as a result.

The Foreign Service Reserve grew younger in the same period, and older at the same time. Those aged 31–40 increased by 11.0 percentage points, and those above 60 increased by 3.2 percentage points, at the expense of the 41–60 ages. The Reserve also grew drastically in size during this period because of the need for specialists who could not be found among the orthodox Foreign Service Officers of the time. Specialists in economics, administration, labor relations, and science were added with a consequent emphasis in the 31–40 group.

The most striking change occurred among those General Schedule officials still working in the State Department after the merger of domestic and foreign staffs. They are growing older, perhaps dying off. Only Foreign Service Officers have a promising future in the State Department under the present scheme; only they among permanent officials will receive the good jobs that deal with policy. Young men who did not merge into the Foreign Service no longer reach the higher grades in enough numbers to show much weight in percentage of the total.

For this General Schedule service of the State Department the group under 30 years old fell 2.0 percentage points to zero in the eight years from 1952 to 1960. Those of age 31–40 fell 25.2 percentage points to 6.1 percent of the total. Those 41–50 increased 9.1, to account in 1960 for 50.5 percent of the total; those 51–60 increased 11.1 points to account for 30.3 percent of the total; and those above 60 increased 8.0 points to account in 1960 for 8.5 percent of the total. The old-time State Department crew is growing old.

Only the Foreign Agricultural Service approaches the General Schedule of the State Department for maturity. It has no young men under 31 in its upper echelons, and has only 10.0 percent in the 31–40 group. Those 41–50 years old account for 41.7 percent of its officers; those 51–60 for 35.0 percent; and those above 60 for 13.3 percent of the total in 1960.

Except for the unmerged civil servants in the State Department and the Foreign Agricultural Service the nation's work in foreign affairs is in the hands of young and middle-aged men, as might be expected. Most of the young men are not exactly beginners. They range from 31 to 40. The middle-aged are between 41 and 60, a time held by some philosophers to be prime. Youths under 31 and old men above 60 provide almost identical, and small, percentages of this personnel.

V

As might be expected in this day when a college degree is customary for nearly any kind of job with a future, nearly all these officials have been to college. The significant question has now become to what extent they went to college. And the answer is surprising. Almost two-thirds of the officials in foreign affairs have gone beyond the bachelor's degree.

TABLE 6. LEVELS OF EDUCATION OF HIGHER OFFICIALS IN FOREIGN AFFAIRS (PERCENTAGES)

High school only	6.3
Attended college, no degree	14.6
Bachelor's degree only	22.9
Graduate work, no degree	17.4
Master's degree, no higher degree	23.4
Law degree, no higher degree	5.4
Other professional degree	1.2
Doctor of Philosophy	8.8

The level of education is fairly uniform from agency to agency. The only striking exception to the norm is the 26.7 percent of Ph.D's in the Foreign Agricultural Service, compared to the 8.8 percent for all agencies. So far as comparisons can be made with 1952, the prevalence of graduate work has not changed much since then.

VI

The colleges attended by American officials in foreign affairs have always drawn attention, probably from a concern that no one type should prevail. Now that almost two-thirds of the officials have had graduate work, the places where they took graduate degrees become as relevant as the places where they took bachelors' degrees.[3]

Officials who received degrees got them in a total of 540 different colleges and universities. This, however, is not the whole story.

When graduate and undergraduate degrees are combined, 27 universities grant half of the degrees held by officials in all the agencies. This should be emphasized. We are considering now all kinds of degrees for the civil agencies in foreign affairs whose officials are listed in the *Register*. Twenty-seven universities have given both bachelors' and advanced degrees to officials in all the agencies.

Within the group of 27 universities, seven have granted almost 25.0 percent of the degrees.

All this is shown in Table 7, where rank, percentage of total degrees granted, and the cumulative percentage are shown for the first 49.19 percent of degrees. After 49.19 percent come five institutions each granting 0.66 percent of all degrees to put the halfway mark up to 52.49. The five are Michigan State, Nebraska, Oklahoma A.&M., Pennsylvania State, and the University of Utah.

There is some variety among the agencies in the origins of their officials, but not much. When a university ranks high as a source of officials for one agency, it tends to rank high as a source for the others.

The four agencies that account for by far the most officials are the Foreign Service, Foreign Service Reserve, U.S. Information Agency, and the Agency for International Development. All four are staffed with officials who have either or both bachelors' and graduate degrees. Two kinds of degrees for each of four agencies makes a total of eight categories in which a university might appear. The first ten universities for all degrees appeared in three-fourths of the categories possible for all degrees, all agencies.

[3] In the analysis of 1952, *Op. Cit.*, we were able to find the proportion of officials who had attended private rather than public high schools. (It was higher in all agencies than for the population at large.) In the 1960 *Register* the preparatory schools were left out of the biographies, and we can no longer shed light on this point.

TABLE 7. Universities that Grant Half of all Degrees to Officials in Foreign Affairs

Rank	University	Percentage of all Degrees	Cumulative Percentage
1.	Harvard	5.91	5.91
2.	Columbia	4.96	10.87
3.	California System	3.30	14.17
4.	Yale	3.01	17.18
5.	Georgetown	2.98	20.16
6.	George Washington	2.30	22.46
7.	Wisconsin	2.19	24.65
8.	Chicago	2.06	26.71
9.	Minnesota	1.90	28.61
10.	Princeton	1.87	30.48
11.	Michigan	1.66	32.14
12.	Cornell	1.61	33.75
13.	New York University	1.50	35.25
14.	Ohio State	1.50	36.75
15.	Stanford	1.43	38.18
16.	Pennsylvania	1.19	39.37
17.	Fletcher School (Tufts)	1.16	40.53
18.	Illinois	1.11	41.64
19.	Iowa State	1.08	42.72
20.	University of Washington	.92	43.64
21.	Boston University	.90	44.54
22.	Syracuse	.84	45.38
23.	Northwestern	.82	46.20
24.	City College, New York	.77	46.97
25.	Missouri	.77	47.74
26.	Texas A. & M.	.74	48.48
27.	Southern California	.71	49.19

No difference worth considering appears between the standing of one of the first ten universities for the bachelor's as against the graduate degree. If a school ranks among the first ten for the bachelor's, it will usually rank among the first ten for the graduate degree.

Differences appear, at least tentatively, in the relative standing among the first ten universities when compared by services. Thus Harvard ranks first for the Foreign Service and Foreign Service Reserve but twentieth for the Agency for International Development bachelors' degrees and second for the same agency's graduate degrees. Wisconsin ranks nineteenth for the Foreign Service bachelors' degrees but seventh for Information Agency and fourth for International Development. Princeton ranks fourth for the bachelors' in the Foreign Service but fourteenth for the Information Agency and not among the first ten for International Development. The California system (the University of California in all its branches plus the state colleges), is among the first ten for all agencies.

It is too soon to conclude anything from these differences by agency. One hypothesis that is suggested is that certain universities among the first ten are turning out graduates who are more interested in either the older or newer services, and perhaps better qualified to pass the entrance exams.

Nothing much can be concluded either about why certain universities show up in the list and not others. For some to show up at all is no doubt an accident of the sample and the year. The percentage of degrees granted by any particular institution, except perhaps for Harvard and Columbia, is not high enough to signify much beyond the fact that for this sample the school was among the first 27 of a slowly declining curve.

Two of the universities can be explained in part by their location. Georgetown and George Washington are both in Washington, D.C., and both draw students who are already working for the government. Georgetown in addition has long offered a special course for students interested in the career Foreign Service. (Georgetown ranks second for bachelors' degrees in the Foreign Service and Foreign Service Reserve but does not rank among the first ten for the Information Agency and ranks nineteenth for the bachelors' degrees of the Agency for International Development.) One other school among the first 27 specializes in training for this work. It is the Fletcher School of Law and Diplomacy, a branch of Tufts University.

Good reputations may be the answer. All the first ten schools have good reputations in general. So do some of the next ten and the ten after that and so on until all the 540 schools are exhausted. Experienced educators do not indulge in rating colleges, for they know that competence varies from decade to decade and department to department. Still they also know that some schools maintain their reputations through lean and fat years alike, and students know this too. Students who want this kind of work may well go to the schools of top reputation.

Answers would come easier if enrollment seemed to govern. It does not. Counting undergraduates only, Harvard and Columbia, both small, match California, Wisconsin, and Minnesota, all large. Nor does the kind of management seem to be clearly decisive. Of the first ten, seven are private and three public universities, but of the first 27, that grant half the degrees, twelve are private, and fifteen are public (if we count Cornell and Syracuse public as parts of the New York State University system).

About the only clear conclusion is that American officials in foreign affairs come from universities headed by Harvard and Columbia and declining steadily but slowly through a long list of 540. The list declines with mainly the same schools holding their place for all the services.

VII

The amount of experience in jobs other than the ones held in foreign affairs at the time of this count sheds some light upon whether a tight career group exists. A tight career group is one in which all recruits enter directly from college and stay within a particular service until death or retirement, in the stereotype of the secure and changeless civil servant, and the members successfully fight off any attempt by outsiders to infiltrate. All the agencies have been at work long enough, under one name or another, to have gone far in the creation of tight career services if they had started to do so twenty years ago. None has done so, not even the career Foreign Service.

In all the agencies a majority of officials have had experience outside the government or within other agencies of the government than the one they are now in. There is much overlap, too. An individual has had experience both outside the government and in some other government agency.

TABLE 8. PERCENTAGES OF OFFICIALS WITH EXPERIENCE IN WORK OTHER THAN GOVERNMENTAL FOREIGN AFFAIRS

	Outside Government		Other Government Agencies	
Agency	1–5 Yrs.	6+ Yrs.	1–5 Yrs.	6+ Yrs.
Foreign Service	39.3	24.8	55.9	17.2
Foreign Service Reserve	40.1	29.6	45.0	44.3
General Service	26.3	48.5	46.9	37.8
Agency for International Development	19.6	63.6	34.7	47.9
U.S. Information Agency	28.0	55.4	49.7	21.9
Foreign Agricultural Service	21.7	61.7	21.7	65.0
U.S. Mission to the United Nations	33.0	44.0	67.0	00.0
All These Agencies	29.3	46.4	44.7	34.0

These figures show considerable versatility among the higher officials who handle foreign affairs. To take the oldest, most career-conscious group, the Foreign Service, 39.3 percent of its members have had from one through five years experience outside the government, some of it no doubt no more than marking time between their selection and their appointment, but some kind of different experience nonetheless. More significant is the fact that 24.8 percent of Foreign Service Officers have had six years or more of work outside the government. All such work counted here was significant enough to be listed in the officials' biographies. It does not include summer jobs or other such experience.

As should be expected, the newer agencies show more experience than the Foreign Service in jobs outside the government. The nature of the work also has something to do with the amount of experience. Thus the Agency for International Development, which is newer and engaged in technical assistance, has 63.6 percent of its officials with six or more years experience outside of government, compared to the 24.8 percent of the Foreign Service Officers.

Because military service is counted as experience in other government agencies, the figures for this category may not be as significant as they first appear to be. Those now in mid-career, and middle age, were employed in the Second World War or Korea, while many of the younger men have served in peace. The significant column under other government agencies is the one for six or more years' experience. A full third, 34.0 percent, of all the officials have had six or more years in some other government agency, more than the usual term that might be due to military service.

Experience in government work in foreign affairs is probably the most important kind for these officials. Many federal agencies have some part in this kind of work. A career service in the total field appears to have developed among those individuals who have worked in several agencies. When the total years of experience in government work in foreign affairs are cast for individuals, the results for all officials, all agencies is that in Table 9.

TABLE 9.   PERCENTAGES OF OFFICIALS BY YEARS OF EXPERIENCE IN GOVERNMENT FOREIGN AFFAIRS

Years of Experience	Percent Officials
0–1	8.2
2	6.2
3	8.0
4	7.0
5	6.1
6–10	27.0
11–20	32.9
21–30	3.2
31 or more	1.7

Almost 60 percent of the officials in 1960 had 6 through 20 years of experience in government work in foreign affairs. Almost 5 percent had 21 years or more.

Despite the movement from private to government jobs, despite the movement from one government agency to another, these officials have developed careers in government foreign affairs. The United States has elevated to its higher positions in the conduct of foreign affairs men of varied experience but men who, in a majority, have had most of their experience in government work in this field. The result is a career service that is not a career service in the usual definition of one in which young men enter one service and remain in it for their lives. This service has mixed with the long-term government men some men with long terms in work outside government. Here is a service in which two-thirds are long experienced in government work but with no tight fence around them.

This combination of experience and mobility may be something new in public bureaucracies. Unconsciously we may have begun to mix experience in government with experience outside it. More of this same trait will appear later when we analyze the political chiefs who preside over foreign affairs.

Finally, it is possible to say in what fields the officials had their experience outside the government. It is assumed to be significant only for those who had six years or more of such experience. Table 10 presents the results.

The distribution of officials with experience varies little from one agency to another with these exceptions. More officials, relatively, came from Education and Agriculture, Mining, or Lumber to enter the Agency for International Development and the Foreign Agricultural Service; more from Films, Press, or Radio to U.S. Information Agency, and more from the Professions to enter the General Service of the State Department, this last no doubt because lawyers are counted in this category. Of the fields, only Education can be said to have any edge, and this is not considerable. Business men do not prevail, nor do journalists, lawyers, clerks, or farmers. Nor do teachers and school administrators.

TABLE 10. Percentages of All Officials Who Had Six or More Years Experience Outside Federal Government, by Fields

Field	Percent All Officials
Education	12.2
Agriculture, Mining, Lumber	8.7
Films, Press, Radio	5.7
Clerical Work	5.7
Professions	5.1
State & Local Government	2.7
Social Work	2.0
Foreign Governments & International Organizations	1.4
Research	1.3
Other	1.8

VIII

For years the State Department has moved its men around overseas so often that few true experts in areas have developed. Its main reasons have been five. First, an officer does not make too close ties, does not get committed, does not lose his perspective toward a country if he stays in it only a short time. Second, men deserve to be moved out of hardship posts into pleasanter posts. Three, the chances of promotion are simply better at some posts than at others, and a good man should be moved to those places where he can prove his merit. Four, the work consists of specialties that vary little from one country to another; the skills and poise are more important than special knowledge of an area. Five, men must be moved to the posts where they are most needed; the work does not divide neatly and stay the same. Some laymen think that men should stay in one post until they become throughly familiar with the people, but professionals do not agree.

The result of this policy showed in 1952 and again in 1960. The United States has few Foreign Service Officers who have stayed in any region of the world long enough to be called true experts in the region.

For this count, Mr. Thiele went through the biography of every fourth Foreign Service Officer, the same sample as was used in all other counts above. To avoid distortion that would come from including younger officers who have not had time to build up experience, he considered only officers of Class 5 and above, when Class 8 is the beginning level and Career Ambassador is the highest.

Two years earlier, and we assume still about the same in 1960, half the Foreign Service Officers could be considered old-timers.[4] These had entered by passing an examination or had been taken in under several acts of Congress between 1924 and 1946. The other half had entered by Wristonization, a scheme recommended by a committee headed by Henry M. Wriston and in force from 1954 through 1957 in the Eisenhower administration. People Wristonized were members of the State Department service who were taken into the Foreign Service. They had considerable experience if they were in Class 5 by 1960, but their experience was probably not gained overseas. These Wristonees make the practice of assignment to posts less clear for the next few years than we could desire. A statement of the years of experience in regions by percentage of Foreign Service Officers in 1960, therefore, should be considered subject to change by 1972 as the Wristonees may establish a new pattern for longer tenure in a country.

Up till 1960 certainly the policy has been to move men not just from one country to another within the same region but from one region to another after short terms. In the 1952 analysis, before Wristonization, we found that 84.2 percent of all assignments of officers in comparable classes were for less than six years in any region. In 1960 we find for officers, rather than assignments, the results in Table 11. Adding within the column, we find that two-thirds, 68.0 percent, of the officers have had a maximum of three years in any one region of the world.

A region in this definition is one in which cultural traits and

4 Derived from Appendix 11, "Classification of Foreign Service Officers According to Mode of Entry into the Foreign Service," William Barnes and John Heath Morgan, *The Foreign Service of the United States, Origins, Development, and Functions* (Washington: Department of State, 1961), p. 366. (Data of June 30, 1958).

TABLE 11. PERCENTAGES OF FOREIGN SERVICE OFFICERS, CLASS 5
AND ABOVE, BY MAXIMUM YEARS OF EXPERIENCE IN
ONE WORLD REGION

Maximum Years in One Region	Percent of Officers
1	17.9
2	26.8
3	23.3
4	11.7
5	7.8
5+	12.5

political and economic concerns are the same. With one exception, the region is in one part of the world. The exception is Great Britain and the white dominions of the Commonwealth. These were counted as one region although the nations are not contiguous. Other nations of the Commonwealth, where the people are not of white European origin, were counted in their geographical regions.

The percentage of officers who have had years of experience in regions is shown in Table 12.

Not much can be made from these statistics. There is no precise way to decide how many Foreign Service Officers ideally should be stationed in what regions. Many factors govern. In some countries the host would resent too many officers; in other countries the work is not heavy enough to require many men. Size of staff is no indication of the importance of a mission. When the Middle East is tense, Jidda may be a more important post than Paris, requiring great skill but few numbers.

Further, Foreign Service Officers do not get all their experience from work abroad. They spend time in the Department of State, and in training, or at work in international organizations, or on loan to other agencies of the government. The percentages in these categories are shown in Table 13.

Some of this experience undoubtedly was concerned with regions of the world, though there is no way to tell how much.

TABLE 12. PERCENTAGES OF FOREIGN SERVICE OFFICERS, CLASS 5

Region	Years of Experience	
	1	2
North Africa	2.1	3.7
Mid- and South Africa	2.1	3.6
Central America	2.7	2.8
Caribbean and Mexico	3.9	5.8
West Coast, S.A.	1.9	4.0
East Coast, S.A.	1.8	2.8
Latin America	10.3	15.4
United Kingdom and White Dominions	4.2	5.5
North Europe	4.0	4.8
West Europe	4.6	9.7
West Germany and Austria	5.7	5.7
"Free" Europe	14.3	20.2
East Europe	2.1	4.0
U.S.S.R.	.6	.6
East Europe and U.S.S.R.	2.7	4.6
China	1.5	1.9
Northeast Asia	2.5	3.9
Southeast Asia	4.5	6.9
South Asia	1.8	4.3
Asia	10.3	17.0
Southwest Pacific	.2	.2
Near East	1.5	3.4
Greece, Turkey, Iran	3.2	4.3
Middle East	4.7	7.7

One impressive fact can be extracted from the percentages of officers in various regions and in other assignments. It is that a single officer of Class 5 and above will have served in different regions of the world and perhaps in an assignment in Washington as well. The subtotals for the Africas, Latin America, Britain and the white dominions, "Free" Europe, Eastern Europe and the Soviet Union, Asia, Southwest Pacific, and Middle East in Table

| | Years of Experience | | | |
3	4	5	5+	Total
3.1	1.3	.7	.3	11.2
1.9	1.5	.7	1.3	11.2
1.9	.7	1.0	1.1	10.2
3.9	1.8	1.3	4.3	21.0
3.4	1.6	.9	1.3	13.1
2.8	2.5	1.3	1.6	12.8
12.0	6.6	4.5	8.3	57.1
3.3	2.8	2.1	2.7	20.6
4.6	1.2	1.2	1.8	17.6
8.6	6.1	3.7	4.3	37.0
6.6	2.7	4.0	4.2	28.9
19.8	10.0	8.9	10.3	83.5
3.4	6.	.5	1.2	12.2
.9	.2	.3	.7	3.3
4.3	.8	.8	1.9	15.5
2.1	.2	1.0	1.5	8.2
4.5	1.5	.9	1.9	15.2
6.9	1.5	1.6	1.3	22.7
3.4	2.1	.7	.9	13.2
16.9	5.3	4.2	5.6	59.3
.2	.2			.8
2.1	1.3	.7	1.9	10.9
3.1	1.5	1.0	1.2	14.3
5.2	2.8	1.7	3.1	25.2

12 above add up to 284.4 percent. If other assignments than those overseas are included, the total becomes 441.2 percent. There are four times as many different experiences as men. It is possible that each man has had four different experiences in regions and other assignments. No doubt this should be qualified by "on the average" for an escape.

We conclude that it means, at the least, that many Foreign Serv-

TABLE 13. PERCENTAGES OF FOREIGN SERVICE OFFICERS,

Assignment	Years of Experience	
	1	2
Department	11.0	13.8
Training	37.2	10.6
International Organization	5.4	2.4
Loaned	6.0	4.2

ice Officers have served in different regions of the world and have not spent their careers becoming specialists on one culture, one language, or one set of concerns. Note that we are now talking about the big regions of the world, Asia, Latin America, and the others, and not about regions within one of the big regions. Each of these regions has its own culture and politics. Conceivably a man who serves in Southeast Asia will learn something of use in South Asia, but it is hard to see how a man who serves in South Asia will learn much to help him in Latin America or Eastern Europe. Yet the figures seem to show that many men made these jumps.

Again we see that Americans are trained in work more than in region. For a Foreign Service Officer the important thing is to acquire skill at diplomatic and consular routine, which remains the same in any country and any region. He must be calm and gracious no matter the country or region. His work and his manners are set, not by one nation, but by centuries of professional history.

The routine is the same anywhere. The peculiarities of national cultures and creeds, the individuality of particular statesmen, and all other data that comes only from long experience in a place, all these may be important to an understanding of foreign policy, but they are not essential to the performance of the diplomatic and consular routine. Our Foreign Service Officers, key figures though they are, are not trained to think about policy, as we have said earlier. They are expected to be good Foreign Service Officers in the performance of routine. This they can be in one place as well as another. While doing it, they can be given pleasant assignments

	Years of Experience			
3	4	5	5+	Total
17.1	11.3	8.8	22.0	84.0
.9	.2			48.9
1.3	.5	.2	1.8	11.6
1.2	.5	.2	.2	12.3

to offset unpleasant ones and be given experience in several different parts of the world.

IX

Such counting tells much and yet tells little about the kind of people who serve the United States in the higher posts of career. Certainly these permanent officials come from all parts of the United States. They are the right age to be vigorous and inventive. They have more education than might be expected, at least more college work, which is not always the same as education because the outcome depends upon the use to which a man puts his knowledge. In Yiddish a *phudnik* is a *nudnik* with a Ph.D.

When one walks into an American mission overseas, whether it be an extension of the State Department or one of the other agencies, one finds in the higher posts competent and varied Americans just as one finds them at home. All will be intelligent; most will be courteous, even helpful. If one stays for a month in the office, one begins to see the usual variety of types beneath the surface of such officials who have reached high status among their kind. Some will be more serious than others. A few prothonotarial keepers of the rule will work alongside a few who will flex the rule wherever they can help a fellowman. Some stuffed shirts develop after appointment, perhaps encouraged by wives who were not interviewed at the time of selection. Some men of deceptive affability appear, and some of pretentious, but obvious, habits acquired in pathetic attempts to hide weak points.

Mostly, though, these Americans are first-rate people. They have both knowledge and good sense, along with good manners. They have skill in their work and a high level of ethics in serving their nation. Their attitudes toward others are, on the whole, those to be found among successful people who have that inner sense of security that comes from the prestige of being in the higher levels of a pyramid.

The very nature of the work in most places requires courage. Disease, accident, and civil disorder threaten in so many foreign posts, and diplomatic immunity is not much use in the middle of a riot when passports are not examined. Americans working overseas meet death in line of duty oftener than most of their fellow citizens at home ever realize; and they catch disease with regularity. As good people, they accept danger as part of their work. This is as true of civilians as military men who are expected to be in a dangerous profession.

These people who work in foreign affairs, in the higher positions, know that they are doing important work and feel a dignity that is proper for it. Only the exceptions, one might say the pathological aberrations, take on the burlesque qualities so often attributed to Americans abroad by mischievous, ignorant, or plain slanderous publicists.

Whatever limitations hold down the performance of Americans in foreign affairs come from sources other than the innate quality of the people. One source is the nature of international relations. Another is the nature of bureaucratic behavior, whether public or private.

No one man can with wisdom take too much initiative in any action in international relations. He might start a chain of other actions that no one wants. In this work, men deal not with other men alone but with nations whose governments have interwoven problems of their own in status and security. Not even a self-serving, arrogant ruling family of some Oriental land can be offended save by decision in many and ever higher conferences among American officials. By the very delicacy and intricacy of international relations, American officials are framed at every moment by what they may and may not do in responsible behavior.

Our men are not helped either by the confusion of instructions from Washington concerning their main purposes. When they are told to be forceful, using America's power ruthlessly, at the same time they are told to win friends everywhere, they can hardly be expected to be certain what the large goals are.

Bureaucratic behavior by its demands for conference and agreement produces in the higher levels a conformist type. If government officials share certain habits, so do Sears Roebuck store managers. Both groups have proved to their fellows in the same organization that they respect the rules and each other and that they can carry out orders from above responsibly at the same time they can give advice with dignity. They are men who can be reasonable in a difference of judgment, yielding without abjection in order to find a solution. So long as organization men are not stupid, craven conformers, they can be as useful as anyone can be expected to be in bureaucracy. The iconoclast, the belligerent innovator should stay outside all organizations.

On the whole, again, we can conclude that the government gets for all its agencies in foreign affairs the best qualified officials from among those Americans who want this kind of work and apply for it.

CHAPTER 15   POLITICAL CHIEFS

Should perfection ever break out in federal organization and personnel, the question of its use would remain. Men, not units, work in organizations, and if there is any place where men are more human than in the federal government, no one has found it.

The men who set the tone of administration and the quality of results in the conduct of foreign affairs are politicians in the noble definition that belongs to that word in a republic. They make public policy and are responsible for it. They are known as political executives, to distinguish them from permanent, or career, officials. Together they form an "Administration," as the Eisenhower Administration or Kennedy Administration.

First is the President who is chosen by free citizens and given more power by them than any other executive of a democracy on earth. Our peculiar institution of the electoral college still cannot cloud the distinction that the President usually wins more than half of all the popular votes cast, and more than half of all eligible voters take part in a presidential election. Our President is no prime minister elected by only one constituency but moved to first place by his party's leaders, nor is he the first man in a one-party state who gets his post by removing opponents. A President chosen by the millions who voted for him is allowed his great power by all citizens, friends and opponents alike.

Moreover the checks and balances of the Constitution work out in practice to make the President the nation's leader in policy.

When the young, who are taught catch phrases of American government, tell us that Congress hamstrings the Executive, let us remember that nearly all important foreign policy of the new era was proposed by the President and approved by Congress. The very names given the decisions tell the story. Economic aid and containment were carried out in the *Truman* Doctrine, the *Marshall* Plan, the *Eisenhower* Doctrine.

When no name was given, the facts remained the same: The President proposed; Congress agreed. Mr. Truman ordered the armed forces to help South Korea, and Congress put up the extra money needed. Mr. Eisenhower proposed that atoms for peace be given to other nations, and Congress made it possible. Mr. Kennedy proposed more money for defense and the exploration of space; Congress gave it. All three men year after year got most of what they asked for in money for foreign aid even though members of Congress had good reason to question many of the fallacies in policy and execution of this program. A more honored, more trusted, more powerful politician than the American President is hard to imagine.

Below the President are appointed politicians, some of whom worked in his campaign, and some of whom never helped a candidate in their lives but who begin to act politically as soon as they take a Cabinet or Sub-Cabinet post. These Secretaries, Under Secretaries, and Assistant Secretaries of State and Defense, the Directors of U.S. Information Agency, U.S. Arms Control and Disarmament Agency, and the Agency for International Development, these and the heads of other agencies on occasion, and their assistants in the first degree, are all politicians with the fate of the nation in their hands. They make decisions of their own; they work up the policies which the President in turn either accepts as his own or proposes to Congress if he needs approval. Politics is the decision of policy within the bounds of what is possible. All the men who think of things that ought to be done, then get them done within the possible limits set by voters, Congress, press, interests, and the competition within the Executive Branch, are politicians in the noblest definition.

II

Political chiefs in America have to be competent. The cliché that men of little talent enter politics is simply wrong (at least at the national level). More skill, agility, and knowledge are required to win a nomination and campaign for President than to become head of any corporation. A Secretary of State or Secretary of Defense has an incomparably larger job than do the heads of the largest corporations. They direct more people, make decisions of greater consequence, and decide the use of greater amounts of money. So do the Directors of United States Information Agency and Agency for International Development, and so do all their deputies. No President, unless by error, will appoint a stupid man to a post in foreign affairs. The work is much too delicate to trust any but the best available men.

This much is easy to say, and true. More difficult is to say how competent men become good political executives. Theirs is a unique occupation. They can never be certain that their policies will work out as expected. Their rewards and punishments are never so simple as profits and losses. They can never know firsthand all the facts upon which they base conclusions but must rely upon parades of subordinates stretching to anonymous dimness in the outer ranks of career men. The brightest, most disciplined person may fail as a politician in foreign affairs unless he masters the skills of government.

First of all, the successful political chief learns to listen. He listens to experts, to other politicians, to his own hunches. After a time he knows that he has heard enough to allow a conclusion. He has heard facts and arguments for both sides. If wise, he has listened critically, alert to ask the right questions, skeptical of too-easy answers. He needs an educated mind with a blend of information and ability to apply facts to answers and to see the whole if it can be seen.

Second, the competent policy chief needs to be conscious of purpose. He can be a good man, full of fellowship, and still be a nought. The awareness of purpose is what counts. A politician wants peace, of course; who doesn't? A competent politician wants peace with a list of difficult subheadings such as national security, economic growth for all people, at the least cost and for the least difficulty of administration. He has a system of purposes, all related to each other. By his system he becomes known in our inadequate language as a liberal or conservative, a realist or idealist, a hard or a soft man. The words are too loose to mean much. They show, however, that a man who has no system of purpose has no identity, and this is justice, for a politician without identity is not to be trusted with an important assignment. Franklin Roosevelt's system was to save freedom; Harry Truman's to contain Communism; Dwight Eisenhower's was to create a sense of tranquility after storm; John Kennedy's to get back into action to strengthen defense. Unless a President and his political executives have purpose, they are no more than pompous clerks.

Third, the political executive needs courage to make decisions and to see that they are carried out. He has to take risks every time he signs his name. The press may attack; other nations may retaliate; members of Congress may jump on him; superiors may be displeased. A weak man evades decision. Sometimes subordinates have to be pushed to execute policies. Weak men dislike the necessity of command. They prefer to overlook disobedience or lethargy as the easiest way to get along without tension. Only strong and brave men make good politicians.

Fourth, a political executive needs to be flexible enough to recognize merit in change. The needs of society change. Techniques change. Attitudes change. Change is certain and normal. Public policy changes too if the politicians are flexible. Damage is done by politicians who refuse to anticipate social growth and who resist change instead of guiding it.

Fifth, the political executive needs to be tough. This is a vague and overworked word, but it covers an element of personality that sophisticated practitioners of either public or private administration recognize as a plus attribute of those executives who have it. A tough executive is willing to take the hard way if the goal is worth a hard trip. A tough executive defines his goals boldly, in the light of his own definition of public purpose, knowing that he will never get full support from all citizens, nor from all subordinates, for any decision. He expects opposition. He will try to lessen it, for politics is the decision of policy within the bounds of what is possible, but he will not compromise his purpose so far that he loses it. He will, instead, fight with confidence and skill to overcome the opposition. The quality of toughness does not mean that a man is ruthless, cold, or deceitful. The tough executive who is respected never has these nasty traits. He just won't run from fights, and, once involved, he fights with more agility than the average.

III

Our national method has produced presidents of high quality most of the time. None has been a complete failure; only a few have left doubts in history about their competence. In the time of people now alive only Warren G. Harding was a mistake. Harding's own weakness was offset by the high quality of some good department heads. While the office of the President had many of the odors of a dirty courthouse, Agriculture was under command of Henry C. Wallace, father of Henry A. Wallace, Commerce was led by Herbert Hoover who was making a reputation that helped him to become President, and State by Charles Evans Hughes, who later closed his career with distinction as Chief Justice. The rotten apples were Interior and Justice. For the rest of the barrel, any hardheaded businessman, as one would have called himself in Harding's time, should have been glad to meet a payroll with the names of Wallace, Hoover, and Hughes on it.

Among appointed politicians, consider the Secretaries of State since the second war began.

Cordell Hull and Edward Stettinius as the wartime Secretaries laid the path for such elements of postwar policy as the occupation of Germany and Japan and the creation of the United Nations. They should be counted as members of the crisis. Both were run-of-the-mill men when measured against the outstanding Secretaries; for example, Thomas Jefferson, James Monroe, John Quincy

Adams, William H. Seward, Elihu Root, Henry L. Stimson, or George C. Marshall.

Hull was so dedicated to his one great purpose of reciprocal tariff reductions that he never took firm grasp of the startling innovations of the war, and he lost the mastery of foreign policy to the President's staff, the War and Navy Departments, and other agencies created to handle foreign relations that an alert and flexible State Department should have handled.

Stettinius was the perfect organization man. He trusted his fellowmen, wanted to use the Department, held, not firm purpose, but good intentions, and lacked the tough fiber to make any difference. The best, and saddest, example of the nice guy in Washington was Stettinius in his effort to reorganize the Department. He believed very much that it should be made efficient. At the time he took office, it could hardly have needed reorganization more. He tried. But he also tried to avoid trouble. After a year of his reorganization, 32 more units existed than before; the chart had grown from 62 units to 94, when consolidation was needed. Four more persons reported directly to the Secretary than before; the number had risen from 21 to 25. Either number was too many.

These men were good in all the attributes of political executives, except flexibility for Hull and toughness for Stettinius.

James F. Byrnes, who served from July 3, 1945, until January 21, 1947, lacked all the attributes save courage to make decisions and toughness of fiber. He listened not, neither did he flex, and his purpose was so obscure that his identity was never certain. Perhaps his trouble came from success in South Carolina politics and his apparent assumption that small matters of reward and revenge were just as important among nations as among the people who were for him or against him down home. Byrnes' only clear success had been in the Senate. He quit the Supreme Court before he had made a record. He was not memorable in the Executive Office of the President, where he served as coordinator of domestic affairs during the War.

This man may have had ability that never showed. He worked so much alone that it is possible he never got credit among associates. The history of his day shows so far only that the conditions that produced the Cold War developed irrevocably during his term as Secretary of State without plan or apparent foresight of consequence. Whether they could have been avoided, we will never know. All that seems certain is that we did not plan this kind of costly foreign relations and Mr. Byrnes lacked the greatness to grasp the significance of his own actions. He was a man of small scope in a time when his work had shattering results.

George C. Marshall, Byrnes' successor, was the great man who approved and secured policies that gave some hope for winning the Cold War. During his time containment and economic aid were begun. Apparently Marshall never had a petty reaction in his life.

Dean Acheson, John Foster Dulles, Christian Herter, can all be classed as ministerial. They managed programs already started and tried to live with the good and the bad left by their predecessors. All were competent.

Acheson and Herter could hardly be expected to start great new programs since they succeeded Secretaries under whom they had served as Under Secretaries.

Dulles was a different matter. He came in with a clear opportunity and a free hand. His President had just been elected by a large majority, and the same President wanted his subordinates to decide most matters for themselves. No one ever doubted Mr. Dulles' purpose and toughness. A good many thoughtful people doubted his ability to listen and his flexibility. His opportunity to shift to more emphasis on economic and political measures in the Cold War was unused. His freedom to make most decisions by himself, without direction from the President, seemed to make little difference in results.

Dean Rusk appeared to be a competent man who worked under a strong President. He did not surrender control to the President's staff or the military, but he did not show distinction as a Secretary of State either. President Kennedy did not leave him in charge of foreign policy but rather included him in the groups that made suggestions.

The conclusion of this brief survey must be that Secretaries of State are poor, average, and great. Presidents appoint the best men they can find who are willing to take the job. The way men perform has to be seen later in the results of their tenure. Politicians at this level are as competent as any in our society but not perfect.

There is no way in our system to guarantee that only great men will become either Presidents or Secretaries. About all we can be sure of is that our men will do their best. Some will lack the ingredients and the recipe for greatness. Some will squat to rise and bake on the squat, as older cowboys said of flat biscuits. Others will be overcome by the great volume of small things that threatens any man in public office. And a few will rise above the level, learn the skills of statesmen, and achieve bright purpose.

IV

One characteristic of political executives in the State and Defense Departments is little noted in discussions of American government. It is their previous experience in government. Without design, indeed with some loud laments that we do not have it, the United States has developed in both parties a group of noncareer career diplomats who resemble those British professional politicians so admired by some Americans.

Our partisan executives, further, are joined in the conduct of foreign affairs by career Foreign Service Officers, and once in awhile by career civil servants, who serve for periods as political executives at the pleasure of the President. In 1960, for example, in the last year of the Eisenhower administration, of 22 political executives in the Department of State, nine were career Foreign Service Officers. In 1962, in the first years of the Kennedy administration, of 25 political executives in the department, seven were career officers.

One expects the career men to show experience. The notable and largely unrecognized fact is that most partisan executives, proud Democrats and Republicans, have had experience in the federal government before they were appointed as partisan chiefs.

Recent Secretaries of State head the list. All of the postwar Secretaries had had considerable experience in government before they became Secretaries of State.

James F. Byrnes was head of economic stabilization and war

mobilization in the Executive Office of the President from 1942 to 1945. In this work he dealt for the President with any and all economic programs at home during the war. He became acquainted with wartime supply programs and with the people who ran them.

George C. Marshall was a career army officer who, as Chief of Staff of the Army, managed the vast military alliances of the Second World War. After the war he was a special ambassador to China in 1946, before becoming Secretary of State in 1947. He had had at least six years' experience at the top in foreign affairs, including conferences with chiefs of state, before he became Secretary of State. In addition he had a life career as a military officer.

Dean Acheson was appointed Assistant Secretary of State early in 1941, became Under Secretary of State in 1945 and served until 1947. Then for two years he was a private citizen. He became Secretary of State in 1949 and served until 1953. All told he had six years experience in high posts of the State Department before he became Secretary of State. During the Republican administration from 1953 to 1960, he worked as a lawyer. In 1961 after his party had elected the President, he became a member of the Advisory Group of the North Atlantic Treaty Organization and occasional special envoy of the President.

John Foster Dulles, Republican, had been in and out of both public and private work in foreign affairs since the age of nineteen when, in 1907, he was a secretary of The Hague Peace Conference. He was a special agent for the State Department in Central America in 1917, assistant to the chairman of the War Trade Board in 1918, counsel to the American mission to negotiate peace in 1918 and 1919. Between wars he worked on international economic matters.

After the second war he was a member of the United States delegation to the San Francisco conference to establish the United Nations. Next he was a member of United States delegations to four meetings of the United Nations General Assembly and adviser to the Secretary of State at four meetings of the Council of Foreign Ministers. As a cap to his training he represented President Truman in the negotiation of the Japanese Peace Treaty and the Australian, New Zealand, Philippine, and Japanese security treaties in 1950 and 1951. President Eisenhower appointed him Secretary of State to assume office in January of 1953. He had spent some seventeen years in government service before he became Secretary.

Christian A. Herter began his career at age 21 on the staff of the American Embassy in Berlin in 1916 and 1917. He continued with the State Department, with the American mission to the Paris Peace Conference, as secretary of the European Relief Council and as an assistant to Secretary of Commerce Herbert Hoover until 1924. Thus he had eight years as a young man in government work. Then came six years of private vocation, as journalist and as lecturer in international relations at Harvard. Next he entered the Massachusetts Legislature as a representative, then Congress, then the post of Governor of Massachusetts for a total of 22 years in state and congressional elective office. He was appointed Under Secretary of State in 1957 and served until 1959 when he became Secretary. Eight years as a young man and two as Under Secretary made ten years of training in foreign affairs, not to mention some acquaintance with the subject in the House of Representatives where he served for ten years.

Dean Rusk entered the State Department in 1946 after six years in the Army. He remained until 1952. During the six years in the Department, he had varied experience, as assistant chief of International Security Affairs, director of United Nations Affairs, and Assistant Secretary for Far Eastern Affairs. Before the war he had been a professor of government and academic dean. When he left government, he became President of the Rockefeller Foundation, from 1952 to 1960. President Kennedy brought him back to Washington in 1961 as Secretary of State.

V

The pattern of experience holds true for Assistant Secretaries of State as well. It is in this rank that a number of career Foreign Service Officers come and go as political executives, but their experience is not necessary to make the point that most top officials of the postwar Department of State have had government experience before they entered their present jobs.

Two examples will illustrate. Both have held the same job, Assistant Secretary for International Organization Affairs.

Francis O. Wilcox, before the war a political scientist specializing in international affairs, worked in 1942 in the Office of the Coordinator of Inter-American Affairs, followed by an interlude in the Office of Civil Defense. Next he was an international organization analyst in the Bureau of the Budget, 1943–1944. For two years, 1945–1947, he was head analyst in international relations for the Library of Congress. Then he became chief of staff for the Senate Committee on Foreign Relations for eight years until he became Assistant Secretary of State in 1955. He had spent twelve years in government foreign affairs before he entered the Eisenhower administration.

Harlan Cleveland, who took the same post in the Kennedy Administration, went to Washington in 1939 when he was 21, as an intern in the National Institute of Public Affairs. His first work was with the Farm Security Administration as a writer in the information division. Then he got into the middle of wartime international economic relations, with the Board of Economic Warfare and the Foreign Economic Administration, with the Allied Control Commission in Rome, with the United Nations Relief and Rehabilitation Administration in Rome and Shanghai, with the Economic Cooperation Administration and the Mutual Security Agency, where he was working in 1953 when his party lost the election and he turned, for the first time since he was 21, to private work as executive editor of *The Reporter* and later as Dean of the Maxwell School at Syracuse University. When the Democrats won, he became Assistant Secretary of State for International Organization Affairs. He had spent eleven years getting government experience for the job.

VI

A summary for all political executives of the State Department from 1946 through 1960 can be shown in Table 14. To get these

TABLE 14. YEARS OF GOVERNMENT EXPERIENCE PRIOR TO APPOINTMENT AS POLITICAL EXECUTIVES, DEPARTMENT OF STATE, 1946–1962

Years of Experience	Number of Executives by Years									Total	Percent
	1946	1948	1950	1952	1954	1956	1958	1960	1962		
None	0	0	0	0	3	4	0	2	2	11	7.2
1	2	1	0	0	1	1	0	0	1	6	3.9
2	1	3	1	1	0	1	0	0	0	7	4.6
3	1	0	1	0	3	2	4	0	1	12	7.8
4	1	0	0	1	1	1	1	1	1	7	4.6
5	2	0	3	1	1	0	1	0	2	10	6.5
6–10	1	2	2	2	1	3	3	6	4	24	15.7
11–15	1	1	2	5	3	1	3	1	5	22	14.4
16–20	1	3	3	2	1	1	1	2	0	14	9.6
21 and more	0	1	3	5	3	3	6	10	9	40	26.1
Total Political Executives	10	11	15	17	17	17	19	22	25	153	100.4

figures, Robert W. Thiele, who also made the earlier analysis of permanent officials in foreign affairs, went through the biographies of all officials of Assistant Secretary rank and higher in the Department of State's *Biographic Register* for each year shown in the table. When the *Register* did not account for a man's full career, he went to *Who's Who in America* as a supplement. Years of experience in government prior to appointment to a man's current high post are shown. Mr. Thiele counted as experience all employment by the federal government except in posts which were obviously of no more than clerical nature and in military service of limited duration except when the man had clearly been engaged in military government in occupied nations or in some other kind of international work. Career military officers had all their service counted as government experience. Experience with international organizations was counted as experience in government. Professional Foreign Service Officers were included when they were in top positions in the Department; that is, when at the rank of Assistant Secretary or higher.

Foreign Service Officers assigned to top positions in the State Department account for the number having more than 21 years experience. Below 21 years, partisan executives are mixed with career government men. In either case the answer is the same. Most political executives of the Department of State in the postwar years are experienced in the federal government. Of the 153 such officials since 1945 only 11 had no federal experience before appointment. Of course these 11 were qualified even though their training may not have been in federal experience. Presidents simply cannot afford to take the risk of appointing incompetents to these jobs.

The pattern seems to be set for three Presidents. It is also clear for the beginning of two new presidential administrations, those of Dwight D. Eisenhower, which shows in the table in 1954, and John F. Kennedy, which shows in the table in 1962. Experience is distributed among the years without showing any great variation from the pattern.

VII

In the Department of Defense the Secretary, Under Secretary, and the Assistant Secretary for International Security Affairs can be said to have a full-time concern with foreign affairs. Other political executives in Defense have military duties more strictly defined, and occasional concern in foreign affairs.

Secretaries of Defense have not all had government experience prior to appointment as recent Secretaries of State have had, but the majority are experienced. Of eight Secretaries of Defense from 1947 through 1962, six had worked in the federal government, for terms ranging from one year to a life career.

Under Secretaries show similar experience. Of seven since 1950, through 1962, six had government experience ranging from one year to twelve years. All the Assistant Secretaries for International Security Affairs have had experience, ranging from one year to the 36 years of a retired career officer who occupied the post under the title of Assistant to the Secretary in 1950.

VIII

The myth that political appointees are all amateurs is raised most often when ambassadors are mentioned. Too many think the myth is truth. They may have heard some of the horror stories, carefully preserved by career men, including one recurring account of a political ambassador in Central America years ago who walked naked through the Residence followed by a local alien maid bearing a pitcher of cool gin, which was an interesting though not a prudent way to live. The myth never mentions Franklin, Jefferson, the Adamses, and other political ambassadors of their kind all through history who kept their clothes on and stayed sober most of the time.

One point in answer to the myth is that career men have been appointed ambassadors increasingly since 1924. Table 15 shows

TABLE 15.   CAREER CHIEFS OF MISSION AS PERCENTAGES OF TOTAL,
1924–1962

Year	Career Chiefs	Non-career Chiefs	Total	Percent Career Chiefs
1924	18	33	51	35
1928	30	28	58	52
1932	31	28	59	53
1936	29	32	61	48
1940	31	27	58	53
1944	33	20	53	62
1948	41	24	65	63
1952	49	25	74	66
1956	49	28	77	64
1960	63	26	89	71
1962	67	27	94	71

Sources: *The Foreign Service of the United States,* 1961, and *The Foreign Service List,* 1962, publications of the Department of State (Washington: Government Printing Office).

the percentages of career men who headed missions at four year intervals after 1924.

All Presidents and Secretaries of State since Harding's administration have either promoted the career Foreign Service or failed to damage it, Warren Frederick Ilchman found in his superb administrative history, *Professional Diplomacy in the United States, 1779–1939.* The Rogers Act of 1924 founded the modern Foreign Service in a merger of the consular and diplomatic staffs. It directed the Secretary of State to recommend career men to the President for promotion to the grade of Minister. As a result, career men were named more and more to be chiefs of missions abroad and higher officials in the Department of State in Washington.

Charles Evans Hughes was Secretary of State in the beginning under the Rogers Act. His President, Calvin Coolidge, was no more enthusiastic about the Foreign Service than he was about other aspects of government, all of which he suspected, but he relied upon Secretary Hughes to run the Department, and Hughes was friendly to career men. So was Secretary Frank B. Kellogg who followed him. So were later Secretaries and their Presidents.

Even Franklin Roosevelt, who did not admire career men as a type, ended his time having increased the number of career men as chiefs of mission. In his first term, he had leaned just slightly more on political than upon career ambassadors, but in later years he appointed more career men than his predecessors had. Dwight D. Eisenhower, as the first Republican President in 20 years, might have been expected to appoint more political ambassadors, as Franklin Roosevelt had done in his first administration, when he was the first Democratic President in 12 years. Mr. Eisenhower did so, but barely enough to show. The percentage of career men dropped from 66 in 1952, the last year of Harry S Truman's administration, to 64 in 1956, the third year of Eisenhower's. But it had risen to 71 by the end of the Eisenhower administration in 1960.

One can argue long and deep over whether career men always make the best ambassadors. One cannot argue that they have not been used increasingly since 1924, with only nominal setbacks, by all Presidents and Secretaries of State of both parties.

IX

A second answer to the myth is, again as in the case of political executives in Washington, that not all non-career ambassadors are amateurs. In fact, only one in five non-career ambassadors in the postwar years has had no previous government experience in foreign affairs before receiving the appointments held at the time Mr. Thiele analyzed their biographies. Table 16 shows the number of years of experience for all non-career ambassadors from 1946 through 1962. Mr. Thiele found this data too in either the *Biographic Register* or *Who's Who in America*. Only experience in the federal government in foreign affairs or in international organizations was counted. In the case of military career men who became ambassadors, their entire military career was counted as

TABLE 16. Years of Government Experience in Foreign Affairs Before Appointment as Non-Career Ambassadors, 1946–1962

Years of Experience	Number of Non-Career Ambassadors									Total	Percent
	1946	1948	1950	1952	1954	1956	1958	1960	1962		
None	3	3	4	3	10	4	5	5	7	44	21.4
1	3	3	1	4	1	2	3	1	0	18	8.7
2	0	1	2	3	3	3	3	1	2	18	8.7
3	1	3	2	2	3	3	2	3	3	22	10.7
4	2	1	0	2	3	3	1	1	1	14	6.8
5	2	0	1	0	0	1	1	1	0	6	2.9
6–10	1	2	5	5	3	6	6	8	2	38	18.4
11–15	3	3	3	4	1	0	1	2	3	20	9.7
16–20	0	1	1	1	1	1	1	0	3	9	4.4
21 and more	6	3	1	1	1	2	1	1	1	17	8.3
Total	21	20	20	25	26	25	24	23	22	206	100.0

experience. Others who had served for only temporary terms in the armed forces did not have their military experience counted.

Almost as many had six through ten years as had no experience. A sub-total of 40 percent had six years or more. This most experienced group includes career military men.

Admiral Alan G. Kirk, for one, as a Navy officer was in and out of diplomacy all through his career, first on a gunboat at Canton during the Sun Yat Sen revolution, next on the presidential staff as executive officer of the official yacht for both Wilson and Harding, next as Naval Attaché in the embassy in London in 1939–1941, then as Chief of Staff for American Naval Forces in Europe in 1942 and 1943, not to mention commanding naval task forces in the invasions of Sicily and Normandy. He retired from the Navy in 1946 and in the same year became Ambassador to Belgium and Minister to Luxembourg. Next he was the American representative on the United Nations Committee on the Balkans. All this diplomatic experience, as a Navy man and as a civilian, preceded his appointment as Ambassador to the Soviet Union, where he served from 1949 to 1952. Then in May, 1962, he returned to diplomacy as Ambassador to Taiwan.

Another military man in the count is Walter Bedell Smith, who had served as secretary of the Combined Chiefs of Staff (British and American) in 1941–1942, then as Chief of Staff for Allied Forces in North Africa and Europe, 1942–1945, and for American Forces in the early stages of the occupation of Germany. He became Ambassador to the Soviet Union in 1946 and served until 1949. General Smith shows also among the political executives in the State Department. After serving as ambassador, he became Director of Central Intelligence Agency then Under Secretary of State.

Among non-career civilians, W. Averell Harriman spent most of his time after 1941 in top posts as ambassador and as a political executive at home. (He took time out from diplomacy for one term as Governor of New York.) Mr. Harriman became the President's Special Representative in London in charge of economic aid to Great Britain for the first two years of lend-lease, beginning in March, 1941. As chief of all economic programs, he dealt with shipping and joint planning for British and American production, as well as with all the wide variety of lend lease supply. He also headed a mission to the Soviet Union in August, 1941, to plan supply. In 1943 he became Ambassador to the Soviet Union, then Ambassador to Great Britain in 1946. Next for two years he was Secretary of Commerce, at a time when international economic affairs were foremost in the work of Commerce. He served next with the rank of Ambassador as chief in Europe of the Marshall Plan 1948–1950, next as a Special Assistant to the President, 1950–1951, next as American Representative on the North Atlantic Treaty Organization committee to study defense plans, 1951, and as Director of the Mutual Security Agency which handled foreign aid, from 1951 to 1953. Later when his party won again, he returned in 1961 as a Special Assistant to the President, then as Assistant Secretary of State, this time handling for the President the hot spots in Southeast Asia. Mr. Harriman is hardly an amateur. Yet he is certainly a political appointee, a partisan who serves his party as well as his country.

Other civilians not so experienced, and less prominent as partisans, also illustrate the point. J. Kenneth Galbraith, an eminent economist and writer who was appointed Ambassador to India in 1961, had spent a year with the Defense Advisory Commission just before Pearl Harbor, had been director of the Strategic Bombing Survey in 1945, and had been director of the Office of Economic Security Policy in the Department of State in 1946. Edwin Oldfather Reischauer, appointed Ambassador to Japan in 1961, a professor of Far Eastern languages and author of books about the Far East, served during the War as a research analyst in the Departments of State and War, as a Lieutenant Colonel in Military Intelligence, and as Special Assistant to the director of the Office of Far Eastern Affairs in the Department of State.

X

This assault on the myth that non-career men are amateurs, based as it is on the evidence that most political executives and ambassadors have had government experience, should not be interpreted to mean that those without government experience are incompetent. Some extremely successful ambassadors got their first government experience in foreign affairs in their first posts, although they may have had international experience in journalism, business, or civic affairs. In this postwar period, we need mention only such examples as Clare Boothe Luce, Arthur Dean (before his appointment as negotiator at Pammunjon), or Eugenie Anderson to suggest that good ambassadors come out of Congress, journalism, law firms, civic groups, and political parties.

No President in these times, to repeat, will appoint an incompetent person to a high post in foreign affairs if he can find a good person to take it. Party workers are also able diplomats if they get these jobs, or at least the President thinks they are able and makes a mistake if they are not. Party contributors cannot buy ambassadorships. They have to appear to be competent and prove to be so if they stay in the work. Foreign affairs are too important to the reputation of any President to play loose with the choice of either political executives or ambassadors.

XI

The political chiefs provide leadership in the conduct of foreign affairs. Their job is to decide high policy. If they were ignorant, inexperienced, mean, or stupid, the nation would be in a bad way. But they are not. They are chosen for their qualities in this kind of work, qualities which they have demonstrated already, in striking refutation of the myths about patronage that linger in our discourse.

They are, it is safe to say, the most competent people in our society to do this kind of work. This statement requires some explaining.

Clearly, it does not mean that all the political chiefs are geniuses but only that they are the ablest people who are interested in this kind of work. But this statement in itself has profound significance, for in a free society only those who are interested in public work should be considered eligible for that work.

Once a democracy begins to select its political leaders for their skill alone, disregarding their attitudes, it will soon find that it has some skilled men who do not appreciate the peculiar traits of a free society, all of it and not just some chosen segments. The wrong men will not be servants but either crooks or tyrants, either men who exploit their positions for personal gain or men who hope to use power for control. Politics in a democracy is a strange and wonderful calling. Its practitioners want many different things, including personal importance and the excitement of big events, but politics is the last place a smart man would go to make money or to boss other people around.

The man who wants the political post, certainly at this level of cabinet, sub-cabinet, and ambassadors' posts, is pre-selected as someone who can be trusted to be a political executive in a democracy. He is eligible to be a leader. Only his kind should be eligible.

Therefore if our system of choosing political leaders gets the most competent from among the only ones who are eligible to be chosen, it is the best system we can find. In this case of leaders for the conduct of foreign affairs, the system has worked better than we think. The quality of political chiefs is high.

PART FOUR CHANGES NEEDED

CHAPTER 16   THE NEED

FOR THINKERS

Recent change has brought more action than thought to the conduct of foreign affairs. The move from traditional diplomacy into operations abroad diminished the old central work of scheming. Without scheming, without the incessant analysis of what other nations were up to and how our nation should move, the conduct of foreign affairs became almost entirely routine.

Only very rarely did a flash of diplomatic analysis light routine operations. One such was a single paper in which George Kennan predicted in 1944–1945 what the Russians would want after the war. The Russians behaved as he said they would, and our policy of containment was adopted. But Mr. Kennan's kind of analytical reporting was so rare that no similar analysis was made of the containment policy after it was begun, to see if it needed revision.

From the outside, at least, the policy appeared to be neglected by thinkers, and the doers were in full gallop. Possibly other papers were written behind the secrecy of security and never had the same influence as Mr. Kennan's work. And possibly other insight just as keen as his got stranded in the doldrums of committees that found the easiest way in no change. To outsiders the containment of communism by military deployment appeared to be working in the main, but no one seemed to work on containment by political means. Those who worked on economic means seemed mostly to act from the latitude of our wealth more than from careful schemes of how to use wealth to get the most for our cause. There was no one whose job was to plan a shift from military to political and economic emphasis in containment.

The practice of diplomacy itself had become almost entirely response, not foresight. Men who worked in the political affairs divisions may have thought they were diplomats in the mold of de Callieres. They were, in fact, no more than reporters of events, assemblers of views, drafters of replies, attenders of meetings.

Foreign policy was made in answering the mail.

So far as anyone could tell from results, the truly big questions were not considered. What policies, for instance, can we make now to adjust to the oncoming development of underdeveloped countries? Do we wait until the time, perhaps within one generation, when Red China and India become industrial competitors, then react in surprise?

What should we expect from future accelerated technical change and what policy can be decided now? Unless foreign policy is made in the light of technical change, always accelerating, all nations are sinking in quicksand. They only struggle when they should build bridges. The rate of change is already alarming. A child born in 1948, the year the Department of Defense first reported research underway on a possible earth satellite, was only 13 in 1961 when Russia sent the first men into orbit and unmanned satellites were commonplace. There was still no international law for space.

By the time the new citizen reached 21 he would see more wonders of the universe and less international order unless planning had begun. Technical change is inevitable and can be foreseen by those who look ahead from what is already known, from space science to entomology, the stars and the insects both being matters of American foreign relations today.

How should we prepare for the time when population in the Far East breaks out of present national boundaries? Do we try to accommodate the overflow in this hemisphere, or do we make the wall higher? Do we talk with other nations in this hemisphere about policies of immigration, or do we wait for the crisis? Has the time come, in view of the threat to Soviet Asia of the multiplying, hungry Chinese, to talk with Russia about an alliance against China?

The most serious question of all is this: What is the future of Russia? Will that troublesome adolescent grow into a civilized member of the adult community when it has enough industrial and agricultural production not to feel subconsciously inferior to the Western nations? What happens to the drive of evangelical communism when the comforts of mature industry spread to all members of the ruling elite in Russia and, later, to the masses? Do the Soviet communists then relax about their status in the world and seek peace so that they may pursue pleasure? (One can speculate idly, alone in a cloister, about the outcome if the United States had spent all its billions of foreign aid on soft automobiles and suburban houses for every member of the Russian Communist Party, when nothing else seems to discourage communism so much as a drive home to the suburb and hard labor on a bourgeois lawn.)

Such questions have to be answered if the nation in the future is to devise basic policies from which the smaller, daily policies derive; such basic policies as, for example, the Monroe Doctrine or containment, both of which shape subordinate decisions.

One defense of the present system is to say, again, that "policy is found in the cables," or "you can't make policy except as incidents arise." And here, in the attitude that produces these statements, is the defect. Men who take answering the mail as the only purpose of their work are not men who can think of the larger issues from which the mail comes. Men who cope with daily events and fail to see that events reflect the great unfolding patterns of change in the world are unable to think ahead. They fight swarms of gnats, and no one looks for higher ground where a breeze might solve their problem.

II

The solution is to stress general foreign policy more than incidental decisions in the mail, foreign policy more than foreign relations. Foreign policy can be practiced successfully by men who think broadly of causes and consequences of every move, by themselves and by others, and who see the past and the future as part of each decision. Not all men, by any means, who hold posts in the diplomatic service or in Washington are qualified. Some are and always have been. Franklin, Jefferson, John Quincy Adams, Elihu Root, Henry L. Stimson, are ready names from the past of men unmatched in this work. Those competent to see patterns were the more useful because they were—and still are—always rare.

Because of the new boom in foreign operations, the career Foreign Service, as it operates, has small chance to develop any true diplomats. It always discouraged broad or original thinking, as all career services do, and a paper such as George Kennan's took courage and great self-confidence to write. In the early 1950s, the environment practically forbade candid, much less bold, thinking by career men. By then two developments had made the work different for an untold future.

For one, espionage became more prevalent. The trustworthiness of government men was checked before employment and was subject to repeated checks as a constant possibility and as a certainty whenever the least suspicion was raised. Security officers became as customary on our side as the threat of spies from the other side.

For the other, accusers and haters gained such standing that they could endanger any man's career simply by calling his name. These wreckers were recurrent in our society, from the time of witch hunters, through Know Nothings, foes of Bolsheviks in the early 1920s, the Ku Klux Klan of the 1920s, to the White Citizens Councils and the John Birch cells of the 1960s. They had been represented in Congress since the 1930s by the House Committee on Un-American Activities, but in modern times they had been more a latent threat than a major force in national affairs until the tensions of the 1940s and 1950s.

In a fearful time of cold war the accusers became a major force. A press that was not clear about its purpose gave space freely to their most preposterous accusations. A sufficient number of public officials encouraged, and very few discouraged, the practice. The immunity of words in Congress from action in court was used with no restraint from Congress, and the accusers could say whatever they chose without fear of suit for libel.

At the deepest moment of moral sickness, the Attorney General,

Herbert Brownell, and his chief of police, J. Edgar Hoover, Director of the Federal Bureau of Investigation, appeared before a Senate committee and national television to name former employees of the government as spies. Their larger purpose was to claim that the former President, Harry S Truman, was "soft on Communists," as the peculiar language of the cult described anyone who did not share their view. They had been unable to get the accused men indicted because, the Attorney General said, his evidence was obtained by wire-tapping and the federal courts would not admit it. But he called names in public, and the victims could not cross-examine or introduce their own evidence, nor even testify in their own cause. They could not sue for slander because the government officials were wrapped in Congressional immunity.

Career government workers were in such danger during this terror that they were afraid to say or do anything that mattered. For them the police state existed. Security officers might be listening on tapped telephones; associates might gain merit by reporting unwise remarks. Some of the fear passed away in time, but never all of it. The accusers always threatened to surge up again. Then always the very real existence of spies for the other side made security necessary, and men who knew secrets had to be watched for this good reason.

Today circumstances demand that at least some career men be free to think candidly and fearlessly about basic policy, with originality and all the wisdom that our culture can muster. For the career men are now in charge.

III

Foreign Service Officers occupy nearly all the State Department's posts where decisions are influenced below the very top echelons where political chiefs rule. In 1954, as reported earlier, on recommendation of the Wriston committee, the overseas and departmental services were merged. A Foreign Service Officer now would serve both in Washington and in missions abroad. (Military career men for years had been used this way and had occupied policy

posts below their civilian political chiefs in the military departments.)

The logic of Wristonization was clear. Men who had worked
abroad would be more competent to work in the State Department
than men who had not, and men who had worked in headquarters
would serve better in the missions. Periodic returns to America
would keep Foreign Service Officers in touch with their own
people. When the world grew smaller by the day, and the United
States was only a telephone call from anywhere, our staffs for
headquarters and the field should be interchangeable as members of
the Foreign Service of the United States. In this logic lay trouble
due to faulty grasp of the facts that supported the premises. One
error was the failure, already mentioned, to see that work abroad
was different from work in Washington. Another was the failure
to understand the nature of the Foreign Service.

The career Foreign Service was not in 1954 or later nearly so
much of the United States as it was of the State Department and
more, of itself. It did not consider the operations of economic aid,
secret intelligence, and propaganda to be part of its responsibility.
When these operations affected general foreign relations, the
Foreign Service wanted to control; otherwise it was satisfied to
define its role in the ancient trilogy of reports, negotiation, and
representation. The agencies that handled grants, loans, technical
assistance; military aid; espionage and subversion; information and
propaganda had their own separate staffs in Washington and
abroad.

More seriously, the Foreign Service represented itself. With the
exception of a few who took the broad view, Foreign Service Officers when change threatened thought first of how change might
damage the security of the service. They found high principles to
justify their concern. Their group, they said in public, maintained
the professional skill and, equally necessary, the professional attitude toward work abroad. Its members were the only men in government service who were specialists in foreign relations and willing to work wherever needed no matter how unpleasant. They
talked among themselves of threats to their chance of promotion
if new numbers were admitted. Other professions do the same.

Physicians rationalize that what is good for their incomes is the best of all medical care for patients; plumbers argue that the beneficent provisions of the building code are essential for public health; professors find that no matter how high the price, the rule of tenure is the way to protect academic freedom.

Men with a stake in the status quo are hardly the ones to promote change. Instead they resist change, then, finding that change continues in spite of their efforts, they move to protect their own interest. When change was needed after the war, the career Foreign Service Officers built a stronghold for their own group in the Foreign Service Act of 1946. Harold Stein showed this unmistakably in his superior case study of the genesis of the act in *Public Administration and Policy Development, A Case Book.* Their shelter was soon penetrated and surrounded by change, however, for change usually penetrates and surrounds cysts built against it. As often happens, the invaded group assimilated the invader. The number of Foreign Service Officers grew by three times in ten years, and manners changed some as a result, but the career Foreign Service remains a self-contained island. Its members are experts at what they do. They do not do much of the new foreign relations of military aid and advice, economic aid, propaganda, and secret operations.

IV

Part of their shield against the new men was their control over foreign policy, justified quite properly by the clear need for someone to be in charge. The executive orders said that any agency in foreign affairs should make its operations conform to the foreign policy of the United States as interpreted by the Secretary of State in Washington and the Ambassador in another country. Career Foreign Service Officers held the influential positions in the Department of State and in all the embassies and so they kept control over policy.

The kind of policy they meant was not the large, foresighted policy that will guide American operations for the long haul. By foreign policy the Foreign Service Officers meant routine decisions. Foreign policy was whether we paid one price or another for uranium, or bought from one seller or all sellers, or held firm in our demands under a contract when important foreigners would be annoyed.

Nearly anything that a man in the career service wanted to question became foreign policy simply because he questioned it. Men in other services who had to submit to the questions, and the delays, resented the overemphasis on trivia which comes invariably when authority lacks large purposes and large ideas to go with it. Foreign Service Officers are, regardless of questions, interpreters of policy, as they define it. They provide the permanent staff to advise political chiefs.

Their definition of foreign policy is so distant from the answers to large questions that the present group should not be expected to plan ahead. The present men who control, below the top chiefs, are hired because they are good at foreign relations, not because they are interested in the large questions of foreign policy. They are chosen by examinations, as we saw earlier, that find aptitude for routine work that can be handled only by the most intelligent, most responsible, and most dedicated of men, but both the written and oral examinations fail to test a candidate's interest or ability in foreign policy. In truth, strange as it seems, the United States in its years of anxiety has no experts specially chosen, trained, and experienced in foreign policy.

V

To handle the new version of diplomacy we need about 400 specialists in policy in the career service; stationed, roughly, 320 in missions abroad, 20 at the center of decision in Washington, probably in the Executive Office of the President under the reorganization suggested earlier, and 60 in training at intervals throughout their careers.

These specialists would form a new and distinct unit, called here, for the purpose of referring to it, the Policy Corps. Members of the Policy Corps would be free of routine work but would have access to any papers they want to read. They would not be obliged to attend office meetings but could do so when they might learn something they wanted to know. Sometimes men can learn easier and quicker from listening than from reading.

As a rule, though, members of the Policy Corps will waste their time when they spend it reading cables or attending meetings just to keep informed of the routine flow. The Policy Planning Staff of the State Department, as described earlier by Robert Ellsworth Elder, is the sad example. Its members spend too much time at keeping informed ever to lift themselves above the routine and see a pattern. To be plain, any policy thinker caught reading all the mail should be fired. He has the office man's worst malady, routine for the sake of routine with boondoggle complications.

Policy men worth their salt would have three main tasks. They would write analytical papers on the large issues. They would read critically the proposed basic policies to come from the analyses of large issues. They would advise political chiefs on policy for the long run.

They would work in the missions abroad and the central office in Washington, never in large numbers, for the more people involved in this kind of work, the more talk and the less result, but only in number enough to whet and test each other. When the 320 are divided into 80 missions the result is an average of 4 to a mission. They would not be divided this way in practice; Moscow might have ten and Ottawa two, while the consulate in Hong Kong might also have ten because, while it is not a capital, it is an outsider's center for Communist China. Some missions would have one, and some perhaps none. The 20 in Washington may be too many. Only trial will show in Washington and abroad how many are needed, and all will need to fight the easiest way, which is to add numbers rather than to drop old work when it is no longer needed.

VI

A member of this staff would come to work in the morning at the embassy in, let us assume, Cairo. He works there with four other professional members of the Policy Corps. They are assisted by stenographers and interpreters as needed. Officers and staff occupy a block of rooms that includes a conference room where all the officers can gather quickly. The conference room might double as a small library of reference books and maps. All rooms will be studies more than offices, dominated more by bookshelves than by telephones. The job of this officer is to analyze continuously American relations with Egypt, to think ahead and propose changes, to see a long-range American foreign policy for Egypt, as part of the Middle East, as part of the world, then to watch developments to see how they conform to the large policy or to suggest that it be changed to fit the developments. To do such work, the officer needs most a place to read, talk, and write. He need not be in the flow of mail or in the welter of office conferences.

Most of his dealing will be with his associates in the Policy Corps in Washington. Because the ambassador in Cairo under present doctrine has no discretion over policy, the true authority is in Washington, divided in practice now among several agencies but to be located in the Presidency when that institution becomes competent through reorganization. To be influential in any bureaucracy, private or public, the first rule is to locate the real center of power and work there. A new Presidency will have in it the control over all decisions of large policy, and the foreign policy men in Washington and in missions abroad will be part of the central control.

The man in Cairo may be working this day on a significant development, say on a fundamental technical change, as, for example, the changing of sea water to fresh water and the use of atomic fuel to pump it from the coast to inland reservoirs. He is not a chemist nor an engineer. He gets his information from reading and from talks with technicians. As any good journalist does, he checks his information to make sure that he is not led into error.

Anyway, his interest is not technical but political. He needs to know whether it will work, when, at what cost; but his main task is to say what new irrigation will mean ten or twenty years hence to Egypt, Syria, Israel, Saudi Arabia, and all other nations in the region. Fresh water will make a new Middle East. Nations there will have to make new adjustments to each other, and nations elsewhere will need new policies. Our man in Cairo will prepare a policy to recommend to his colleagues in Washington.

His next task may be to propose a long range policy to exorcise the nonrational demagoguery of Arab nationalism, which is a potent and dangerous weapon against the West no matter how silly it is. A whole generation has matured without ever knowing the heel of the British Colonial Office, which was never heavy or cruel in any case. Englishmen who travel abroad are now more diffident than not, wondering how they lost the empire so suddenly. Yet the young Arabs can riot against a Western imperialism that does not exist. One safe assumption is that the Arab nations (or the South Asian nations for that matter) will never be safely held in friendship for the West so long as their battle cry is churned-up hatred for the West of a past century.

If a bright foreign policy man can invent the antidote to this hysterical ideology, he will do more for world peace than a dozen conferences. He will not find a ready answer, for there is none. He will consider various means. Can the American Declaration of Independence be identified with the Middle East, perhaps in a twentieth century document? Without hurting Britain any more than she is already hurt? Do we choose an old reliable monarch and support him in a counterrevolution, then supply him with our military protection to keep him loyal?

Do we demand more political concessions from the new men of power before we grant economic aid? Do we revive old-style imperialism and move in with troops? Do we offer economic aid without strings? Do we agitate a holy war among the Moslem sects and so divert attention from the war of words against imagined Western crimes? Do we encourage the latent feuds among the nations of the Arab world and thus weaken the psychological union of paranoiac nationalists? Do we simply wait for time to cure the malady?

All these questions and others will be tested by the policy man in Cairo. He will read, listen, talk, and write, trying ideas on his colleagues in Cairo and in other Middle East posts, until in the mystifying way of the mind at work, he produces a paper that makes the most sense to all concerned.

This paper goes to Washington where the central policy staff sees it in relation to all the other regional questions. Finally a fundamental policy toward Arab hostility would be adopted. Daily decisions could be made to conform to the fundamental policy. No longer would each new event be a crisis to be met with improvisation.

We have no employees now hired and assigned to such work, and we risk much. If it is important to get men who specialize in policy, it is equally important to get the men most skilled for the work.

VII

The first recruits for the Policy Corps will be found in the present foreign service and State Department. Let present officers who are interested apply for the new corps. Then let people who have no commitment to the present service and its habits examine the applicants. Enough can be gathered about the personal traits of these applicants by analysis of their behavior on the job. Their skill in policy thinking can be ascertained from papers they will be asked to write on large questions.

Teachers have discovered that the way to get students to think in alternatives and consequences is to give them problems for which there are no black and white answers. This forces them to analyze goals, facts, choices, and consequences. If a recommendation of policy is required, each student has to use judgment based upon the analysis. Such is the decision of foreign policy: choice of goals, analysis of facts, choice of alternatives, choice of means, analysis of consequences, and judgment to reach a conclusion. There is nothing new about this technique.

For several years after the Second World War, the Brookings Institution used it for its annual conferences on problems of foreign policy. For several years the Midwest Universities Seminar for citizens has done the same. The State Department uses it for the smaller questions with which it deals as routine. It can be used for the large questions, and foreign service officers can be selected for the new corps by their showing of vision and skill in handling the method.

A brand new recruit just out of college can be chosen by an examination very different from the one now given.

He will spend two or three days, not just one day, in the written examination. Questions will test his ability to understand, to analyze, and to think creatively. They will expose his knowledge of the factors to be included in the solution of a problem, not in detail, because detail always has to be searched out for each new question, but in the general contours of political, economic, military, and cultural considerations and their place in large policy.

The interview too will be different from the one now held. Instead of an hour or two before a board, the candidate will spend about a week in a "house party."

We should keep the mind sweepers, as A. P. Herbert once called house party psychologists, out of the whole affair. Their tests discover no more than goes into the tests. Since no expert in test construction can also be an expert in the work that the candidate will do, the tests include a lot that is irrelevant to the real purpose of hiring a good hand. Worst of all, the tests reveal standardized traits, when the best candidate may not be a standardized person. To use analogy, if William Faulkner wrote as he did to win the Nobel Prize, he could not pass the standardized test in English composition for admission to any first rate American college—not, for example, by using those flooded paragraphs about the spawning of his doomed county, each ending quite improperly with a semicolon, in the intervals of *Requiem for a Nun.*

The only way to discern the creative thinker is to watch him at work.

The main purpose of the house party will be to see what kind of person each candidate is and how well he can handle a problem. Candidates will form into groups of five or six. They will be given a problem. One of the unanswered questions listed above will serve. Each candidate will write a paper on some phase of the problem, economic, military, political, or cultural. Working with these papers, in question and answer, in check and balance, each group will present recommendations of policy. A dissenter, who might have a good idea, should be allowed to submit separate recommendations and so avoid the damage of smothering consensus.

Elders with experience in diplomacy, drawn from government and from outside, will listen to these group reports and will read all the papers. Any older man who has been through the mill should be willing for the sake of his country to spend a week in this testing of beginners. He can do nothing more important in his life.

All through the week the candidates will have eaten meals and talked with the senior hosts, in as natural a meeting as can be arranged, without strain and speed that obscure. If an older man of good sense and full experience cannot size up a younger man accurately under such conditions, he has not learned much from life. His judgment of character and competence will, nine times out of ten, be worth more than the findings of tests devised by technicians.

Ratings will be necessary as usual. Here another heresy can enter. Instead of measuring each candidate against one set of criteria, ranging from "no good" at the bottom to "outstanding" at the top, let each candidate be analyzed in terms of his own performance. Grade each of them as a professor grades an essay paper and not as a machine grades the graphite marks placed by a student on alternative answers in an "objective" examination.

Each candidate will write his evaluation on the other candidates with whom he has worked in his group; each elder will write his report on each candidate. The chosen ones will be found from analysis of these reports, each man measured in terms of himself. It should not be necessary to say that elemental good manners require that all evaluations be anonymous to avoid the obscene behavior at such house parties when conducted by personality evaluators instead of gentlemen.

VIII

The future policy specialist is now ready to go to work. He will need about two weeks to learn enough about how the government is organized and what its various units do. This fellow is, after all, a grown man who knows how to acquire information rapidly. He does not need the eight dull weeks of instruction in organization and practice that he now gets in the Foreign Service Institute.

Get him to work as soon as possible. He will learn most on the the job. Put him to work in the State Department for a year. Send him to a mission abroad for three years. Assign him to various kinds of work. He should learn political and economic reporting so that he can evaluate it later when he has to make policy. He should do some conventional diplomatic and consular work to learn how this honorable profession forms the backbone of foreign relations and requires the utmost reliability. He should do some work in aid and information and in the military offices too. He will get the feel of working abroad. His supervisors will be able to watch him at work so that if a mistake was made in his admission it can be corrected. The personnel office must remember, though, that he is destined to be a policy-maker and not just another member of the foreign service. It must move him around during these first four years so that he gets broad training from experience.

At least one year in ten of a policy man's career should be spent away from his job. It can be at a university, in a business firm, in a research outfit, in a military college, in any place where the man will get away from his own work and be required to study with people who specialize in other work than foreign policy. It is a platitude, but no less true, that men need a change periodically to gain perspective on their own work. The present Foreign Service releases men to study as much as it can with the money it gets. For the Policy Corps, as suggested above, the total number from the outset should be large enough to allow a good portion to be assigned to training.

IX

Any new group in bureaucracy, no matter how fine its initial press or how high its promise, can be killed a few months after birth by subtle, quiet murder. Old hands can starve it by denying office space, vehicles, secretaries, and funds. Other groups steal its work and deprive it of blood until it drains to death. A few members of Congress strategically placed may take a dislike to the whole idea and reduce the money. The federal government is no peaceful meadow where sheep may safely graze.

Executives from the President down who want a special group to work on long-range policy will have to be tough shepherds, vigilant against many foes. Only executives from the top down can guard a controversial new activity. They have to want the new to thrive; they have to use it and let all others know that they use it. They cannot simply sign an order to create the Policy Corps, issue a laudatory press release, then expect the new creature to grow strong without further help.

Executives can insist that the new policy men have the same promise of career as any others who work at foreign affairs. One of the truly iniquitous ideas of the State Department's career Foreign Service Officers in the present disunity is that only they should be eligible to rise to the top posts of Ambassador or Assistant Secretary of State. A career man in information or economic and military aid can never hope to reach the top posts in a mission or in the State Department in Washington. Because Foreign Service Officers are most concerned with the limited kind of foreign relations which they are trained to handle, they produce Ambassadors and Assistant Secretaries who perpetuate an emphasis on routine. The new policy men will threaten this comfortable habit. If they do their job well, they will become known to executives who will begin to seek their advice.

Members of the old guard will resent the change. They will use their initial control, as superiors in Washington and abroad, to keep the upstarts in their place. One sure way to do this is to hold promotions to top posts open only to members of the old guard, as we now do. Only the chiefs who were appointed from outside the Foreign Service, the political executives, can break this system. They can insist that all good men, including policy men, information men, economic men, military men, and Foreign Service Officers, be eligible for promotion to the top.

In addition, political executives can abolish all differences in pay, benefits, and privileges that remain among employees of the various agencies that work in foreign affairs. These are not always in favor of the old-line career men. We need to practice as soon as possible the theory that all work in foreign affairs is equally important, whether it be the oldest protocol or the newest purchase with counterpart funds. All who work should stand equal before the regulations, no matter the kind of skill they use at work.

This break from the favored place held by the Foreign Service, as we have known it for years, will be easy if we establish the one civil department for foreign affairs with one service abroad, both recommended earlier.

Executives will have to fight hardest, probably, to keep the new policy men away from the immediate and the routine. The threat will come from the men themselves and from their superiors. Thinking is the hardest of all work, and the loneliest. To read, collate, analyze, and write with long perspective is torture compared with the easy task of drafting cables and discussing them in congenial groups.

Policy men will be tempted to smother themselves in reading all the mail. They will have to be forbidden such ease. Executives themselves will be tempted to pull a good man away from policy in order to fight a fire that roars through the routine papers. "Flaps," these were called in the slang of government during the 1950s, to mean that hell had broke loose and everyone had to work up a fever until the crisis passed. Flaps are routine in the conduct of foreign affairs. Still executives, being human, forget this. To them a flap, as other routine work, is immediate and just as important as any more distant fundamental policy. They will call all hands to put down the flap or keep up with the flow of routine. They will do this unless they agree not to do it, then fight temptation as much as they insist that the policy men fight their natural desire for the easy way.

Executives have one task in any new enterprise which is just as essential as their obligation to protect the new. It is to check on results and to kill the new agency if it fails. No one can ever say in administration exactly how a new unit will work. Much depends upon the competence and attitudes of the people who start the work. If the Policy Corps fails to produce answers to the awesome questions with which it deals, it should be dropped in honesty to taxpayers and integrity to public service.

In a way, the kindest, most protective duty that executives can perform for the new policy men is this one of holding them responsible to produce results. If any subject is undefined, it is foreign policy. Some good men now think they make all the policy that is needed when they answer the daily mail. Others think that the fundamental questions can be isolated and answered by mortal men who are hired and trained to do this and nothing else. No creature is less worthy than one who pretends to be doing something when he isn't. Society already has enough of these living dead without preserving another group that failed.

If the Policy Corps follows some other new groups of specialists, it need not fear that it will fail. The chances are that executives will use it more and more as its advice proves to be better than the kind of advice that was available before. Once upon a time economic analysts, statisticians, and management specialists were new to public administration. Their services are now established. The new men too will be used if they do the job that needs to be done.

CHAPTER 17   CULTURE AND
THE STRONG EXECUTIVE

THE MACHINERY OF GOVERNMENT IS ALWAYS used by men. No easy cure for national lags can be found in the reform of machinery alone.

But to return to an earlier theme and repeat it here, men can accomplish more when the machinery helps rather than hinders them. Certainly when more time has to be spent tinkering, keeping informed, or pushing administrative papers than in thinking about the foreign policy of the United States, the machinery is less help than hindrance. When the best career men are spent on routine and not on foreign policy the machinery is not working. Politicians great and small could be served so much better than now if they would only take the time to rebuild their caves into houses.

II

New machinery is easy to design and has been proposed in earlier chapters. All who make the study of administration their profession can do this as easily as an architect makes freehand sketches of the layout of rooms for a house. In their shoptalk with each other specialists in administration get much more abstract and inconclusive, dwelling upon theories of the structure and behavior of groups as the cells of organization, but when hired to design an agency, they all come out with much the same chart.

The difficulty comes when design has to change into the marvelous intermixture of people who make an organization. No architect ever had to work with such inconstant and retaliatory material. These structural parts are ambitious and fearful; they obstruct and undermine. Sometimes they are big about reorganization and do their best. Usually, though, the builder has to be wary lest his materials cut his throat from behind his back. Men of experience do not expect much altruism from human nature when reorganization looms.

Despite all this, reorganization takes place all the time. It occurs within departments and within the Executive Branch as a whole. Compare a federal chart of today with one of a year ago and the chance is good that difference will appear. Most reorganization is in pieces and never adds to truly big change. Yet deep, drastic change is needed in the machinery for foreign affairs if the nation is to gain in security.

We need, in short, a political theory that blends organization, men, and culture to guide those who are responsible for the conduct of foreign affairs in this new time when the world is more dangerous than it has ever been and change is faster than ever.

III

Men and organization both reflect the culture in which they grew, and here is the most difficult part of a diagnosis. It is easy to look at charts and prescribe changes. Then the uneasy thought intrudes: Our forms of organization and the behavior of our men reflect our way as a society, or what W. W. Rostow in *The United States in the World Arena* calls the national style.

Especially relevant to foresight, or the lack of it, in handling foreign affairs is Mr. Rostow's perception that large bureaucracy as now organized does not create new ideas or suggest new alternatives that have not come through the mill of organized thinking. Mr. Rostow suggests five American traits that are reflected by present American bureaucracy. They are, paraphrased:

1. An empirical attitude that says do not deal with a problem until it becomes so acute that it has to be noticed.
2. A tendency to organize staff work on such specialized lines that the overall view is lost.
3. A tendency to put so many men on staff work that no executive has time left for coherent thought and reflection and the insights of specialists get diluted by a flood of conference and clearance.
4. A tendency to give all units of an organization a voice in any decision that affects them.
5. A result: policy decisions which are formed by compromise and which strengthen the inertia that is already found in large bureaucracy.[1]

The description and analysis earlier in this book of the way men behave in the present machinery for the conduct of foreign affairs bear out all five of Mr. Rostow's hypotheses, if one may use that so often misused word to describe the conclusions of a sensible and observant man. These traits of the American culture are the reason for so much of what has been called in preceding pages the lack of long-range view, or the decision of policy by answering the mail. Men are able, but they are caught in the machinery until they cannot show their best.

Some broader traits too are reflected by the conduct of the new diplomacy, broader than Mr. Rostow's traits that define bureaucratic behavior, as broad indeed as fundamental characteristics of the nation. These broader traits also account for the flaws of administration and give partial answer to why more action is not taken to change things. We Americans are not unique in possession of these traits. The British are twins with us. Other nations have them too. In any case to speak of national characteristics is at best a loose way to describe nations. Science has not proved that national traits exist as distinct elements of personality. But people nonetheless see national traits all the time, or think they do, and talk and act accordingly. In this sense broad traits of a national style are as real as faith and as influential.

[1] W. W. Rostow, *The United States in the World Arena, An Essay in Recent History* (New York: Harper & Row, 1960), pp. 497–500.

(It should be said also that many of the American traits are positive and account for the strong features of administration; such traits, for example, as generosity, honesty, kindness, acceptance of science and the scientific attitude, willingness to reach agreement, courage, forgiveness, friendliness. These agreeable traits are passed over here, and also by Mr. Rostow, because, true as they are as other causes of administrative behavior, they are not relevant to a diagnosis of what is wrong.)

The broad national traits that contribute to our weak side are these: (1) We have too much confidence that pluralism, the incessant competition and resolution of interests, will produce the greatest justice for all, and that decisions reached as the conclusion of debate are the best because they are more democratic than decisions reached by one man on the weight of evidence. (2) We are too bound, too much held to certain practices, by technology. (3) We are too tolerant of public officials and do not hold them strictly to account when they make mistakes.

IV

One must be careful in talking about overindulgence in the faith that justice comes from pluralism and the more pluralism there is the more justice. To question this article is usually construed as an attack on democracy. "This means a dictator," people say. It doesn't, nor does it mean a self-chosen single-party elite or a bureaucratic elite. If a label is wanted, and it probably is in this age of slogans, it means a constitutional democracy that works as ours is meant to work.

The American Constitution deserves confidence. It allows pluralism to operate and provide all its benefits of freedom, yet it also provides in the separation of powers the means to keep the system from floundering impasse. If Congress fails to show initiative, the President may. If the President falters, Congress can carry the load. The Court will sometimes take the lead, as in the desegregation cases, when President and Congress have both been reticent; and at other times the President and Congress will be ahead of the Court, as in the New Deal days.

In the conduct of diplomacy the President, and his civil and military subordinates, have by the Constitution a special responsibility to take initiative. The President is Commander in Chief. He is head of the Executive Branch. He makes treaties subject to the consent of the Senate and executive agreements with other nations without referring to the Senate. He appoints American ambassadors, ministers, and consuls with the advice and consent of the Senate. He gives Congress information on the state of the union and recommends measures that he thinks necessary and expedient, including civil and military measures that affect foreign affairs. He receives the representatives of other nations.

When the Constitution refers to the President, practice means that the President plus all the executive apparatus, civil and military, carries out his powers. All those parts of the apparatus that hold responsibility for the conduct of diplomacy share in the President's power and responsibility to lead in foreign affairs. The first responsibility for the wise conduct of diplomacy rests then in the President and in all his subordinates who work in this field.

When all these executive agents in all their units of bureaucracy bow too low in obeisance to the faith that conflict and resolution, debate and compromise, produce the wisest decision, the nation may be in danger. When executives falter in the conduct of foreign affairs, for which they have first responsibility, they cannot be corrected easily by Congress and Court. In the ultimate sense in the nuclear age only one mistake is allowed; if the executive makes it, there is not much left to correct. But one need not worry about the ultimate to say that the quality of decisions made by executive agents in the conduct of diplomacy is as important for the national welfare as the quality of any other decision concerning any other aspect of our national life, public or private. And one may worry about too much collegial, pluralistic faith among executive agents.

Certainly executive agents take account of various interests, for such are facts in evidence. But executives also have a larger purpose, at least to an adherent of the Constitution. They should analyze other evidence than the interests of various groups. Special interests in conflict are only part of the evidence to be analyzed, not necessarily the main part. Executive agents should, for example, take the national, not a sectional view. And they should act when action is called for without waiting for a consensus of approval.

When executive authority itself is used to express no more than the muted decisions of compromise, the nation's ability suffers. This is true especially in the conduct of foreign affairs, where the executive is responsible for most decisions of policy and has less immediate check from Congress or public groups than in domestic affairs. What the Secretary of State does at a Conference of Foreign Ministers on the Berlin crisis is much more his own choice than what the Secretary of Agriculture decides to recommend as a change in the support program for wheat.

Too much faith in pluralism produces decision more by consensus than by evidence. Executives make foreign policy that is acceptable to all the agencies involved, not because it is the best policy that comes from all the facts but because it is the policy that has the most support within the Executive Branch. Organization is diffused to reflect the special interests of the diplomats, the military men, and the new men of economics, propaganda, and secret intelligence. If pluralism is the accepted way in the national culture, it becomes the way of executive organization. Committees form to provide the consensus needed, and staff conferences produce agreement when no committee exists. Decisions that come from agreement by all members of a group are more likely to represent the average than the wisest men.

The initiative of bold individuals fades in the radiance with which groups are lighted. Men who work well with other people are most sought for executives, and men who have strong and different ideas are doomed to trouble. To march to a different drum is rude. It steals time from the reaching of agreement.

Another, and contrary, result can come from the diffusion of organization, and the politeness that comes from administration by consensus. Unobtrusive individuals and enterprises can escape notice for years at a time. If they are competent and trustworthy, this may be good for the cause of government. Some fine work is done by Foreign Service Officers who avoid the system. If the lost men are no good, however, they waste time and do harm. All over the world in all our foreign enterprises there are people and activities that should be stopped. They continue because executives who should stop them are too busy in coordination and too polite in group work to pay attention to such unpleasant tasks as cancellation.

Weak executives too can escape responsibility by shifting all decisions to the group. And strong executives can use the confusion that comes from too scattered organization to do as they please without proper attention to the evidence that should be sent up by subordinates. The wiliest President of this century, Franklin D. Roosevelt, created a hell's cauldron of confusion among his subordinates, then made his own decisions. He was strong and sometimes wrong, but he was clearly the one to be held responsible.

Faith in pluralism lies deep in our culture. It comes from a misunderstanding about democracy. By now the term democracy seems to mean for many Americans that as many people as possible should be satisfied. Apparently it no longer means with equal force the freedom for a man to be different. It means to some a simple majority rule and not the checks and balances of the Constitution. Good manners impel others to trust to the formation of consensus as the only polite way to settle disputes.

The Golden Rule may be invoked. It calls for understanding the viewpoints of others. Industrial psychologists since Elton Mayo and public relations advisers since Ivy Lee have preached that good will is more found in tolerance than in conflict. Production and profits go up too, a fact that does not escape some psychologists in their study of the Lord's message, until politeness, conference, agreement, and the unintrusive executive become principles of the new dogma of groupism.

Add to these feelings shared by kind people, the fact that the quickest and easiest way to be an executive is to get the most possible agreement and therefore the most possible support. Decisions reached in maximum agreement may not be the most sensible ones, but they tempt executives. They are safe and relatively tranquil.

The question is whether the American executive can overcome the culture on this point. If he cannot, we will continue in diffused organization and diluted action, avoiding the firm and sharp conviction. Weak men will not restore the executive function to strength, for weak men thrive on conference and consensus. Only the strong—perhaps the unpleasant—need try.

V

"Give me a little time, can't you?" said Eugene Manlove Rhodes' proud sheriff. "If you . . . would just tear down that damned telephone line, that would be a start. I'm tied to it." He was talking about the first line to reach Hillsboro, N.M. By now we are tied to all the new lines, and wrapped in them, until we can barely move. Technology uses us as much as we use it. We have lost the upper hand.

The new communication by wire, wave, and photography, added to faster delivery of persons and written messages, is the technology most relevant to the conduct of diplomacy. It includes mimeographs and other fiendish devices that duplicate rapidly and profusely the slightest words that anyone thinks are worth spreading. It includes, too, the new filing systems, and typewriters, carbon paper, tape recorders, and nearly anything save a thoughtful man chewing on a pencil until he gets an idea clear in his mind.

Change comes so fast and is so exciting that most men think it valuable. So they add more men to handle the new volume of work that comes from faster communication. Older men have doubts. Once I asked a Permanent Under Secretary of the British Foreign Office what he considered to be the biggest difference in diplomatic work between now and when he began 30 years before. He was as high in career as a professional can go, knighted, invited to the palace for small parties, in direct touch with a Minister who talked with the Prime Minister who talked with Queen and Commons. The Permanent Under Secretary had not reached his station without good judgment and accurate reporting. His answer to my question was immediate. It required no contemplation, for the man had suffered. "It is," he said, "the enormous amount of unnecessary work we do now."

The work comes from the very existence of technology. Arabian princes, let us say, begin to look to the West as being more the source of what they want than any Arab federation can ever be. Without so much technology, and massive communication, an American diplomat in the Middle East could negotiate quietly and secretly until he had a firm offer. Then he could cable in code to his government. The princes are willing to renounce Arab union for a 10 percent bigger share of oil royalties, 3 new hospitals, 300 Parker pens, and 50 litres of French perfume.

Next the western governments would begin to dicker secretly with each other and with the private firms that have to agree. Oil royalties involve the British and American governments and firms; hospitals the American government; Parker pens the American government and the pen company in Janesville, Wisconsin, where this prestige symbol of literacy is made; and the perfume involves the British, American and French governments and a French business firm.

Officers with gumption would know whether this offer was as good as they could get. Certainly men of experience would not question the sense of the list. Each item is important to the princes; the royalties for big money, the hospitals for popularity, the pens for gifts in lieu of raises to civil servants, and the perfume for wives and friends as evidence of the skill of their men in securing the good life.

With today's technology, by contrast, the first intimation that the princes are susceptible will be cabled to Washington by our man because, since the cable exists, Washington expects to be notified of the smallest change. In Washington the abominable duplicator scatters copies of the message. Agriculture will try to substitute wheat for the hospitals. Commerce will try for a mixture of all the makes of American fountain pens in hope of opening new markets, although the magic overseas of Parker is long proved. Treasury will object to spending dollars for French perfume.

State will try to find common ground. Many cables will be exchanged. Our man in Araby is told in detail what he may suggest to the princes. During the delays and arguments between our man and Washington, spies have told Cairo and Moscow, and probably Peking, what is going on. It is next to impossible to keep secret the subject of much communication.

News reporters too have learned about the negotiation, without being spies in any sense but rather part of the process of foreign relations, as Bernard C. Cohen shows in *The Press and Foreign Policy*. The good reporters usually learn about big developments that get into prolonged discussion. They share information with diplomats, other reporters, and princes. Being outside official responsibility, newsmen are free to talk to anyone. They can ask questions that diplomats dare not ask because Washington has not authorized it. Then news reporters are able sometimes to help causes along. Princes use them to reach Americans who read news and watch television, hoping that some officials will be impressed. Officials and private interests try to make the kind of news that will be reported and used in media.

Once the news is out about the possible deal with the princes, complications double. Now members of Congress declaim, and private interests cry outrage. The Representative from Southeast Iowa speaks for Sheaffer pens, made in Fort Madison. Leaders of the opposition recognize in the deal for perfume headlines that will hurt the President. That much perfume at that cost can be made to sound preposterous to the average citizen, and the high stakes of diplomacy be damned. Other agricultural exports are added to wheat as being more desirable than hospitals. The chances are good that the negotiation will fall through. Few Arabian princes will enjoy the notoriety they now receive for what they began as a simple sale of their power for things they wanted from the West.

Technology rides the back of news media. It means large investment in the machinery of communication and high salaries for the specialists who use the machinery. All have to be fed. So much space and time has to be filled all through each day. Anything that may interest an audience has to be considered. Reporters in the Middle East should tell all they know, and so should reporters in Washington. Their loyalty is to the institutions of press, radio, and television, all of which are enslaved to the cost of technology.

But life can never be the same again in diplomacy once technology takes control of both the work of diplomats and the news about it. Only a few aging gentlemen remember a time when tempests were not created in teapots, simply because so many different people now get involved. Younger men think that all the busy work is necessary. It reflects the only world they have known, one in which technology makes work and people make livings from doing jobs that are made necessary only because they exist.

It is hopeless to talk of a return to the old days. Not even more automation promises yet to reduce the number of handlers and talkers in diplomacy. Probably the only way to revive contemplation and the old secrecy in negotiation is to appoint some people who can work outside the whirling cage that is created by technology, the Policy Corps suggested earlier. So long as American diplomats, and those of other nations too, are kept busy with the damned telephone line, they will not have time or ability to handle surely the big results of technology, such as deadlier weapons and the conquest of space.

VI

No matter what we think, we are much too nice to hold our leaders strictly responsible. Some examples from the British side of the family will show this; it is easier to see the illusions of kin than our own.

One unorthodox and startling way to visit Westminster Abbey and St. Paul's is to pass by the truly great, then read carefully the gravestones of the many others buried there. The majority of these forgotten eminences had little to recommend them while alive yet they somehow passed the selection committee for this ultimate club. If one studies especially the generals and admirals, one begins to suspect that the British Empire began to be lost 200 years ago, and one wonders how it ever got established in the first place. Cornwallis' errors in the American colonies were not his only record. He had a whole career of failure. It is reported favorably on his monument.

Or take the late Lord Halifax as a twentieth-century example. He was praised in obituaries, and he was, without reservation, a good and sincere man who worked hard when he could have idled life away. As a political leader he was accountable, at least in part, for he was a policy-maker, for four shattering events; the rise of Gandhi and Indian passive rebellion, the rise of Hitler, the appeasement of Hitler at Munich, and the Second World War. With the exception of winning the war, the events were failures of British policy. In his autobiography Lord Halifax does not think this way, in terms of his success or failure as a diplomat. Only once in his life, according to his book, did he recognize failure and get annoyed. That was when mutiny broke out in the pack of harriers at his country home. British citizens did not call him a failure at foreign affairs nor hold him responsible.

Douglas MacArthur and Harry Truman are examples at home. Both were commendable for much that they did—and also censurable, though neither was criticized for the right reasons. After a good record as commander in the Pacific and as military governor of Japan, MacArthur failed as supreme commander in the war for South Korea. There was no other word for it in the old-fashioned sense that a commanding officer has authority over tactics and also has responsibility for mistakes. This general mistook the intentions of the Red Chinese, and his troops were set back in great damage when the Chinese attacked. His later claim that he could have won the war if he had been allowed to bomb inside China obscured the fact that he was in command when China caught him unaware and pushed his forces south.

Mr. Truman was held responsible in press and Congress for withdrawing MacArthur after the general went too far in his political effort to argue policy against his superiors. In the doctrine of military command, Mr. Truman as Commander in Chief should have been criticized for not questioning MacArthur's ability as a commander in the field.

The tenor seems to be that so long as popular men try to do their best, most people allow them to proceed without criticism.

All our leaders are nice fellows. They would not be chosen if they weren't. All of them can appear to be doing the best they know how. They have access to the media and can report favorably on their own stewardships. Most of us in the electorate will be more interested in something else, anyhow, and will be tolerant when we do notice the actions of political leaders.

We are this way, no doubt, because the leaders act much the way most of us would act, so there is no need for us to get concerned. (One study shows that non-voters are more satisfied than voters with the way the government is run and feel no motive to vote; it makes sense.)

When we change Presidents, at least since 1932, it is not from dissatisfaction with the man in office, or even strict accounting of his acts, but from a combination of things. An amendment bars a President from three full terms. Incomes increase and old party appeals grow weaker or stronger to the independent voter. Population shifts to city to suburbs to certain parts of the country with changes in party strength. Moods of the people change. Certain men draw more votes than others because of their personal traits. We do not measure results first when we enter the secret booth.

While they are in office, Presidents and their subordinates are free to do anything reasonable in the conduct of foreign affairs. So long as they do not affront us, we will give them support.

VII

These traits, then, account for the way we conduct foreign affairs. No President, no Secretary of State made our system. No single person, no group can be blamed much or praised much.

Because we are the way we are, we have developed executive machinery that perpetuates habits, allows pluralistic debate to delay and dilute decisions, and discourages the strong executive. We hold on to old concepts of diplomacy long after they are dead in practice. When we reorganize to take on the new jobs, we add new agencies rather than reform the old. We become absorbed in answering the telephone, and other artifacts, and spend our energy on busywork with too little left for thought. We allow officials to fail without censure so long as we like them.

VIII

Still, if these traits of culture slow up action, they can equally allow freedom to public officials to make decisions. This pluralism also has open spaces in which free men can run their own course, just at it has thickets of conformity and clearance and the leaden norm. The man who knows how to operate in American bureaucracy, because he knows where the holes are, is familiar to all who observe federal administration from the inside.

Unless those who manage government recognize the difference between their inclinations as members of the national society and their duties as public officers faced with other realities, when the two are in conflict, there is small reason to expect them to change. Public officials need to be efficient in the conduct of foreign affairs even though the national style, the traits of culture, discourages efficiency.

Only the naive argue in today's complex issues that public agents should be no more than wind vanes of public opinion. Often in decisions of foreign policy they cannot know what public opinion is in time to respond to it. In any case, the opinion will be held only by those individuals who are paying attention to the issue, while the public agent's duty is to serve all the people whether attentive or not.

We elect a President to make decisions for us. He appoints political executives to help him. They direct permanent civil and military subordinates who share the duty. All these have to recognize that organization and the behavior of men may need to depart from habits of the national style. This is the first step toward a new theory for the conduct of the new diplomacy.

In this case, of the conduct of the new diplomacy, the nation needs, first and inevitably, Presidents who can and will operate. Strong Presidents are also admired in practice under the remarkable

American Constitution. From the usual list of great Presidents, all were men who used the office in strength. Washington established the independent strength of the office. Jefferson used his power to extend the national boundaries and conduct exploration beyond the new boundaries. Jackson made the federal government reflect the masses and the frontier. Lincoln saved the Union, but in the struggle he made decisions that today would cause shudders among members of the Civil Liberties Union. Theodore Roosevelt shook the big stick, blasted malefactors, and established conservation more than any man before him. Franklin Roosevelt established welfare as a national concern and opened the era of American economic aid to friendly nations before America was at war with unfriendly nations.

For the years after the Second World War, Harry Truman and Dwight D. Eisenhower were both committee men. They depended upon the slow, sometimes remote, debates of the National Security Council to produce the advice they heeded. Of the two, Mr. Eisenhower made teamwork a virtue. In the end, for some important action for which he got the blame, he appears to have lost control to subordinates who were running free in the clearing while he listened to orderly plodders in the thicket. Operators running free, and not the Security Council, made the decision to send the U-2 plane over Russia at that sensitive time.

John F. Kennedy showed in the first three years of his administration that he did not like committees as executives and did not intend the President to be a chairman. He brought in to advise him people he wanted regardless of their relevance in the hierarchy of foreign affairs, including his brother, the Attorney General. He kept little more than the name of the National Security Council as it had existed under Truman and Eisenhower. He called in advisers at times in the name of the Council; or a creation of his own called the Executive Committee of the Council which included some men who were not members of the Council. One suspected that the use of the Council's name at all was more for reasons of legal and public assurance than for accurate reporting. One of the President's Assistants was called director of the Council's staff. In practice he was much more than this. Certainly he was, as

McGeorge Bundy defined the post, the center man next to the President for pulling together a foreign policy from its many sources in the military and civil sprawl. He was a long way from the previous concept of the Council as a committee and its staff as another committee, all working for coordination among departments until many things were left aside because the Council and staff were absorbed in handling those matters that had happened to come to their attention.

IX

A strong President's next job in the conduct of diplomacy is twofold.

First, he can reorganize the Executive Branch for this work. He can do much within the fences set by Congress. Mr. Kennedy had done this to some extent by using certain members of the National Security Council, which is defined by Congress, and not others for his advice in crises. Presidents can in so many ways do as they please within the tolerances of pluralism. It matters little whether they announce a reorganization if they get the same results by their practices with small regard for the old forms.

Beyond his own practices, he will need reorganization approved by Congress. Most of the changes recommended earlier in this book will require acts of Congress. A strong President by definition is one who can get from Congress approval for most of those measures that he thinks most important. Before Congress's attitude toward reorganization for the conduct of diplomacy can be tested, a President has to propose the measures to Congress. Until a President does so, there is little point to saying that Congress will or will not approve.

Second, he can make sure that the new organization is given a chance. Once reorganization is obtained, the President's subordinates have to be as tough as he is to make the new system work. Deputies to the President, proposed earlier, with clear authority to make decisions and not merely to suggest, will have to establish their authority in practice. So will the new Secretary of Foreign

Affairs and the Secretary of Defense over all others in Washington who will try to chip off pieces of work and decision. Practice is what counts always, not the paper that defines jurisdictions and authorities.

Over all, the President, and only the President, can demand that all his agents abide within the new structure, chastising unambiguously those who do not. All need to persist until the reorganization is working, the wounds healed or their bearers dead, the new men no longer excluded by the old. Then executives need to check on how the new scheme works. Some unexpected outcome will always show because designers can never anticipate everything. New change is needed, hopefully not in as drastic degree as the first.

Executives can direct deep reorganization and supervise the result if they want to. Until now they have thought that other jobs came first, so they have left undone, or only partly done in small pieces, the reorganization that is needed. By now the loose structure may be as great a threat as megaton bombs, but not as recognizable. If the machinery of government fails, the nation fails. It is this simple.

Any President who wants can seize the big job.

BIBLIOGRAPHY

Adams, Sherman. *Firsthand Report, The Story of the Eisenhower Administration.* New York: Harper & Row, 1961.

Albertson, Maurice, Rice, Andrew E., and Birky, Pauline E. *New Frontiers for American Youth: Perspective on the Peace Corps.* Washington, D.C.: Public Affairs Press, 1961.

Almond, Gabriel. *The American People and Foreign Policy.* New York: Harcourt, Brace & World, 1950.

American Academy of Political and Social Science. "Congress and Foreign Relations," *Annals* V (1953) 289.

American Assembly. *Cultural Affairs and Foreign Relations.* Englewood Cliffs, N.J.: Prentice-Hall, 1963.

American Assembly. *The Representation of the United States Abroad.* New York: Columbia University Press, 1956.

American Assembly. *The Secretary of State.* Englewood Cliffs, N.J.: Prentice-Hall, 1960.

Barnes, William, and Morgan, John Heath. *The Foreign Service of the United States; Origins, Development, and Functions.* Washington D.C.: Department of State Publication, Government Printing Office, 1961.

Barrett, Edward W. *Truth Is Our Weapon.* New York: Funk & Wagnalls, 1953.

Bauer, Raymond A., Pool, Ithiel de Sola, and Dexter, Lewis Anthony. *American Business and Public Policy, The Politics of Foreign Trade.* New York: Atherton, 1963.

Berding, Andrew. *Foreign Affairs and You: How American Foreign Policy Is Made and What It Means to You.* New York: Doubleday, 1962.

Binkley, Wilfred E. *The Man in the White House: His Powers and Duties.* Baltimore: Johns Hopkins University Press, 1959.

Brines, Russell. *MacArthur's Japan.* Philadelphia: Lippincott, 1948.

Brookings Institution. *Administrative Aspects of United States Foreign Assistance Programs.* Washington, D.C.: Government Printing Office, 1957.

Brookings Institution. *The Administration of Foreign Affairs and Overseas Operations.* Washington, D.C.: Government Printing Office, 1951.

Brown, William Adams, Jr., and Opie, Redvers. *American Foreign Assistance.* Washington, D.C.: Brookings Institution, 1953.

Buck, Philip W., and Travis, Martin B. *Control of Foreign Relations in Modern Nations.* New York: W. W. Norton, 1957.

Boyce, Richard Fyfe. *The Diplomat's Wife.* New York: Harper & Row, 1956.

Cardozo, Michael H. *Diplomats in International Cooperation: Stepchildren of the Foreign Service.* Ithaca, N.Y.: Cornell University Press, 1962.

Carroll, Holbert. *The House of Representatives and Foreign Policy.* Pittsburgh: University of Pittsburgh Press, 1958.

Carroll, Wallace. *Persuade or Perish.* Boston: Houghton Mifflin, 1948.

Cerf, Jay H. *Strategy for the 60's, Summary and Analysis of Studies Prepared by 13 Foreign Policy Research Centers for the United States Senate.* Washington, D.C.: Foreign Policy Clearing House, 1961.

Cheever, Daniel S., and Haviland, H. Field, Jr. *American Foreign Policy and the Separation of Powers.* Cambridge, Mass.: Harvard University Press, 1952.

Childs, J. Rives. *American Foreign Service.* New York: Holt, Rinehart & Winston, 1948.

Cleveland, Harlan, and Mangone, Gerard J. *The Art of Overseasmanship: Americans at Work Abroad.* Syracuse, N.Y.: Syracuse University Press, 1957.

Cleveland, Harlan, Mangone, Gerard J., and Adams, John C. *The Overseas Americans.* New York: McGraw-Hill, 1960.

Cohen, Bernard C. *Citizen Education in World Affairs.* Princeton, N.J.: Princeton University Press, 1953.

Cohen, Bernard C. *The Political Process and Foreign Policy: The Making of the Japanese Peace Treaty.* Princeton, N.J.: Princeton University Press, 1957.

Cohen, Bernard C. *The Press and Foreign Policy.* Princeton, N.J.: Princeton University Press, 1963.

Committee on Foreign Affairs Personnel. *Personnel for the New Diplomacy.* New York: Taplinger, 1963.

Corwin, Edward S. *The President: Office and Powers, 1787–1957.* 4th ed. New York: New York University Press, 1957.

Craig, Gordon A., and Gilbert, Felix (eds.). *The Diplomats, 1919–1939.* Princeton, N.J.: Princeton University Press, 1953.

Crane, Katherine. *Mr. Carr of State: Forty-seven Years in the Department of State.* New York: St Martin's Press, 1960.

Dahl, Robert A. *Congress and Foreign Policy.* New York: Harcourt, Brace & World, 1950.

Dangerfield, Royden, and Gordon, David. *The Hidden Weapon: The Story of Economic Warfare.* New York: Harper & Row, 1947.

De Conde, Alexander. *The American Secretary of State, An Interpretation.* New York: Praeger, 1962.

Dizard, Wilson P. *The Strategy of Truth: The Story of the U.S. Information Service.* Washington, D.C.: Public Affairs Press, 1961.

Donovan, Robert J. *Eisenhower: The Inside Story.* New York: Harper & Row, 1956.

Egger, Roland (ed.). *International Commitments and National Administration*. Charlottesville, Va.: University of Virginia Press, 1949.

Elder, Robert Ellsworth. *The Policy Machine; the Department of State and American Foreign Policy*. Syracuse, N.Y.: Syracuse University Press, 1960.

Elliott, William Yandell. *United States Foreign Policy, Its Organization and Control*. New York: Columbia University Press, 1952.

Farago, Ladislas. *War of Wits; The Anatomy of Espionage and Intelligence*. New York: Funk & Wagnalls, 1954.

Feis, Herbert. *The China Tangle: the American Effort in China from Pearl Harbor to the Marshall Mission*. Princeton, N. J.: Princeton University Press, 1953.

Feis, Herbert. *Churchill, Roosevelt, Stalin*. Princeton, N.J.: Princeton University Press, 1957.

Feis, Herbert. *Seen from EA; Three International Episodes*. New York: Alfred A. Knopf, 1947.

Feis, Herbert. *The Spanish Story: Franco and the Nations at War*. New York: Alfred A. Knopf, 1948.

Finer, Herman. *The Presidency: Crisis and Regeneration*. Chicago: University of Chicago Press, 1960.

Fischer, John. *Master Plan U.S.A.; An Informal Report on America's Foreign Policy and the Men Who Make It*. New York: Harper & Row, 1951.

Forrestal, James. *The Forrestal Diaries*, ed. Walter Millis. New York: Viking Press, 1951.

Friedrich, Carl J., and Associates. *American Experiences in Military Government in World War II*. New York: Holt, Rinehart & Winston, 1948.

Glick, Philip M. *The Administration of Technical Assistance: Growth in the Americas*. Chicago: University of Chicago Press, 1957.

Goodfriend, Arthur. *The Twisted Image*. New York: St Martin's Press, 1963.

Goold-Adams, Richard. *John Foster Dulles; A Reappraisal*. New York: Appleton-Century-Crofts, 1962.

Grassmuck, George. *Sectional Biases in Congress on Foreign Policy*. Baltimore: Johns Hopkins Press, 1951.

Hall, Edward T. *The Silent Language*. New York: Doubleday, 1959.

Hammond, Paul Y. *Organizing for Defense: The American Military Establishment in the Twentieth Century*. Princeton, N.J.: Princeton University Press, 1961.

Haviland, H. Field, Jr. *The Formulation and Administration of United States Foreign Policy*. Washington, D.C.: Brookings Institution, 1960.

Higgins, Trumbull. *Korea and the Fall of MacArthur; A Precis in Limited War*. New York: Oxford University Press, 1960.

Hilsman, Roger. *Strategic Intelligence and National Decisions*. New York: Free Press of Glencoe, 1956.

Hirschman, Albert O. *The Strategy of Economic Development*. New Haven: Yale University Press, 1958.

Hitch, Charles, and McKean, Roland N. *The Economics of Defense in the Nuclear Age.* Cambridge, Mass.: Harvard University Press, 1960.

Hobbs, E. H. *Behind the President: A Study of Executive Office Agencies.* Washington, D.C.: Public Affairs Press, 1954.

Holt, Robert T., and van de Velde, Robert W. *Strategic Psychological Operations and American Foreign Policy.* Chicago: University of Chicago Press, 1960.

Huntington, Samuel P. *The Common Defense: Strategic Programs in National Politics.* New York: Columbia University Press, 1961.

Huntington, Samuel P. *The Soldier and the State: The Theory and Politics of Civil-Military Relations.* Cambridge, Mass.: Harvard University Press, 1957.

Hoopes, Roy. *The Complete Peace Corps Guide.* New York: Dial Press, 1961.

Huzar, Elias. *The Purse and the Sword: Control of the Army by Congress Through Military Appropriations, 1933–1950.* Ithaca, N.Y.: Cornell University Press, 1950.

Ilchman, Warren Frederick. *Professional Diplomacy in the United States, 1779–1939: A Study in Administrative History.* Chicago: University of Chicago Press, 1961.

Janowitz, Morris. *The Professional Soldier; A Social and Political Portrait.* New York: Free Press of Glencoe, 1960.

Jones, Joseph M. *The Fifteen Weeks, February 21–June 5, 1947.* New York: Viking Press, 1955. [Account of the decision of the Truman Doctrine.]

Kent, Sherman. *Strategic Intelligence for American World Policy.* Princeton, N.J.: Princeton University Press, 1951.

Kintner, William R. *Forging a New Sword: A Study of the Department of Defense.* New York: Harper & Row, 1958.

Kissinger, Henry A. *The Necessity for Choice: Prospects for American Foreign Policy.* New York: Harper & Row, 1961.

Koenig, Louis W. *The Invisible Presidency.* New York: Holt, Rinehart & Winston, 1960.

Koenig, L. W. *The Presidency and Crisis: Powers of the Office from the Invasion of Poland to Pearl Harbor.* New York: King's Crown Press, 1944.

Lasswell, Harold D. *National Security and Individual Freedom.* New York: McGraw-Hill, 1950.

Lederer, William J. *A Nation of Sheep.* New York: W. W. Norton, 1961.

LeFever, Ernest W. *Ethics and United States Foreign Policy.* Meriden, 1957.

Lincoln, George A. *Economics of National Security: Managing America's Resources for Defense.* West Point: U.S. Military Academy, 1953.

Liska, George. *The New Statecraft; Foreign Aid in American Foreign Policy.* Chicago: University of Chicago Press, 1959.

Litchfield, Edward H., and Associates. *Governing Post-war Germany.* Ithaca, N.Y.: Cornell University Press, 1953.

London, Kurt. *How Foreign Policy Is Made.* Princeton, N.J.: D. Van Nostrand, 1949.

McCamy, James L. *The Administration of American Foreign Affairs.* New York: Alfred A. Knopf, 1950.

McCloy, John J. *The Challenge to American Foreign Policy.* Cambridge, Mass.: Harvard University Press, 1953.

McGovern, William M. *Strategic Intelligence and the Shape of Tomorrow.* Chicago: Henry Regnery, 1961.

Macmahon, Arthur W. *Administration in Foreign Affairs.* University, Ala.: University of Alabama Press, 1953.

Markel, Lester, *et al. Public Opinion and Foreign Policy.* New York: Harper & Row, 1959.

Martin, Edwin M. *The Allied Occupation of Japan.* Stanford, Calif.: Stanford University Press, 1948. (Supplemented by Fearey, Robert A. *The Occupation of Japan, Second Phase: 1948–50.* New York: Macmillan, 1950.)

Masland, John W., and Radway, Laurence I. *Soldiers and Scholars: Military Education and National Policy.* Princeton, N.J.: Princeton University Press, 1957.

May, Ernest R. (ed.). *The Ultimate Decision: The President as Commander-in-Chief.* New York: George Braziller, 1960.

Millis, Walter, Mansfield, Harvey C., and Stein, Harold. *Arms and the State: Civil-Military Elements in National Policy.* New York: Twentieth Century Fund, 1958.

Mosher, Frederick C. *Program Budgeting: Theory and Practice with Particular Reference to the U.S. Department of the Army.* Chicago: Public Administration Service, 1954.

Nelson, Otto L. *National Security and the General Staff.* Washington, D.C.: Infantry Journal Press, 1946.

Nero, Alfred G. *Americans in World Affairs; Studies in Citizen Participation in International Relations,* Vol. I. Boston: World Peace Foundation, 1959.

Neustadt, Richard E. *Presidential Power; The Politics of Leadership.* New York: John Wiley & Sons, 1960.

Nicolson, Harold. *Diplomacy.* New York: Harcourt, Brace & World, 1939.

Parks, Wallace Judson. *United States Administration of Its International Economic Affairs.* Baltimore: Johns Hopkins Press, 1951.

Pettee, George S. *The Future of American Secret Intelligence.* Washington, D.C.: Infantry Journal Press, 1946.

Platt, Washington. *Strategic Intelligence Production: Basic Principles.* New York: Frederick A. Praeger, 1957.

Plischke, Elmer. *Conduct of American Diplomacy.* Princeton, N.J.: D. Van Nostrand, 1950.

Plischke, Elmer. *American Foreign Relations; A Bibliography of Official Sources.* College Park, Md.: University of Maryland Press, 1956.

Plischke, Elmer. *American Diplomacy; A Bibliography of Biographies, Autobiographies, and Commentaries.* College Park, Md.: University of Maryland Press, 1957.

Plischke, Elmer. *Summit Diplomacy: Personal Diplomacy of the President of the United States.* College Park, Md.: University of Maryland Press, 1958.

Ransom, Harry Howe. *Central Intelligence and National Security.* Cambridge, Mass.: Harvard University Press, 1958.

Robinson, James A. *Congress and Foreign Policy-Making; A Study in Legislative Influence and Initiative.* Homewood, Ill.: Dorsey, 1962.

Rossiter, Clinton. *The American Presidency.* New York: Harcourt, Brace & World, 1956.

Rostow, W. W. *The United States in the World Arena: An Essay in Recent History.* New York: Harper & Row, 1960.

Rovere, Richard H. *The Eisenhower Years: Affairs of State.* New York: Farrar, Straus & Co., 1956.

Rovere, Richard H., and Schlesinger, Arthur M., Jr. *The General and the President and the Future of American Foreign Policy.* New York: Farrar, Straus & Co., 1951.

Satow, Sir Ernest. *A Guide to Diplomatic Practice,* ed. Nevile Bland, 4th ed. New York: Longmans, Green & Co., 1957.

Schilling, Warner R., Hammond, Paul Y., and Snyder, Glenn H. *Strategy, Politics and Defense.* New York: Columbia University Press, 1962.

Sherwood, Robert E. *Roosevelt and Hopkins; An Intimate History.* New York: Harper & Row, 1948.

Snyder, Richard C., Bruck, H. W., and Sapin, Burton (eds.). *Foreign Policy Decision Making; An Approach to the Study of International Politics.* New York: Free Press of Glencoe, 1962.

Sorensen, Theodore C. *Decision-Making in the White House, The Olive Branch or the Arrows.* New York: Columbia University Press, 1963.

Stein, Harold. *Public Administration and Policy Development; A Case Book.* New York: Harcourt, Brace & World, 1952.

Stein, Harold (ed.). *American Civil-Military Decisions, A Book of Case Studies.* University, Ala.: University of Alabama Press, 1963.

Steiner, Zara S. *The State Department and the Foreign Service; The Wriston Report—Four Years Later.* Princeton, N.J.: Center of International Studies, 1958.

Steiner, Zara S. *Present Problems of the Foreign Service.* Princeton, N.J.: Center of International Studies, 1961.

Stephens, Oren. *Facts to a Candid World; America's Overseas Information Program.* Stanford, Calif.: Stanford University Press, 1955.

Stimson, Henry L., and Bundy, McGeorge. *On Active Service in Peace and War.* New York: Harper & Row, 1948.

Stuart, Graham H. *The Department of State.* New York: Macmillan, 1949.

Stuart, Graham H. *American Diplomatic and Consular Practice,* 2nd ed. New York: Appleton-Century-Crofts, 1952.

Szulc, Tad and Meyer, Karl E. *The Cuban Invasion, The Chronicle of A Disaster.* New York: Ballantine and Praeger, 1962.

Thayer, Charles W. *Diplomat.* New York: Harper & Row, 1959.

Thomson, Charles A., and Laves, Walter H. C. *Cultural Relations and U.S. Foreign Policy*. Bloomington, Ind.: Indiana University Press, 1963.

Thomson, Charles A. H. *Overseas Information Service of the United States Government*. Washington, D.C.: Brookings Institution, 1948.

Truman, Harry S. *Memoirs*, 2 volumes. New York: Doubleday, 1955, 1956.

Tugwell, Rexford G. *The Enlargement of the Presidency*. New York: Doubleday, 1960.

◦ U.S. Bureau of the Budget. *Organization and Coordination of Foreign Economic Activities*. Washington, D.C.: Government Printing Office, 1961.

U.S. Commission on Organization of the Executive Branch of the Government, First Hoover Commission. *Reports*. Washington, D.C.: Government Printing Office, 1949. [The following separate reports are the most relevant: *General Management of the Executive Branch, Foreign Affairs, Task Force on Foreign Affairs, The National Security Organization, Task Force Report on National Security Organization*, and *Overseas Administration*.]

U.S. Commission on Organization of the Executive Branch of the Government, Second Hoover Commission. *Intelligence Activities, Overseas Economic Operations*, and *Task Force on Overseas Economic Operations*. Washington, D.C.: Government Printing Office, 1955.

U.S. President's Committee on Administrative Management, Brownlow Committee. *Administrative Management in the Government of the United States* and *Report of the Committee with Studies of Administrative Management in the Federal Government*. Washington, D.C.: Government Printing Office, 1937.

U.S. Senate, Committee on the Armed Services and the Committee on Foreign Relations, 82nd Congress, 1st Session. *Hearings to Conduct an Inquiry into the Military Situation in the Far East and the Facts Surrounding Relief of General of the Army Douglas MacArthur from His Assignment in that Area*. Washington, D.C.: Government Printing Office, 1951.

U.S. Department of State. *The Biographic Register*. Washington, D.C.: Government Printing Office. [See various revisions.]

U.S. Department of State. *Career Opportunities as a Foreign Service Officer* and *Sample Questions from the Foreign Service Officer Examination*. Washington, D.C.: Government Printing Office [latest revision].

◦ U.S. Department of State. *The Foreign Service of the United States; Origins, Development, and Functions*. Washington, D.C.: Government Printing Office, 1961.

U.S. Department of State. *Toward a Stronger Foreign Service* [report of the "Wriston Committee"]. Washington, D.C.: Government Printing Office, 1954.

U.S. Government Organization Manual. Washington, D.C.: Government Printing Office [revised each year].

U.S. Senate Committee on Foreign Relations, 85th Congress, 2nd Session. *Recruitment and Training for the Foreign Service of the United States* [Staff Study]. Washington, D.C.: Government Printing Office, 1958.

U.S. Senate Committee on Foreign Relations, 86th Congress, 1st Session. *The American Overseas: Hearing* [statement and answers by Dean Harlan Cleveland and others from Maxwell Graduate School of Syracuse University]. Washington, D.C.: Government Printing Office, 1959.

U.S. Senate Committee on Foreign Relations, 86th Congress, 1st Session. *United States Foreign Policy.* Washington, D.C.: Government Printing Office, 1960. [See especially No. 6, "The Operational Aspects of United States Foreign Policy," by the Maxwell Graduate School of Syracuse University; No. 8, "Developments in Military Technology and Their Impact on United States Strategy and Foreign Policy," by the Washington Center of Foreign Policy Research of The Johns Hopkins University; No. 9, "The Formulation and Administration of United States Foreign Policy," by The Brookings Institution; and No. 12, "Economic, Social, and Political Change in the Underdeveloped Countries and Its Implication for United States Policy," by the Center for International Studies, Massachusetts Institute of Technology.]

U.S. Senate Committee on Foreign Relations, 86th Congress, 2nd Session. *Administration of the Department of State.* Washington, D.C.: Government Printing Office, 1960.

U.S. Senate Committee on Foreign Relations, 86th Congress, 2nd Session. *Events Incident to the Summit Conference; Hearings.* Washington, D.C.: Government Printing Office, 1960.

U.S. Senate Committee on Foreign Relations, 86th Congress, 2nd Session. *Events Relating to the Summit Conference; Report.* Washington, D.C.: Government Printing Office, 1960.

U.S. Senate Committee on Foreign Relations, 87th Congress, 1st Session. *Organization for Economic Cooperation and Development.* Washington, D.C.: Government Printing Office, 1961.

U.S. Senate Committee on Government Operations, 86th Congress, 1st Session, Subcommittee on National Policy Machinery. *A Bibliography.* Washington, D.C.: Government Printing Office, 1959.

U.S. Senate Committee on Government Operations, 86th Congress, 2nd Session, Subcommittee on National Policy Machinery. *Organizing for National Security; Hearings.* [Released in parts, with subtitles, in order of appearance: "Organizing for National Security," "Mobilizing Talent for Government Service," "The National Security Council," "The National Security Council and the Departments of State and Defense," "The Department of State, the Policy Planning Staff, and the National Security Council," "The Executive Office and Public Support," "The Budget and the Policy Process," "State, Defense, and the National Security Council."] Washington, D.C.: Government Printing Office, 1960 and 1961.

U.S. Senate Committee on Government Operations, 86th Congress, 1st and 2nd Sessions, Subcommittee on National Policy Machinery. *Reports and Studies.* [In order of appearance, "National Policy Machinery in Communist China," "National Policy Machinery in the Soviet Union," "Selected Materials," "Intelligence and National Security," "Science

Organization and the President's Office," "The Secretary of State and the National Security Policy Process," "Organizational History of the National Security Council," "The Bureau of the Budget and the Budgetary Process," "Super-Cabinet Officers and Superstaffs," "The National Security Council," "Final Statement of Senator Henry M. Jackson, Chairman."] Washington, D.C.: Government Printing Office, 1959–1961.

U.S. Senate Committee on Government Operations. *Organization of Federal Executive Departments and Agencies* [with Chart]. Washington, D.C.: Government Printing Office [published annually].

U.S. Senate Special Committee to Study the Foreign Aid Program, 85th Congress, 1st Session. *Foreign Aid Program; Compilation of Studies and Surveys.* Washington, D.C.: Government Printing Office, 1957.

Vagts, Alfred. *Defense and Diplomacy: The Soldier and the Conduct of Foreign Relations.* New York: King's Crown Press, 1956.

Westerfield, H. Bradford. *Foreign Policy and Party Politics: Pearl Harbor to Korea.* New Haven: Yale University Press, 1955.

Wildes, Harry E. *Typhoon in Tokyo; The Occupation and Its Aftermath.* New York: Macmillan, 1954.

Wise, David, and Ross, Thomas B. *The U-2 Affair.* New York: Random House, 1962.

Zink, Harold. *The United States in Germany.* Princeton, N.J.: D. Van Nostrand, 1957.

INDEX

Hoover, Herbert, in Harding Cabinet, 230
and overseas dispersion, 57
Hoover, J. Edgar, 253
Hoover Commission, and reorganization, 73, 87
Hughes, Charles Evans, and career men, 240–241
in Harding Cabinet, 230
Hull, Cordell, 230–231
Human nature, and reorganization, 268
and staff correction, 46–49

Ilchman, Warren Frederick, 240
India, need for cultural change, 176
variety of languages, 180
Intelligence, evaluation of, 123–125
in new diplomacy, 157–159
Intelligence and Research, Bureau of, 95
International Organization Affairs, Bureau of, 91–92
International conferences, 160–161

Janowitz, Morris, 204
Japan, occupation policy, 144–145

Kellogg, Frank B., 241
Kennan, George, 249, 252
Kennedy, John F., and Adlai Stevenson, 92
and Cuban invasion, 7–8
and coordination, 34–35
on Presidency, 106
as President, 106–107, 110, 115, 116, 229, 281–282
use of Vice-President, 118
Kirk, Alan G., 243
Koestler, Arthur, 126
Kraft, Joseph, 6–7
Khrushchev, Nikita, and U-2 affair, 12–19
visit to United States, 10–12

Labor leaders, and Khrushchev, 11–12
Languages, methods of teaching, 181–182
needs for, 177–183
Layering, 130–131
Luce, Clare Boothe, 245

MacArthur, Douglas, 278
McNamara, Robert, 107
use of budget, 76, 98–101

Management, administrative, as control of policy, 135–136
See also Staff units
Marshall, George C., background of, 234
as Secretary of State, 232
Maverick, Maury, 169–170
Maxwell School, 199
Mergers, 69–72
Midwest Universities Seminar, 260
Military, see Armed forces; Defense, Department of
Military aid, and foreign policy, 148–149
Military Assistance Advisory Groups, 71
Military deterrence, success of, 8
Missions, environment in, 172, 173
need for unity overseas, 183–184
Multi-headed agencies, 32–33
Murphy, Robert, 145

National Aeronautics and Space Administration, 21, 35
National Security Council, and recent Presidents, 281–282
and cabinet officers, 58
and U-2 affair, 21–22
use by President Kennedy, 131
Neustadt, Richard E., 32
News media, and technology, 276

Office of War Information, 71
Ogburn, Charlton, Jr., 59
Operations Coordinating Board, 131
Organization, importance of, 6–9
and institutional memory, 49–52
and integration, 69–72
present, 31–37
purpose of, 44–53
risks of, 38–44
rules for, 54–72
units in foreign affairs, 35–36
See also Reorganization

Peace Corps, 156–157
Pei, Mario, 179
Personnel, competition for, 50–51
and U-2 affair, 25–26
Planning, need for, 39–42
and policy, 250–251
proposed group for, 92–93
staff for President, 127–129, 136–137